What Now?
Boggles - Musings
Rants – Macksims

By: Mack Mahoney

Published by: C.S. Ramahon 2023 ©

ISBN: 978-1-955736-13-8

To Stephanie

and everyone mentioned herein
and those I didn't remember

Also, by Mack Mahoney

Novels:

"Race For the Money"
"Blood and Bluebonnets"

Nonfiction:

"F-5 - Assault on Waco
When the Legend Died"

INTRODUCTION

None of the writing herein has been previously published. It has been created as original material, from the wanderings and wonderings of my mind. I wish to enthusiastically declare that by way of preparation according to the creation of this book, I have headstrongly scanned dozens of articles, television shows, and comic strips, conducting many minutes of extensive research.

My objective was to make it educational but entertaining, therefore by intention the essays trend to the controversial, or at least thought-provoking. With abrupt self-confidence, I shall bypass outright ideological debate to thrust forward eccentric conclusions and render forth some clearly biased and admittedly haughty assertions. I will assume the guise of devil's advocate sometimes, an irate citizen once in a while, and occasionally prove myself to be a crusty old buffoon. But, I promise to always keep my tongue firmly in cheek while offering up my homespun brand of social criticism as a proverbial provocateur. If at times I appear to you to be a nut, I can only compliment your astute observation, because I certifiably am.

Unlike my cards, there aren't many rhymes. There won't be any limitations either. I shall attempt to offer up a droll look into my silly and well-used mind. By that—I mean that it's got quite a few miles on it. If it were a car I'd have traded it in a long time ago. It is quite likely that many of these subjects will have been embraced before. So be it. All writing is plagiarism of a fashion. There are only so many words jogging around in our brains, and each of them has been employed innumerable times over the eons. That also applies to most phrases, metaphors, and even ideologies. It would be naive of a writer to believe that his or her every thought was cosmically new and completely original. Since approximately 27,943,782,642,003 people have been on the planet before me, it's a bit presumptuous to think one might have a previously unused thought.

All a writer can ever be is everything they have read and learned, pieced together into combinations of what they remember or imagine. Therefore, the various essays, commentary, and assorted illogicality herein represent what I know—would like to know—or think I know.

Believing a book's title to be a pithy glimpse into the abyss of its author's psyche, I judiciously searched for an appropriate designation, generically establishing the working designation of simply *Nonfiction*. I naively considered utilizing that for the final manuscript but discovered it'd already been claimed every which way. I envisioned using the name of one of the essays considering both *My Thing* or *Unfunking*. They didn't quite zing.

By way of baring my soul a bit, I confess that each of the following sort-of-appropriate descriptive phrases was also contemplated: *Rages and Rationalizations, Gnomic Persiflage, Dreams and Dribbles, Brain Boogers, Consternations and Contemplations, Delights and Discomfits, Acerbic Assignations, Chunks of my Mind, Morsels of Me, Shards and Fragments of a Mind Under Matter* or *Confusions and Delusions*. None fundamentally worked.

In a moment of marketing brilliance, I thought of *Worth Every Penny*. But then, in a separate but similar moment of introspection, it dawned on me that the gist of the book was often inordinately bodacious and its bent was atrociously boastful. So, I briefly considered *Bodacious and Boastful*. About then is when a perfect name smacked me in the brain like I'd been whacked in the gourd with a hyped-up-thesaurus on steroids. I stumbled on an ideal defining title. Because this book is without a doubt *Vaingloriously Pedantic*.

I put that admittedly eccentric title on the shelf and let it seep and stew whilst I reflected. I gave it the taste test, and the weight test, and allowed my mind to rest. I drug my feet, pondered it a bit, slept on it, kicked it around, and bounced it off the wall. I ran it up and down the mental flagpole and unsuccessfully attempted to give it the Rorschach Ink Blot test. I let it dangle in the breeze, and played the waiting game. I contemplated, ruminated, meditated, cogitated, and ideated as I procrastinated. I mulled until my muse was sore, but it didn't quite soar.

Then one day my better half was playfully chiding me for something I'd neglected to do. Thinking quickly, I withdrew my rapier wit to excuse away my irresponsibility saying the first thing that sprang to mind: "*You forgot to remind me—so it's your fault*." "Why don't you write a book about it" she quipped back. I think I may already have thought, and decided that would my absolute final title.

But then, as might be expected, some editorial feet-dragging occurred and one-day Peetie inquired if I was ever going to put it to bed. I replied that I was about done, but it just needed *A Few Finishing Touches.* Hey! That sort of even sounds title-ish itself. I set it in print to see how it looked. Hmmm? Not bad.

I leaned it up against a mind post while enjoying a respite to see what the morrow would bring. But in the morrow, it didn't quite take wing. Back to the mental blackboard and tapping into the same vein I came up with *Soon.* A procrastinatory word? Ehhh... guess not. How about *Pretty Soon, Not Too Long* or *I'm Working On It?* After a while they all sunk like badly skipped flat rocks sinking into a dark deep quarry. So I deduced and reckoned and got struck by *Not Much Longer* or *Deal With It.* Try as I may, I just couldn't deal with it. *Ain't It Ridiculou*s? Time passed as titles flicked across my mind like Keystone Cops in an old silent movie. In a "Eureka!" moment *It's Finally Finished* jumped in and hijacked my plane.

But it wasn't over and over time that too fell *By the Wayside.* As I lay gasping for air like a guppy out of water one wee-hour eve I had a sudden burst of enthusiasm when *Breaking Wind* set. It quickly passed and every fish in the sea of titles swam around on my computer screen like the aquarium screen saver I'd recently deep-sixed. It became time to sink or swim. I let it sink in and went down for the third time, while flailing for a lifesaver, in great desperation I reached out and snagged a floating thought which was: *Them's The Breaks*! After a while, that began to smell like an extinguished fish laying out in the sun too long.

I just couldn't nail it to the wall. The title was an elusive ghost that danced through the dim corridors of my cerebral cortex. I deferred, shelved, and delayed until all editing had been done and the manuscript was so sleepy it had to be put to bed. But alas... none of the titles sold my soul. I needed absolution badly and so I asked myself the one question many authors daren't ask themselves. Exactly what the heck was this book? I considered and meekly responded: "Well, it's a... er... er... this is *My Great Book.*

I revealed my momentous decision to my muse, who straightforwardly accused me of being audacious. I slunk away and thunk, admitting to myself that it was indeed a tad impudent. *I Just Couldn't Do It.* About then, *Mental Dysmorphia* sailed across my imagination like a wildly wiggling gigantic

Chinese dragon at a kite-flying contest. But soon it crashed and burned, a shot-down flaming Kamikaze kite. It was simply too self-deprecating. What I needed was something that sizzled. Something that would grab the casual eye and strangle it—something extremely catchy like **Super Hot Sex!**

"What do you mean it's not fair," I said. "It would make people curious and want to read it. At the end of the book, I could simply say that I lied about the super hot sex. That would be clever."

"It has to have some correlation to what is in the book" my driving force replied.

"Oh!" Responded to my meek conscience. I deeply mulled. "How about **A Blissful Dream Like State**? That's mellow enough, isn't it?"

"You truly are in your little world, aren't you?"

Conquered and crushed, I shrugged my shoulders in exasperation and palms-up desperation, surrendered—meekly retorting: **"What?"**

My influencer smiled. "That's the story of your life, isn't it?"

"Why not" my guiding star stated. Seems good to me my conscience concurred. I think it has significance my wireless keyboard commented. Looks fine on my hard drive my computer indicated. Prints up nicely too my LaserJet joshed. Short, sweet, and to the point, which is, that there is no point. My wits-end wept when I discovered that the Oxford English Dictionary dedicated five pages and about 15,000 words to the word "what." I was sold.

I couldn't fight all those forces. So **"What?"** was it. It consists of **Boggles, Rants, Musings,** and Maxsims—ergo with some witty anagrammatic use of my name: **Macksims.** So that is briefly how it became: **What? - Boggles, Rants, Musings, and Macksims.**

It was enjoyable to write and I hope you find it amusing or at least moderately evocative. I strove to make it good bathroom reading material, but feel free to pore any place you like. While these writings may tender no great revelations, there is some semi-soul surfing and a few of my mini-epiphanies. I candidly discuss and examine weird personal experiences, observations of bizarre things, little glitches of odd human behavior, or perhaps mistakes of a life that have scrolled across the vast field of my personal I-Macks vision on this unique little carbon-based planet. Pleasant perusing.

Mack

MY THING

It seems as if everyone has a "Thing" nowadays. You know, some essential enterprise that they make their own. I must admit that for most of my life I was "Thingless." It's not like I didn't have any serious interests or hobbies. I've had some terrific jobs that I took lots of pride in, including my Naval career. But they were jobs—not a Thing. I've always been a compulsive reader and sort of a fanatical movie-savant, having dedicated much of my life to relishing practically every film ever made. I can count on no fingers for all the Lakers games I've missed in the last thirty years. I've also invested tons of time in creative writing and I have seldom missed my daily bike ride for the last twenty years.

But I never actually had a successful "Thing." Not that I didn't want one. I always wanted to do something remarkable—something so unusual or challenging that I could be proud of the deed. This is about my achievement and finding my "Thing." I don't mean to boast like the fellow from Texas that I am, but I can't help it and after I reveal my particular accomplishment, I cordially invite anyone who wishes to duplicate it to feel free to do so.

So what is this "Thing" that I have mastered that I am so proud of? It all began quite innocently, turned into a modest hobby, grew into a total commitment, and eventually became such an obsession that it has now become my "Thing"— which I do by force of habit. It is now such a part of me, it helps me be who I am.

I know—you must be wondering what in the Sam Hill I am talking about. I beg your patience as I try to explain. I suppose I could blame it on love because that's kind of how it all began. It started a couple of decades ago when I began buying love cards for my darling—that is romantic greeting cards or cards with some sort of inspirational message, all to impress my Peetie—at that time my recently acquired significant other. It wasn't my first dance—but I quickly discerned that it would be my best.

At first, it was easy. Every morning, along with coffee, I'd present her with another card. Each of them brought a smile to her face, and I am an absolute sucker for smiles. I'd walk a mile to get a smile any day—especially from her. I loved pleasing her. But alas, after a couple of months, there were no more cards available in the card shops. I'd used them all up. Panic started to develop. What could I do to replace that moment of pleasure I'd been giving her daily?

The light bulb of inspiration flicked on. I'd create a few cards myself—just to keep the good vibes going. I mean, how hard could it be? I'd always been sort of a handy dude with words, and, although I'd never seriously undertaken any great art projects, I did like doodling and had generally stayed within the lines when coloring.

I had always been a sort of night owl, doing my best work late at night. Initially, I took it easy. You know—some hearts and a few flowers—with a sentimental thought of some kind of hastily sketched out in my office on a piece of blank paper after she had retired for the night. It worked. The morning smiles kept coming.

Bit by bit, my little sketches began to resemble actual cards as one might see in a store. The hobby began to take shape as I slowly began to accumulate some actual card stock, along with plenty of watercolors, a wide variety of colored pencils, artists' brushes, acrylic paints, felt tip pens in all colors and sizes, and all the various tools of the trade needed to create handmade greeting cards.

The story gets a little unbelievable here. I began buying art books, or checking them out from the library and doing more and more difficult creations. It didn't take me long to become a fanatic.

Within a few months, I was obsessively working the wee hours, often for several hours on each card. I utilized every possible media except oil paints, which took far too long to dry to be practicable for such purposes. I began experimenting with color washes to create instant backgrounds. I learned how to mix colors and paint pine trees in one stroke with a certain brush. I mastered countless artistic tricks to speed up my work while constantly striving to make it look better. I developed many different speed-painting techniques, which allowed me to swiftly create a small 8 X 10 or 8 X 13 original illustration or painting on card stock every night.

By the time I had done about a hundred paintings, I began writing a poem to go with each one in a theme to the subject of the art. The artwork served as my muse. I'd never written poetry before, but it seemed to come together. The poems flowed into my head like God had created me just for that purpose.

I did paintings using every kind of artistic technique I discovered. I tried it all. There were paintings of nature scenes, flowers, animals, monuments, and people. I think I took a stab at my version of just about every painting the famous masters ever made regardless of whether it was impressionistic, modern, cubist, or a cartoon. Each card was a small painting that some folks thought to be worthy of framing, but I faithfully folded it and added the rhyme and usually another smaller illustration of a similar vein on the opposite side. I used watercolors, pens, ink, charcoals, magic markers, felt-tipped pens, acrylic, crayon, colored pencils, and whatever other media I could devise to create the cards.

Night after night, rain or shine, in sickness and in good health (thank goodness I was seldom ever ill), at home or on vacation, without fail, for over ten years—I painted and created a nightly "morning card" with an accompanying poem for my Peetie.

Then, unfortunately, thanks to Father Time, old uncle arthritis began to kick in and my right (painting) wrist began to ache from all those hours of brush strokes. I realized the end of my obsessive artistic creations was approaching. Then, just as I was beginning to think fate was going to end my card-creating compulsion, I got my first digital camera. Problem solved.

I thus began taking pictures and writing my usual 16-line poem. By the way, all of my poems rhyme and have some metaphorical or cogent message—like this:

On my cards, all poems must rhyme
Each one and every time
And there has to be a sort of meter
No other lover has done it neater
It is the way that I persist
Absent it, I feel I've missed
I do it now with innate ease
For the one, I need to please
And so this challenge I fulfill
I do it thusly and always will
Because I make no compromise

My rhyme must shine in Peetie's eyes

I provide this example to illustrate a typical poem on my cards. Of course, the rhythm and spirit vary with each card. To my way of thinking any poem that doesn't rhyme is prose. I know technically I'm wrong on that point, but I'm stubborn. That's well over 100,000 lines or I'd immodestly estimate about a million words of poetry and still ticking. You might be thinking "how difficult could it be to create a small painting (actually it is two small paintings since there is one on both the front and the backside of each card) and write a meaningful (generally romantic or life-enhancing) sixteen-line rhyming poem every day. I suggest you try it for a few months. You might discover that without proper enthusiasm the paintings won't cut the mustard and that a good poem must flow from inspiration or it doesn't flow at all. If I appear to be too self-promoting and grandiose here, please forgive me and remember that it is ***my thing***!

Nowadays I continue creating Peetie's daily card, mostly with pictures I have taken and processed through my computer. Every once in a while I do the artwork, just to keep my heart in it. As I write this, she has over 8,000 and is still counting—a new one every day.

Each card has been presented to my darling, folded with a crease in it, regardless of the quality of the painting. They express the joy of our relationship and tell the story of our togetherness. They are singularly interesting and in total, a remarkable accomplishment, even if I do say so myself.

An interesting side aspect of these cards is that when I show more than a few of them to people they tend to become overwhelmed by the sheer volume. Most people simply cannot concentrate on many of them at a time. I have discovered that this is a reasonable reaction and that if I show someone only a small sampling they can comprehend and appreciate them much more than marveling at the insurmountable collection as a whole.

The cards have been unfolded and are currently maintained with protective covers in binders that are kept in a display case in my home. They have been scanned, organized, and cataloged on my computer. They are the "world's largest collection of original handmade greeting cards". If you would like to see a small sampling of some of my card art, poetry, and photographs you are invited to visit my website at "mackmahoney.com" and check them out for yourself. There are some pictures of the cards and more information. On the website, you will be able to print your free cards or send free E-cards with only a few clicks. There are no membership fees, login requirements, or passwords needed.

And now that you know, I invite any of you romanticists and would-be gallants out there to feel free to go ahead and duplicate my "Thing" if you feel the urge. Just remember that I've had a 23-year head start on you and I am still turning out a card a day for my Peetie.

I'VE GOT WORDS FOR YOU

I decided to write the essays and other text herein about whatever happens to strike my mood. No problem—I thought; I've got about 600,000 English words to work with. But, according to language exerts only 43 of them make up about half of everything we say. What's even worse is that only nine of them go into a quarter of everything we say. In case you are not familiar, those nine are: and, be, have, it, of, the, to, will, and you. In my case, I'd no doubt have to include "I" and "me", being the narcissistic individual that I am. I don't have much trouble with any of those words.

So what the heck—I figure I might as well put my two cents in. All I'll have to do is crank out a few of those 600,000 thousand words in such a way as to make them interesting to readers. Therefore I'm giving it a shot, even if this complicated communication system we English-speaking humans have devised confuses me at times.

I'm not thinking about oversized words like that 28-letter long one that many of us faithfully memorized, learned to spell, and still remember from our childhood: "antidisestablishmentarianism." It means, of course, a doctrine against the dissolution of the establishment. Later on, thanks to that very famous song, children learned supercalifragilisticexpialidocious, which is some 34-letters long. But that's an old hat. Today's kids are wizards. They're into such monsters as that miner's lung disease caused by the inhalation of silicate or quartz dust, which happens to be 45-letters long: pneumonoultramicroscopicsilicovolcanokoniosis. But that's zilch for the true brainiacs nowadays. There is a chemical compound that when spelled out completely is 1,193 letters long. I'll pass on taking up a page to spell it out for you if you'll take my word that there is such a word.

However, complicated elocution isn't my consternation. My concerns are about the smaller words that "I," pronounced as in <u>eye</u>, tend to trip over on the keyboard. To be honest, many things about English just don't make sense. Stuff like "i" before "e" except after "y." Why? Or how about "a" is pronounced "ah" as in <u>awful</u>, except when it's pronounced "ay as in the <u>day</u>, and "k" is pronounced as "kay" as in <u>okay</u> except when it's silent as in <u>knew</u> in which case it's pronounced like an "n" as in <u>nutty</u>. How come if we change

15

the first letter of "cough," which is pronounced like "off" with an r to make it "rough" it's pronounced like "buff" instead of like "golf" with an "olf." How come "thorough" isn't spelled like "burro" and is pronounced like "bureau"?

How can "peace," "piece" and "peas" sound so similar and be so different? While I'm p'n around what's up with all those silent p's, like the "p" in pneumonia, and the "p" in pseudo? It's messing with my psyche and I think whoever thought it up was psycho, which ought to be spelled "syce" and "syco." What's up with all the dual usage words with completely dissimilar meanings such as "saw" as in "he saw me coming" and "hand me that saw"? Couldn't anyone ever come up with another word, so we just started reusing them? And how can the past tense for one "saw" be "seen" and the other "sawed."

If the 9th letter of the alphabet can be a personal pronoun as in: "I am confused", why can't the 25th letter of the alphabet "Y" ask the question why? Y Not I say? And if the letter "A" can be a word that refers to anything, how come the letter "O" can't mean "oh"? And how come I can't write "How R U?" and save myself 4 letters?

I'm supposed to be a writer and therefore I write, but how come my fingers don't "fing" when they tap the keyboard. Sometimes the rules just go against my instincts. Speaking of which, have you ever wondered why there aren't any "outstincts"? I don't think I have a slim chance, or is it a fat chance, of learning why our language is full of so many paradoxes.

For example: here's a small poem to consider:
If the plural of tooth is teeth
And the plural of goose is geese
How come the plural of booth ain't beeth
And the plural of moose ain't meese

See what I mean? And while I'm at it, what's with "flammable" and "inflammable"? Which is which? And what's the difference between Emigrate and Immigrate? Our language bulges with superfluous stupidity and repetitive resemblance. Imagine some deranged troop inspector saying, "I compliment your fine complement for their concomitant contingent continuity" and the droll reply "our facultative faculty is factually facilitated throughout our entire facility with no factious factions."

How come if you get a tear in your shirt, you spell it the same way as a tear in your eye, but if you fear something it's not spelled the same way as when you go to the fair? Does anybody know, or even care? Exactly when does an oral agreement become a verbal agreement? Are you disinterested in such matters or merely uninterested? Is what I am alluding to eluding you?

How can you "fill out" a form while "filling it in"? And can somebody just explain to me why is there no ham in a hamburger, or egg in an eggplant? If those words are not sufficiently misleading, how come there isn't any pine or apple in a pineapple? Why is it that quicksand is slow working and you can make amends but not one amend? Why must we park on driveways and drive on parkways? How come actors are "in" movies and "on" TV? How come our bottom is in the middle of our bodies? Why do doctors go into "practice" instead of "doctorating"? How come "abbreviation" is such a long word and "all" is so short? One little letter can make all the difference—like if you take an "o" out of good you get God and if you take that same "o" out of hello you get Hell. Confusion abounds.

How come greyhounds aren't always gray? Did you know ladybugs and fireflies are beetles? You do realize of course that very few people still actually "dial" telephone numbers. We conceive a conception and receive it at reception. Could we grieve at a "greption" and believe a "beleption"? How come computers compute, generators generate, and typewriters type, but pistons don't...well...you know? And how come when we send something by truck it is "shipped" and when we send something by ship it is "cargo"? Why are there no English words that rhyme with the colors orange, silver, or purple?

I've always been in the dark when it comes to the "nyms." Those homonyms, acronyms, antonyms, autonyms, eponyms, and tautonyms cause my brain to spinonym.

I remember as a small child using the word "ain't" and being told by my Dad that I shouldn't use that word. When I asked him why not, he replied, "I don't rightly know but thar' tain't no such word as ain't and ya' jus' cain't!"

How can we have "feet that smell" and "noses that run"? Why is it called a hot-water heater and not a cold-water heater? If "night falls" why does "daybreak"? How can "overlook" and "oversee" be different, while "quite a few" and "quite a lot" mean pretty much the same? And what's the story on the temperature in hell? If it's "hot as hell" in July how can it be "cold as hell" in January? How come bookkeepers do accounting and librarians keep books? How come "raze" is the opposite of "raise" and "reckless" is the opposite of "wreckless"? Those (Fr.) words are the worst. Whoever lets "l-e-t" become pronounced, "lay" as in ballet, which causes things like "lot" to be pronounced "lut" as in ballot?

Yes indeed. It is a convoluted language I fracture and it's not getting any easier. Who can remember that a "bigmouth" gossips and a "big mouth" is somebody with a large opening beneath their nose? Perhaps you'll remember a time when you lay prostrate when they checked your prostate. I sure do. How can a "lead" horse be spelled exactly like the "lead" that is a heavy bluish metal? Can you imagine saying "there is no sense in scents made for cents since their essence dissents?"

Thank goodness I'm not alone in this dilemma, or do you prefer dilemmas? And it's a fact that many kids graduating from high school get all glassy-eyed trying to decide between "there" "their" and "they're," or "where" "ware" "were" or "wear," much less the trickier stuff like a marquee, marquis, and marquise.

You may know that "enervate" means to deprive of vigor while "innervate" means to stimulate an organ, or that a "pistol" is a small firearm while a "pistil" is that part of a plant that produces seeds. Perhaps you even know that "minks" are weasel-like animals while a "minx" is a flirtatious young woman. Did some no-account French count make a mistake in pronouncing "faux pas" as "fo pa" which means mistake?

Frankly, our language paradigms stultify me. Ubiquitously lurking innovations such as mnemonic, ptomaine, and xylophone lay buried in our dictionaries creating literary minefields of befuddlement. Our multi-cultured society is replete with a veritable cacophony of multifarious dissimilarities wherein a vast texture of complicated solecistic communication choices are infused, sufficient to perplex any individual not inherently familiar with that explicit terminology. Like that last sentence. Who the heck knows what that means—or even cares for that matter?

But any Blackberry-toting Tweeting, Texting IM-ing cyber-surfing dude will understand the following blog. "An ex-dot-commer working a McJob was listening to some radical headbangers while laying out the last of his dead presidents for a longneck and Frankenfood." In case you missed the cyber train a "headbanger" is a hard rock musician or a fan thereof. A "McJob" is a low-paying dead-end work." Dead presidents" means paper currency and "Frankenfood" is a genetically engineered chow. If you don't know what a "longneck" is, you have led a too-sheltered life and need to upload a new profile. OMG, LOL, and wOOt!

Along those same lines, any enlightened child of the rap—or street-wise homey—will understand a phrase like "I be axing my baby daddy don't dis my bro in the hood get capped." They'll catch that drift right away. Word up. It's all good!

Yes, it's an acute world we write about. Right? And yet, today's youth seem to be able to smack all the curves and cover all the bases with seven simple words that cover all the basis: "Like—whatever—you know what I'm saying." (sic) i.e., etc., and ad Infinitum.

I conjecture that I'm not fully combobulated and peccable—English-wise. In matters of proper language, I am a world-class incompetent. I'm destiny doomed to be a gruntled writer who will end up in an asylum for the Englishly challenged. I don't want to get roily—but I might as well face it. I'm just never going to be a cunning linguist.

TWELVE PEOPLE, YOU WON'T MEET IN HEAVEN

With apologies to Mitch Albom, here are a dirty dozen types you probably won't meet in Heaven. They may not be whom you might suspect. They are not like those easily identifiable bad guys in western movies that always wore black hats. They are instead, chameleon-like predators who live among us pretending to be upstanding pillars of the community, while in actuality they are captives of their egos, bottom feeders who gorge on the generosity of decent people. You will find them on podiums, in front of cameras; in places, there is an opinion to be rendered or a harmful thought to be had. They are especially good at sniffing out weaknesses and money. They like to utilize the first to acquire the latter.

1. <u>Smarmy Politician Types</u>. You know, those fiscally irresponsible gerrymandering charlatans who have probably never earned an honest day's wages in their life, but want you to give them plenty of your money and allow them unlimited abuse of power. They are practitioners of demagoguery, flapping their pompous bureaucratic gums about the mismanagement and incompetence of others while complaining about all the inefficiency and government waste. But, they'll quickly offer copious reasons they need your support for their dim-witted pet project(s). With sheer arrogance, they also sincerely feel that term limits are unreasonable and inappropriate for elected officials such as themselves. They come in many forms and political party affiliations, and like vampires, once they have tasted taxpayer blood they can't get enough of it. They are the masters of sophistic oration and bamboozlers of the masses. They always have some new proposal or plan that will make things better if they can only get the proper support and backing needed to implement it. They've been around since the first village and like cockroaches, will be the last ones to disappear if civilization ever vanishes, which, by the way, would more than likely, be their fault.

2. <u>Religious Opportunists</u>. These effete hucksters make their living by preying on those who pray, amassing their fortune from the gullibility of the vulnerable and meager-minded—offering promises of salvation and spiritual rewards for regular tithing of hard-earned money. They hire puppet boards

of family and friends to redirect ministry funds to personal projects. They are the ones who claim to speak *for* God, (*who insist that they have lots of money to maintain their own lifestyle at the very high standard they purportedly think God desires it to be*) without feeling the need to do any accounting for the millions they amass. I'm talking about the big-money TV evangelists or media ministries, the fundraising conglomerates who operate as non-profit ministries, but never seem to be able to feed enough starving orphans, build enough missions, or save enough sinful souls—the holier-than-thou faith healers who never actually heal anyone, and all the other mendacious hood-winkers who palliate their own insatiably ambitious capitalistic goals under the name of God. God has personally told me that he has a special Hell for their ilk.

3. <u>Creepy Cultists</u>. Another even more conceited snake-oil-selling impostor is the bizarre cult originator who dreams up demented ways to control anyone distrait enough to buy their ersatz brand of baloney. These self-anointed panjandrums will seize control of your brain and never let go if you allow them access. They will employ any obscure obtuse theocratic doctrine or whacko quasi-religion to harvest a following. If you fall prey to one of these types, you'll be lucky if you don't end up participating in a group suicide, or worse. Be exceedingly wary of delusional soul-saving deceivers probing for dithering believers. As Judge Judy often says, "*if it sounds too good to be true, it is probably a lie.*"

4. <u>Whacko Celebrity Elitists</u>. I'm referring to the loathsome licentious limo-lounging Learjet-leasing loopy loudmouth limp-brained lunatics with multiple homes in places like Brentwood, Aspen, South Beach, The Hamptons, or overlooking Central Park. It gets my goat when these self-absorbed narcissistic intellectual posers use their auspiciously obtained popularity to push some ridiculous secularist agenda-driven ideology du jour, which, in egotistical vanity—they see as noble. These moneyed egomaniacs selfishly rip away at the core values and social fabric of society, all the while insisting that everyone else cut back while they stretch extravagance to its outer limits. They demand that we conserve energy as they fly around in private planes and covertly shelter their exotic automobiles in an eight-car garage while having personal assistants buy gas for their Hybrid, which is mostly used by their maid to fetch their dry cleaning, their cook to

shop for groceries, or some other staffer to run an errand. They live the good life never waiting in line to get into nightclubs or for a table in a restaurant. Their unscrupulous agents negotiate their unwarranted ridiculous salaries. Their unprincipled personal managers oversee their portfolio-enhancing investments. Their immoral doctors prescribe their recreational drugs. Their crooked accountant pays their extravagant bills, and their corrupt lawyers cover their smelly behinds when they misbehave. They are often egotistical actors who get lucky enough to score the role of some significant character and then just can't get over themselves as they begin to think that by osmosis they are experts on the occupation or have the intellect of that character. Then they go around like blithering quacks espousing their opinions on things that they know very little about—like war, politics, religion, or whatever the cause of au courant might be.

5.   <u>Environmental Extremists</u>.   These sloth-brained slug-saving tree-huggers see nothing wrong with causing no end of trouble on behalf of every supposedly endangered species, even if they are not endangered. They want to save the world from the large corporations and the wealthy capitalistic individuals that they think are greedy and amoral. They want global warming stopped at any cost, even if it turns out that it doesn't exist. They see oil, coal, or other natural resources as evil, and there must be no trail cuts or fire breaks permitted in national forests. The buried oil and wilderness areas are their private and personal playgrounds and no one is allowed access. Above all, there must be no nuclear power generated. The world must be powered by the wind and sun and of course hot air, which they spew out in abundance. If the sun ever implodes in some unpredicted catastrophe it will serve them right.

6. <u>Animal Rights Activists</u>. These pathetic jerks will happily vandalize a scientific laboratory and cause countless damage to theoretically save some rats that are only alive because they were bred for the express purpose of being participants in important life-saving medical research. The amazing thing is—these boobs just may believe that those lab rats are more important than human beings. They want equal rights for all animals at any cost. They will quickly burn down a building to save any endangered creature and you had better not be inside it. I say let's humor the fools and put them in charge of distributing free condoms for all animals.

7. <u>Extreme Right to Lifers</u>. I'm not talking about the good upstanding citizens who take a firm stand against abortion. I'm referring to the whacked-out nut cases that proclaim that all abortions are murder and they, therefore, feel justified in murdering a physician who performs abortions to put him out of business. These are seriously psychotic dudes— arguably as sick as those who utilize abortion for birth control. If they develop a grudge against you they will keep it for as long as it takes to get their revenge. They can and will strike without warning and are known to be able to hide out in the wilderness indefinitely. So whatever you do, don't jerk their chain.

8. <u>Opportunistic Race-baiting Sharks</u>. These scavengers quickly rise out of the scum to rip away the flesh from the soft underbelly of anyone floating unsuspectingly on the surface of civilization. They are the kind that takes advantage of any quagmire wherein it appears they can gain some media exposure by crying foul. You know who they are. They are the first ones to arrive at the scene of any catastrophe—the first to point fingers and speak out in criticism of everybody else and the last ones to get their own house in order. They are normally the salaried head of some sort of bizarre organization. The physiognomy of their shrill mouths generally reveals spewing venom. These poseurs talk about brotherly love while disgorging vile invectives against anyone brave enough to call them out for their bigotry and vitriolic hatred. And oh yeah, they are generally dumb as a rock.

9. <u>Charity Leeches</u>. These unscrupulous chiselers collect filthy lucre for non-existent charities from unsuspecting good-intentioned folks and keep the vast majority of everything they accrue to stoke their bloated bank accounts. These parasites often spin nasty spiderwebs of deceit with their heart-wrenching stories with a facade of being concerned and charitable citizens. They stink up the shadows they skulk in while conducting their unscrupulous fly-by-night scams out of dingy boiler rooms, in the pretense of representing some ethical-sounding cause as they pay themselves exorbitantly inflated salaries to sit as the honcho of their fake foundations. If I could, I'd cast a pox on them all.

10. <u>Internet Spammers and Junk Fax Scammers</u>. These are the unseen inconsiderate scumbags who hide in the Internet Netherlands while inundating us with useless stock tips and offers of worthless penis enhancement pills by junk fax, using up our paper and telephone time, or

those other inconsiderate creeps who fill up our computer memories with all sorts of valueless and highly irritating spam. We can only hope that when they get to Hades they will be assigned the job of being the Devil's shredder and that they will have to do it all by mouth. And while I'm at it, some of you serial E-mail "joke" forwarders aren't far behind them

11. <u>Internet Sexual Predators</u>. These overly lascivious cretins haven't got the nerve to stalk the parks and playgrounds anymore, so they prowl the Internet (no doubt thinking they are invisible) searching for innocent children or other naive fools to seduce with their lying spiels. More and more of them are being exposed these days. We can only hope they get a sadistic cellmate. Monitor your children's computer usage folks, and know what the heck is going on in their ether world.

12. <u>Slithering Snakes of the Legal Profession</u>. They are the despicable ambulance chasers and other low-life snakes portending to be looking out for us as they slither around within the gray areas of the law filing fake personal injury claims, fraudulent medical malpractice suits, unjustified worker's compensation actions, and ridiculous class action cases that penalize us all, while they get rich. They vigorously fight every type of tort reform while overcrowding our courts and preventing legitimate cases from being heard. They make a mockery of our legal system by utilizing every possible advertising media to beg for every possible kind of lawsuit. The seemingly unaware media earns a fortune from their predatory advertising while they make a fortune from those with the misfortune of being the quarry they unjustly attack. The law should not be used to make greedy unscrupulous lawyers wealthy and fat.

While I'm ranting, as a footnote hereto, some choice *also-rans* would be: identity stealers, crooked contractors, dishonest auto and appliance repairmen, predatory tow truck drivers, rapists, pimps, muggers, arsonists, petty burglars and robbers, habitual drunk drivers, and criminal junkies. The *dishonorable mentions* would be bribe-taking judges and their bribers, welfare queens, crooked boiler room operators, professional burglars and shoplifters, drug smugglers, and mobsters. The *too-evil-to-even-discuss* category consists of murderers, child molesters, late-term abortionists, rapists, and kidnappers. The *way-beyond-evil* group encompasses terrorists, warlords, genocidal dictators, evil kings and sadistic rulers, serial killers, hitmen, and crime syndicate bosses.

I think the eternal bottomless pit will be full of these types. To point them in the right direction, they should all be buried head down in a barrel of their slimy gall. One should use all of their intelligence and abilities to avoid dealing with any of them whenever possible. They have few scruples, little dignity, a minimum of ethics, and practically no morality.

I'm glad I got that off my chest. Who do you hate today?

P.S. - If you are one of these types, please ignore the foregoing, as I am sure you are quite the exception.

OLD CODGER-HOOD

If you consider yourself to be an impatient youth and happen to be reading this, you may opt to go on to the next section, unless you think that one day you just might grow old yourself. It could happen. That warning given, I'm here to tell you that we so-called "old dudes" must find pleasure where we can, as we staunchly embrace—make that seize—the cantankerous portion of our lives. I'm referring of course to the onset of the seasoned citizenry.

I don't know about you, but I am enjoying my old codgerhood immensely. And why not? I earned it, and I intend to fully capitalize on it. No! I'm not referring to obtaining membership in AARP. If you haven't received your invitation yet rest assured, they'll be soliciting you before you hit that half-century mark. Yep! Fifty is their magic number. I think they'd make it forty if they could, but they don't want to be quite that obvious.

Nor am I thinking about those swell Senior Citizen Discounts that are available—though they can be quite fortuitous and anyone over 40 can get them. Perhaps I ought to digress briefly to explain one fact of life that may have thus far eluded you. Any young cashier person and they almost all are, seemingly has no ability whatsoever to judge the age of anyone over forty. Therefore, if you see a Senior Citizen Discount offered and you've got the puissance to ask for it, you'll probably get it—not that I can officially recommend it, of course, seeing how I am so upstanding.

If by some slight chance, they should ask to see your ID and believe me this is about the same odds as winning all the quenelles at the track for the entire next racing season, then I suggest you merely adopt the tried and true formula of fumbledom. Simply begin to browse through the myriad cards in your wallet, (a slight hand-tremor helps) one by one, squinting myopically at them as if you were on your last eyesight legs. Don't quit until that brash youngster who dared question your senior citizen rights, surrenders and says those magic words which are: "Okay. Never mind."

If that technique doesn't work then you have probably slipped into some parallel universe where things don't run right. In this case, an unscrupulous individual might consider a phony Elder ID Card. I've heard tell that they can be obtained for ten bucks on almost any street corner of a major city.

Returning to the subject at hand. For a long time now, I've been having sports with young dudes wearing their baseball caps turned backward. All you have to do to get in on this great fun is learning to maintain a completely straight-faced deadpan look when you approach them. Look them square in the eye and inquire, without flinching and in your best old coot voice: "Skuze me, sonny, I've been looking for one of them backward baseball caps—like you're wearing—for my grandson. Can you tell me where they sell them?"

Just remain silent, allowing your question to mellow and sink in. It may take a while for their toxic substance-addled brain to kick in, but eventually, they will answer you in such a way as to fully demonstrate their utter and complete naiveté. I've had a few of them glare at me like I was batty. But most of them will scratch their head or elsewhere, realize you are putting them on, and stalk off in a huff. Either way, it's fun. If their primary mode of transportation is a skateboard you can also remind them that their "pants are way too big." Inquire if "their pants are a hand-me-down from an older brother?" Then if you want to jerk their fragile emotional chain you can slam-dunk them with the following comment as they are leaving. "Hey! Do you know your crack is showing?"

I feel I must caution you though; to refrain from this sporting activity with any extremely tattooed shaved-headed baggy-short-pants-wearing (possible gang bangers) or other young studs that appear to have been regularly imbibing in steroid cocktails. If they cop an attitude—immediately desist and move on, preferably with a stoop and a limp.

Other fun activities can be experienced in your automobile. Instead of allowing your blood pressure to surge into full-blown road rage, whenever you encounter an unexpected finger-flipping situation while driving, do as I do and shift into geezers. That's right. Slow down to approximately one mile under the speed limit and steer with both hands, while staring vacantly straight ahead. You can sneak a peek at the problem dork and I guarantee—they'll be fuming and spitting fire like an angry dragon of yore.

Rest assured. If you are feeling cantankerous and want to throw another log on the fire, just flick your turn signal on and stay in the same lane. Nothing gets to them like a well-weathered citizen chugging their way down the road blinking. That impatient hyperactive cretin will quickly blast on past, violently stabbing their middle finger in the on-rushing air of their just-opened window, which is scattering around the debris inside their car as it blows the cobwebs out of their mind. But of course, you won't see it. You're in geezer gear.

I will admit there is an extremely slight possibility these days that some lunatic will pull out a rod and cap you, but what the hey, thrills don't come cheap in today's fast-paced society. Whatever you do, don't ever make eye contact with the other driver. If they pull alongside and proceed to glare at you, drooling is recommended. They'll quickly become bored; decide you are just a harmless old fogy and race off to find a more capable foe. Try to refrain from convulsively laughing as they speed away.

Are you getting the idea? Just allow yourself the pleasure of getting ornery. There are all sorts of possibilities. When it's a tie between you and some younger person at a public doorway, smile and say "thank you young person" as you lumber on through, fully aware that as the senior human being you've got rights.

Fumbling through a coin purse in long supermarket checkout lines can be a great jest. I suggest wearing dark sunglasses so you can surreptitiously observe the rolling eyeballs of the intolerant dunderheads behind you. If you want to send them into orbit, manage to drop a few coins and get down on all fours to search. Another delightful diversion is to feign a slow bowlegged crotchety gait in any public walkway such as in airports, bus stations, etc. Additional amusement will be had if you drag an extremely large rolling suitcase behind you. To maximize your merriment, you might opt to wield one with a faulty wheel, stuck so that it tends to dart about recklessly in your wake.

For a vicarious thrill, I sometimes fill out those fifty-cent rebate coupons and spend forty-three cents (it'll probably be more by the time this is published) for the cost of a stamp, plus an envelope to send for them. Imagine how it will tick that company off when someone cuts out the UPC, has an original check register receipt, fills out their inane form, and sends in for his or her ridiculous fifty-cent rebate. At which time, they too have to use a forty-three-cent stamp and write out a check to send it to you.

Such mirthful opportunities abound practically everywhere if you care to seek them out. It will help to elicit repugnance and raised eyebrows of the impatient young if you sprinkle your conversation with some old timely cuss words like "tarnation", "goldang" and "darn tootin".

The main thing is—to dazzle them with your dawdling. Hellfires, you're in no hurry. You got where you are by sheer luck and the good graces of God. Therefore, nothing should provoke an unhurried, mature, sanguine old fool during their bumbling.

Another thing—our ranks are growing. We're living longer and better than any generation ever has. We're the demographic of the future. They've started to take notice of the fact that we've got the votes, the experience, and the chutzpah to go along with it. Let us all vow to maximize our mirth. We're in no hurry and we've got rights.

We're no longer content to sit in rocking chairs and wait for that man in the black robe. We're down at the spa on a treadmill and the over-forties club boogying our buns off on Saturday nights. We have hubris. We don't need orthopedic shoes or Geritol. We need entertainment, and it can be found in the haughtiness and effrontery of the youthful populace.

Lastly, don't stay home. The world is a big beautiful plum, just waiting to be plucked. Get out there and fiddle around. I think I might just go out myself today. I'm still looking for one of those backward baseball caps.

LET'S TALK ... SEX

The battle of the sexes is a long-standing struggle with very few clear victories. Men seem predisposed to promiscuity while most females tend to be somewhat picky about who they bed down with.

No one knows if Homo sapiens have always been faithful. One theory being floated around in the scientific community these days is that our ancient prime-evil (pun intended) ancestors were monogamous. Some scientists believe this to be true because they have been able to compare the size of bones and determined that primitive males were not much larger in stature than primitive females. Ergo—they deduced that early man was monogamous because in non-monogamous societies males are predominately larger than females.

One thing is for sure. We're not all exactly monogamous these days. Aside from all the playing around, there are some cultures where wives take on several husbands at once. In certain areas of Africa and Utah, the reverse is true. Many cultures that pretend to be monogamous have avuncular loopholes; a kid's parental authority is the mother's brother, purely because he's the nearest adult male who is known to be the child's blood relative

The animal kingdom is a virtual carnival of carnality. Begetting among creatures of nature is infinitely complex. There are millions of species of mammals, animals, birds, reptiles, fish, and insects on this planet. A little careful observation reveals that there is every conceivable arrangement in matters of propagation. The methods and processes are limitlessly varied—with factors like estrus, breeding seasons, etc. It's all downright beastly.

All kinds of creatures conduct courtship. Most people know that birds do all sorts of weird things to attract mates. But did you know that a fiddler crab waves his big brightly colored claw as he boogies for the lady of his choice? Many male spiders pour out their hearts and desires by dancing and pirouetting intricately. Have you ever observed a male scorpion take the female scorpion's little hands in his big ones and gently walk backward, pulling her to his chosen place for romance? Crayfish in love grunt a form of a serenade by rubbing their feelers against their beak while male lobsters snap their fingers when they're in the mood.

The animal world proves that males are not by nature monogamous. Take the Pupfish: an ugly little species who breed with frenzy. They live in a stream where the population fluctuates dramatically. When females are scarce, the males hunt down a mate and swim by her side in a faithful monogamous manner. When the population increases and there is a surplus of females, the males puff out their fins and stake out territory on the river bottom, performing little dances to attract the females who drop by to lay their eggs.

Females too have their eccentricities. Female elk are known to copulate with many different males on the same day. We all know what black widow spider ladies do to their male lovers after they've been satisfied. Perhaps you've also watched a female praying Mantis dine on her conjugal partner's head afterward.

Practically all primates are promiscuous. As anyone who has ever visited a zoo can testify—monkeys often copulate like... well, monkeys.

Do you think human beings have a monopoly on transsexualism? If so, you are wrong. Should the male shrimp population in an area grow scarce enough to threaten the survival of the species thereabouts, some of the females simply turn into males. A neat trick huh? Or how about the feat of the hyena where all little ones, regardless of their sex, sport a male penis until they mature at which time the females mysteriously manage to lose theirs. Conversely, all Sheepshead fish are born as females and in response to triggers we mammals do not understand, some of them turn into males.

Among thousands of bees, there is always only one Queen, who exists to produce progeny, most of which are females, with only a few developing into males. The Queen bee is the only female to mate and she does it in the air with many different males, in a very brief time during which, she acquires sufficient spermatozoa to produce all the progeny she will engender during her life. She can lay more than 200 eggs a day. From that time on, whether they are workers, babysitters, guards, or pollen gatherers, all the bees are there to serve their queen. They have no sex life at all. And you thought you had it bad.

The albatross, in addition to being the largest seabird with a wingspan of up to eleven feet, has a terrible sex life. They spend all their time at sea and come to land only to breed. They are kind of like sailors. Egrets, on the other hand, choose their nesting site and enjoy a lengthy four or five-day honeymoon period. They spend countless hours in intertwined ecstasy, cuddling their long supple necks together in a true "lovers knot".

The bull fur seals gather at their Alaska breeding grounds and wait for the cows, which have migrated three thousand miles just for their meet-and-greet time. After that swim, one can't blame those cows for only wanting to party down with the heartiest, biggest, and most popular bulls.

In reptiles and amphibians, all parenting is done on a catch-can basis. Some creatures are sexual catastrophes. The male octopus, for example, doesn't have a penis. Instead, he grasps his little packet of sperm in a tentacle and shoves it down the female's breathing siphon. Naturally, she responds by trying to tear him apart. Sometimes their mating ritual becomes so violent that the female rips the male's tentacle off his body after the sperm has been delivered. Lucky for him it grows back. No humans can do that trick.

Some creatures that are supposedly monogamous are not. Like swans, who most people think mate for life. Many other birds are prone to having affairs. Studies reveal that among songbirds, only one egg in three is sired by the nestmate. Sadly, birds can't file paternity suits or check DNA.

Both cowbirds and the clever cuckoo skip all the fuss and lay their eggs in the nest of other more domestic birds, leaving the involuntary host to rear their young. Unfortunately, the larger cuckoo and cowbird hatchlings will either starve, boot out of the nest, or just destroy any other hatchlings or eggs in the nest. Miraculously the hoodwinked foster parents never seem to notice and raise the ugly chicks, each of them probably thinking it comes from the other one's side of the family.

Opossums, or "possums" to you southerners, are prolific breeders. Thirteen days after the consummation of their marital vows, the female gives birth to as many as fifty-six young. There is a somewhat serious problem though since she only has thirteen nipples. Only those strong enough to latch on to one will survive.

Sex is a powerful attractant. The female emperor moth has a scent gland that disperses her aroma so males can find her from a distance of three miles away. Sex is also music to many lusty creatures' ears. Male crickets aren't singing for the fun of it. A female lingering nearby will keep him in tune and if she likes his song she will eat some ambrosia-like substance out of a cupcake gland just behind the joints of his wing. When she gets full—their nuptials take place.

Sex in the sea is often less than thrilling. The sex of sea urchins is indistinguishable, but miraculously both males and females reach their maturity simultaneously. When the magic moment arrives, the females liberate their secretions at the same time the males are setting their seaman semen free. Their primitive orgy elixir is married by the oscillation of ocean currents and fertilization occurs haphazardly. It was nice knowing you.

Talk about self-abuse. Starfish multiply by schizogenesis. That's a fancy word meaning they divide themselves into two halves, which will each subsequently reconstruct the other half to make two starfishes. That's tricky. And we all know what happens to salmon after they spawn. Eeech!

I guess the "king of reproduction" award would have to go to the plain old Cottontail Rabbit. They get the job done the good old-fashioned way... but they do it very often. For example, if a female's broods all lived and reproduced, after five years she would have established an empire of two and a half million bunnies. And that's a lot of furs.

SECRETS

We both know you have secrets you are concealing that you will never share. Don't be embarrassed. We all do. You know what I'm talking about—those evil little thoughts that sneak into your mind or those things you do when you are alone—those moral ambiguities and strange proclivities known to be possessed by homo sapiens.

You need not worry. I'm not going to delve into the worst of your offenses. We'll just tiptoe around a few of the rough edges. We'll gaze into our crystal ball at some trifling things you routinely do that tickle your conscience. Don't deny it. You do have some fault lines and we both know they are real. It's no big deal. After all, you are only human. So don't feel guilty. We humans have flaws.

Perhaps God built them into us for his amusement. Or maybe it is malfunctioning DNA. Who knows? Who cares? They are there and we really can't do anything about them. Willpower and moral turpitude are horses that can only be ridden so far. They simply can't be relied on to carry us safely across the burning deserts of life without us receiving an occasional sunburn. That's why the dark was made. Practically everyone has some use for a little dab of evil now and then.

I'm not referring to prison-worthy offenses here, although if I'm telepathically reading your mind correctly, in your case I might be willing to make an exception. I have a good idea of what may be slithering around in those deep dark corridors of your cranium. But we'll pass on that, and discuss those not-too-awful but not-completely-innocent offenses you have committed against your fellow men and/or in some cases various other life forms.

These are simply not things one would be willing to discuss with a priest in the confessional, much less with an interrogator from the DA's office. Now don't get all huffy and defensive and become offended by my assertions. Remember—I'm not insensately holding it against you.

But let me tell you, according to various laws, restrictions, covenants, commandments, edicts, rules, policies, regulations, bylaws, contracts, clauses, and a thousand other assorted methods we use to control one another, you have committed some impulsive infractions not to mention the unmentionable misdemeanors, misdeeds, violations, breaches, scandals, scams and swindles, as well as countless wrongdoings and disobedience.

You have been some busy dudes and dudettes, especially when we add religiosity to the mix; in which case, you are guilty as sin. Lord only knows what you've been thinking during your pilgrimage through life. When one enters the realm of the Ten Commandments, they leap off into a fundamental chasm of trouble. My research has shown that if you are an average person, you have broken at least four and in some cases seven or eight of the Big Ten.

Have you practiced any self-abuse lately? Devoured an entire quart of Rocky Road in a spate of TV-watching gluttony? Passed noxious gas in a crowded theater during a particularly loud scene or at the ballet during a crescendo? Picked your nose while driving your car and wickedly flicked it out the window into the oncoming traffic? I just may have an eyewitness to testify to the fact that you were observed pushing the "Close" button on an elevator door instead of waiting for that senior citizen shuffling as fast as they could to catch the elevator.

I also note that you recently averted your eyes from a pathetic-looking homeless wretch holding a cardboard sign when you were stopped at an intersection. The fact that you rationalized giving up a whole buck would only help support their drug or alcohol habit is of little consequence.

Have you ever slightly dinged someone's car with your shopping cart, and after looking around to make sure no one observed you, pretended you didn't notice what you did, and then drove away feeling like you got by with something? How many flashing yellow lights have you sped through that you probably should have slowed down and stopped because the red came on while you were in the intersection?

Have you recently used creative profanity or simple blasphemy? Just as I thought. And Ha! I'm sure you remember the last lascivious impure thought lusted in that iniquitous heart of yours. On a scale of 1 to 10, just how dreadful was it? When was it? A few hours ago, or have you been asleep? If you were, there is just no telling what you dreamed about. Your conscious facade probably has no idea. I wouldn't be surprised if you don't partake in all sorts of licentious and lecherous unthinkable antics when you are alone with that carnal mind of yours. Old President Carter is merely an amateur compared to you.

Then there are the matters of dishonesty, arrogance, faulty rationalization, bad judgment, immature behavior, and dangerous risk-taking. Told any white lies, perhaps to spare someone's feelings, or maybe even cover up your errant behavior? Cheated on your taxes or a test? Wrote a check on a bank account with insufficient funds—just to tide you over until payday? Surely, you realize that from time to time you have been culpable of some of these.

What? Do you mean you have never exceeded the speed limit? You have never attended a "Time Share" presentation just to get the prize with no intention of buying anything? You have never imbibed in excessive use of alcohol or other substances that get one high? You have never practiced gluttony at a buffet? You have never betrayed a friendship? You never cut the line when you recognized someone you knew pretending they were holding your spot? You never got in a fight? You have never engaged in unprotected anything? You probably never even cussed—used the infamous "N" word, the beastly "F" word, the plain-old-vulgar "S" or "C" words, or that notorious "X" word. I believe that.

How about that time when you were out of town and... all right? I know that I'm getting into a sensitive area here. So I'll drop that line of questioning. I guess my point is that all of us, *you included*, from time to time, no matter how much we try and no matter how perfect our moms thought we were, do the things that people do. Our planet is small but there are infinite vices. So whatever your sin—extravagance, lust, gluttony, avarice, greed, sloth, wrath, envy, or pride? Admit it friend—you have dabbled!

It could be that we do such things because of our bad judgment—or lack of proper upbringing—or because somebody pushes us into it. Then again, maybe it's because we simply can't resist the temptation, or even because we need to do it more than our conscious needs us not to do it. But we do it. Don't we?

I guess what it all comes down to, is that the only humans who don't commit an occasional transgression, are those currently residing beneath the ground with a tombstone marker. While we are above ground we just aren't perfect. It would therefore be accurate to say, "Let he who is without a stone cast the first sin."

UNFUNKING

Have you been waking up late to discover that you never went to sleep? Is your psychiatrist having an affair with your spouse and your accountant going to prison because of your taxes? Has your Zoloft prescription expired and the liquor store cut off your credit? Are you perhaps thinking you've become incapable of coping with the overwhelming stresses of simply being? Well friends, perhaps you have been experiencing what I choose to define as a *Lavender Funk*. I think we all find ourselves in one at some time or another. We're rolling along, living well in the fast lane, when all of a sudden it hits us—blam! Everything's mauvish and ennui.

When this happens, there is only one thing to do. Listen to Dr. Mack. You must decompress. You should therefore immediately proceed to your nearest beach for an inspirational walk along the shoreline. You are in dire need of some rehabilitation by the mother ocean. You require the taste of the salty mist on your lips, the feel of tingling cold seawater on your toes as they dig into a million grains of invigorating wet sand. You need to breathe deep and inhale some crisply bracing sea-breeze air. It's a restorative remedy that works every time, at least for me.

Know how come the oceans are filled with salt water and where it comes from? It's simple really. Some came from undersea volcanoes and cracks in the ocean floor. It is also continually washed into the sea by the rain, rivers, and streams eroding rocks containing the compound sodium chloride. Naturally, as the water evaporates, over millions of years, more and more salt is left behind. And, yes, it's the same stuff we use at the table

How about that fine powdery beach sand? Did you ever wonder how it got there? To find that shore it had to make an unbelievable journey in both time and distance. It started hundreds of miles from the sea in the form of massive granite mountains. Changing temperatures continually heat up and cool the immense rock structures, causing small fissures or cracks to form. The wind whips at it, and the rain pounds it, and over the millennia some breaks away to become slabs, which eventually crack off into boulders, and then stones which toss and tumble until they become even smaller granite rocks, that slide down the mountains and into brooks, streams, and rivers running to the sea. Along the journey, the tumbling rocks are pounded and ground into tiny bits of feldspar and quartz. The feldspar is reduced to dark silt and the quartz becomes fine beach sand. Run some through your fingers and appreciate its incredible journey.

There is always something going on along the shore. Beaches are constantly being changed and reshaped by the relentless attack of the ever-constant wind as well as the tides and oceanic waves eternally undulating ashore. The size of those waves is determined far out at sea by wind energy generated in storms moving over the ocean. If you stand there and count them, one every five to ten seconds, you'll ascertain that between nine thousand to seventeen thousand waves are crashing onto the shore every twenty-four hours. The height of every wave will exceed about one-seventh of its wavelength or the distance between the crest of each wave and the next.

The gravitational pull of the moon causes the earth's oceans to routinely rise and fall which produces a high or low tide, delivering hitchhikers from the sea within the frothy foam. Each of the billions of grains of sand is coated with a film of seawater through which countless millions of microscopic creatures such as mites, flatworms, and other animals freely swim, safe from the onrushing waves under their blanket of sand. They live in a world of restless rhythms and continual drama in an unseen universe, struggling to survive in the unique misty macrocosm.

A casual stroll along any coastline will introduce you to an amazing world of mind-boggling surprises. Before commencing your amble, take a moment to stand silently before the vast sea and listen to the ocean singing. Close your eyes and feel the offshore breeze softly pressing against your eyelids. Tune in to the roar of the rolling waves and the calls of the birds. It is a callus person indeed whose soul will not become unfettered in such a place.

To proceed properly, you will next need to find yourself a suitable piece of loose driftwood to serve as a walking stick. It doesn't have to be perfect. Anything even halfway funky will do. It will make you feel like a genuine beachcomber. You will employ it to pry over and examine seashells and investigate clumps of tangled kelp ripped loose from the undersea jungles that grow offshore. Once you have your stick you may begin your journey. Walk slowly and I strongly suggest that you allow the waves to break over your bare feet so you can both feel and observe the miracle of the amazing sea.

The seashore is home to a wide variety of birds, attracted to the habitat, which provides them with shelter, food, and plenty of space to nest. There will be the ever-present gulls, ready to take advantage of any morsel available to them, be it a treat from a passing beachcomber or dead sea life washed ashore by the tides.

You may see sandpipers, plovers, or sanderlings doing their well-choreographed dance with the sea, keeping just ahead of each wave as it unfurls. Or perhaps you'll spot aptly named turnstones flipping over shells and stones in search of worms or insects. You could see terns prowling the water's edge for small fish or shrimp. Or birds like the cormorant diving for food. If you get lucky perhaps just offshore you will spot a migrating whale, a family of seals or sea lions, or a pod of dolphins frolicking in the surf.

As you saunter along allow yourself to be aware of the vivid moment in time. Witness the miracle of the living ocean and all it has to offer. Try to feel the earth turning. There is no need for urgency so take your time and admit to yourself that life is great. Feel the warm sun on your skin and enjoy the saturation of clear transparent light. Savor the sensation of your toes digging into the membranes of wet sand. Observe the play of light and colors reflecting off the blue-green water, the cloud shadows racing across the dunes, and the way the sky floats on the mirror of the distant sea.

Meander in and out of the water line and look for scurrying hermit crabs with bright orange claws sticking out from under their borrowed shell. You may find shells from creatures such as limpets, periwinkle, and mussels as you ramble, or the fan-like shells of scallops, whelks, moon snails, the colorful coquina, and those beautiful but crumbly sand dollars. If you dig through the wet sand you will likely uncover some mole crabs, small shrimp, snails, clams, or ghost crabs but act fast or they will burrow downward into the sand to escape.

There are countless treasures to be discovered along the shore—pieces of sea fan, Staghorn or Elkhorn coral, a rare chunk of brain coral, or some unusual piece of driftwood that reminds you of something else that you simply must take home. There will be strands of kelp, torn from the underwater jungle offshore and cast adrift to wash ashore. It will be bundled into piles and heaps that you will not be able to resist probing through. If you are anything like me, you will find yourself regressing in age and popping the air bubble floats much like you do bubble wrap. Become a kid and let yourself enjoy the adventure. Heck, you might even find a pirate's treasure chest washed up on the sand.

No matter the nature of your troubles, or the status of your sadness, the sea has a way of bringing us back to a state of oneness with the cosmos, especially if we allow our minds to become syncopated to the rhythms of the timeless ocean.

Perhaps it's our old lineage dating back to when our ancient ancestors were a part of the sea itself. After all, each of our bodies holds about five quarts of stuff we call blood, which is composed mostly of salt water, pretty much just like that found in our mother sea. Whatever the reasons, we humans do feel the connection. The tidal force pulls us to the wonder of the sea, and by its power, we are purged.

LONGEVITY

So, you think you want to live to a ripe old age. I'll convey the secret in one sentence. You'll stand a much better chance if you are healthy, good-looking, intelligent, happy, and rich. On the contrary, if you are in poor health, ugly, dumb, depressed, and poor as a titmouse you probably won't be getting one of those birthday letters from the President on your one-hundredth. It's as simple as that.

Oh sure, those dynamic-looking perfect spokespersons who come on TV to advise you on how to live, will inundate you with the basics. But you already know what they are: don't smoke, drink in moderation, practice safe sex, eat sensibly, and exercise regularly. That's all you have to do. And oh yeah...send them heaps of your money for the various products and/or instructions to help you abide by the foregoing.

I say what do they know? They are only offering up placebos. The real secret of living a long time is mostly found in your not-dying too-early effectiveness. To assist you in that regard, I've got some real stuff you need to worry about. Here are my top **100 _don'ts_**—to avoid biting the dust before your time:

1. Don't scuba dive with any blood-alcohol content greater than .014%.
2. Don't yell "hi" to your friend Jack on an airplane.
3. Don't spend your nights in gay bathhouses.
4. Don't engage in the finger-waving game with anyone that cuts you off in traffic.
5. Don't go strolling alone after midnight in darkened streets in the shady parts of town, no matter what you might be desperately looking for.
6. Don't eat unidentifiable food from street vendors in third-world countries.
7. Don't participate in a breath-holding contest while blitzed.
8. Don't hike alone in grizzly bear country unarmed...or armed.
9. Don't hitch rides on the undercarriage of trains.

10. Don't eye-dis gang bangers on the street, even if they are in your territory.
11. Don't smoke poison oak.
12. Don't pet any well-tattooed stranger's pit bull.
13. Don't try to catch a falling meteorite, even with your baseball cap.
14. Don't play chicken with eighteen-wheelers, especially if its driver is wild-eyed looking.
15. Don't snooze while hang gliding.
16. Don't sleep or dine or even just hang with any serial killer.
17. Don't swallow more than 10 Viagra, no matter the special occasion.
18. Don't skateboard down Lombard Street in San Francisco.
19. Don't go to the dentist whose wife you are having an affair with.
20. Don't leap from the platform for a missed train, even if you were a long jumper in high school.
21. Don't get tattooed at the Klu Klux Klan tattoo parlor.
22. Don't attempt to satisfy a drunken nymphomaniac.
23. Don't eat unnaturally colored unidentifiable things from the fridge.
24. Don't go hunting with a bunch of nice mountain men you just met in a bar.
25. Don't ever laugh, or even smile much if a judge says, "you're guilty".
26. Don't let a bank robber borrow your car, even if you are going to stay in it—even for just a little while.
27. Don't try to slam-dunk a basketball (unless you are at least five feet and eight inches tall).
28. Don't lick strange frogs.
29. Don't let ex-girlfriends or inebriated roommates shave you with a straight razor.
30. Don't climb electrical transmission towers, even in a rubber suit.
31. Don't try to surf like Laird Hamilton.
32. Don't do the moonwalk on any building ledges.
33. Don't go to jail in drag.
34. Don't ride in any NYC or TJ cabs.
35. Don't stick your head out the car window to yell while going through a tight tunnel.
36. Don't jitterbug with anyone who weighs more than 500 pounds.

37. Don't ignore signs in a zoo that tells you not to stand too close to the cage, no matter how badly you want that picture.
38. Don't lean way over the edge to see how far your spit will fall.
39. Don't vacation in places where a saber is standard-wearing apparel.
40. Don't pick up a crazy-eyed hitchhiker wearing a "Survivor" buff and carrying a lumpy backpack.
41. Don't tease killer bees.
42. Don't laugh at clown-masked liquor store robbers while they are working.
43. Don't water ski in alligator-infested waters, even if there aren't any stumps.
44. Don't impregnate a boxer's little sister (unless married to her).
45. Don't play catch with hand grenades, even if you are an ex-Marine.
46. Don't hide bullets in your fireplace.
47. Don't tease a bull anytime anyplace.
48. Don't keep poisonous snakes as pets.
49. Don't borrow money from guys named Lefty or Big anything.
50. Don't attempt to outrun the police no matter how badly you want to be on TV.
51. Don't sleep in doorways, under freeway bridges, or on railroad tracks.
52. Don't swallow pills given to you by edgy-looking characters at Rave parties.
53. Don't bathe in piranha-infested waters.
54. Don't stand on a roof with an antenna you broke off someone's car during an electrical storm and shake the antenna at God daring him to strike you dead.
55. Don't practice autoerotic asphyxia.
56. Don't bounce checks to Columbia drug dealers.
57. Don't release the safety bar on roller coaster rides and stand up with your hands held above your head hollering "Whoopee! Look at me!"
58. Don't share needles except for sewing.
59. Don't date vampires.
60. Don't skate on thin ice.

61. Don't screw around with volcanoes.
62. Don't duel.
63. Don't explore abandoned mine shafts.
64. Don't go to cathouses in Botswana.
65. Don't get emotional with a badger.
66. Don't eat unidentified red berries, even if lost in the woods.
67. Don't give mouth-to-mouth recitation to a sick wolverine.
68. Don't surf during a hurricane or tsunami no matter how stoked at the wave sizes you become.
69. Don't play Russian roulette.
70. Don't skip in a minefield.
71. Don't picnic on airport runways.
72. Don't intimidate a cobra.
73. Don't smoke while pumping gas into your vehicle.
74. Don't drink too much at a hanging.
75. Don't dip your toes in fresh lava.
76. Don't play "rock, paper, and scissors" with real rocks, paper, and scissors.
77. Don't participate in "tough man" contests.
78. Don't endeavor to skin a whale with a box cutter.
79. Don't carve on your leg.
80. Don't attempt to perform a self-vasectomy.
81. Don't lasso a rhinoceros.
82. Don't eat fish caught in contaminated waters.
83. Don't date anyone with more than 68 tattoos.
84. Don't pawn your testicles.
85. Don't eat blowfish on Friday the 13th.
86. Don't fake a bank robbery.
87. Don't trim your toenails with a chainsaw.
88. Don't go to a cannibal's hut for dinner.
89. Don't osculate with a Tasmanian devil.
90. Don't huff.
91. Don't chase any wild animal with teeth or claws that desperately wants to get away.
92. Don't try to beat a train to a railroad crossing.

93. Don't try to outrun any charging predators, especially if you have a gun.
94. Don't attempt to enter a dwelling through a chimney, even if there is no fire burning and you are in a Santa Claus suit.
95. Don't party with nitroglycerin.
96. Don't attempt to disconnect any armed nuclear devices.
97. Don't practice safe sex while skydiving.
98. Don't become a mercenary.
99. Don't try to set a new world record for endurance in anything.
100. Don't ever talk politics or religion, with anyone, any time, any place.

MACKSIMS

Occasionally, what I perceive to be pithy, poignant, succinct, significant, insightful, or in some way *sort of worth remembering* aphorisms come flitting into my cranium. Being **vaingloriously arcane** and also unable to think of a more appropriate title, I have ingeniously crafted the anagram "Macksims" utilizing my name.

It's quite possible that I'm not the only person who has ever had some of these particular thoughts, so pardon me if they happen to be analogous to what someone else may have once said. The more pithy and acerbic they are, the more likely it is that some wit has laid claim to their origination. But, I refuse to be deterred by such trifling matters. So if another visionary beat me to the quote, and I'm unintentionally plagiarizing some great philosopher or sage, I'm dreadfully regretful about that. I came by them earnestly and will swear on any size stack of Bibles that I concocted them up all by myself. To quote me: "a fool and his quotes are quite often misquoted" and "a quote is not worth diddly-squat until someone re-quotes it."

Wisdom comes, but slowly.

You can't avoid what you pretend not to see.

Slow gunfighters have short careers.

Discourse with a fool is foolish.

What we don't understand we fear. What we fear we hate and want to eliminate.

Adventures begin where the roads end.

You can't forget what you never knew.

Time is the worst enemy of the seller and the best ally of the buyer.

The one with the fiddle gets to pick the tune.

Every fool can vote, unfortunately.

A loss by any other name is still not a win.

The battlefields of the mind are full of mines.

There is much solace in a warm cookie.

You can't stop a quitter.

Nobody cares about apathy.

In the end—wrinkles don't matter.

Bluff with a smirk.

Don't start dribbling until you have the ball.

Retirement is a full-time job.

Sometimes the best choice of all is to do nothing fast.

Heirs come easy—benefactors hard.

Tolerance is permission.

A wise buyer always gets a receipt and an honest seller always gives one.

Odysseys must be taken before they can be described.

The bureaucracy of democracy is hypocrisy.

Hard choices should be made with a soft heart.

There is always a crack of light in the doorway of possibility.

He who makes the rules tends to win the game.

A strong "I don't want to" is better than a weak "I can't" anytime.

Hatred has no boundaries or limitations.

Sometimes counting to ten before you act only gives your enemy ten seconds more to do you in.

Blame spreads better thin.

Successful daredevils take wiser chances.

Stories come from the mind—poems flow from the soul.

Fools cannot be explained, educated, or reasoned with. They simply are.

Greatness isn't born and doesn't come naturally. It must be created and lived up to.

Softhearted hookers seldom retire.

Your enemy's ideology is their Achilles Heel.

Now belongs to you. If you want to change your life, now is a good time to start.

Blood flows brightly through a happy heart.

Existence itself is a painting that one can only see with their mind.

If you fall off a cliff you have nothing to lose by flapping your arms on the way down. It'll help take your mind off the landing, and who knows, you just might learn to fly.

Practicing political correctness usually only weakens one.

The best place to start is by doing what you know how to do and see how far you can get.

It isn't how hard you paddle so much as it is how smooth you roll.

You can't outrun a bullet or stupidity.

You can't break a cheating heart.

The needs of those who take will always exceed the ability of those who give.

There are no radical pacifists.

A dull brain often controls a sharp tongue.

A small lack of diplomacy has started many wars.

Hints are generally someone's attempt to control you.

Apathy invites domination.

You can't have a good street fight unless someone has a beer bottle.

Incurable addiction is mental fiction.

You can't negotiate with a mad dog.

Answered prayers are often curses in disguise.

The more you speed, the more you'll bleed.

If a theory cannot be reasoned or explained, the likeliness of it being true diminishes to the point of improbability.

No failed experiment is a failure. Many a great invention was not by intention.

You can't outrun someone who refuses to race.

No matter how well it is made, eventually, everything breaks down or wears out.

Being a little bit drunk is like being a little bit schizophrenic.

Lightning is an impatient thing.

Small mistakes often lead to huge catastrophes.

Sweat the small stuff but let God handle the major events.

Trouble doesn't care where it starts.

Be careful what you chase because you just might catch it.

Financial success often goes to one's belly.

Understanding "no" is the first step to becoming a "yes" man.

The person cheaters harm the most is often themselves.

Sure, faith may be able to move a mountain, but you will still need someplace to put it.

Politeness may open a rude door.

Confidence cannot be faked. It must be developed.

Reality is only a state of mind.

The total of everything is *all*.

The best time to bluff is when you only have a few chips on the table.

Doing one's duty should be considered an honor.

The higher you climb the farther you can fall.

PIERCING THOUGHTS

Right up front let it be said that anyone dumb enough to get a body piercing is probably not smart enough to understand all the rational reasons why they shouldn't. But, I am compelled to take a shot at it anyway. So what impels you body mutilation freaks these days? Or better yet, what the heck is your objective? The nauseating thing for me to believe is that you essentially want to appear like that. I know your answer is *that it is your body and you have the inalienable right to do with it, as you will.* In your opinion, I have a close-minded and intolerant mindset.

The conundrum is, my pierce-minded friend, that I believe you to be the close-minded one in your inane interpretation of personal freedom and critical thinking. Your self-mutilation and disregard for your own body make you the target of ridicule and ostracizing by society. You are not a true individual, but rather a non-thinking android guided and controlled by a weak-minded willingness to act in an intolerant fashion. You think your disgusting attitude and repulsive behavior alone isn't adequate humiliation, so you are obsessively driven to make your body even more grotesque. It's your mania and passion. It makes you who you *in reality* choose to be. I see. For recognition and classification purposes—please be aware—that I shall now shift person and hereinafter refer to you bizarre weirdo extremist fanatic nut case self-mutilators as "*They*" "*Them*" or "*Their*".

I know, it's none of my business what someone else does with *Their* body—after all, it is *Their* temple and *They* can violate it as *They* wish. But goodness gracious, don't *They* realize what other people think? No, make that "know!" That *They* (the body mutilators) are idiots?

It's as if *They* are intent on making everyone who chances to see them want to puke. I know I sure do. *They* might as well carry around a big sign that says "Hey—Look at Me—I'm Stupendously Stupid!"

I'm no prude, but for crying out loud—don't *They* have any common sense? Okay, just for the sake of argument, let's agree that perhaps a small earlobe ornament is not too serious a maiming of one's body. Why then, don't *They* stop there? No way! *They* simply must mangle *Their* poor ears with more holes than a McDonald's French fry strainer. Then, as if 47 holes around the exterior rim of their ear aren't adequate, *They* find some pressing need to stretch *Their* poor defenseless lobes until they will easily accommodate a fairly good-sized saucer.

I'm quite certain that if you delve into the annals of history, you will find that the various cultures and tribes that practiced the art of crippling, cutting, and otherwise generally mutilating their bodies, were not particularly civilized or extraordinarily intellectual beings. I'd speculate that they were mostly illiterate uneducated barbaric creatures of the wild—not quite up to the standards of modern-day life.

Let's say that a person is foolish enough to get *Their* (whatever) pierced. That must excruciate comparably to the pain threshold of giving birth or performing self-lobotomy. One might think that experience alone would assuage the urge to further undertake such unnecessary torture and suffering. But no! *They* even have to get *Their* (whatever) punched and then having done that *They* get *Their* (other whatever) drilled. Etc. Quite honestly, it's sordid and unpleasant to even think about.

Do *They* in any way think *They* are endearing themselves to future employers? Or perhaps it is *Their* way of expressing *Their* individuality, which is a weak-minded way of saying "Hey! Notice my world! I'm so incapable of coping I had myself punctured in appalling ways to help others readily identify me as a loser."

(Note to puncturees: the truth is that most non-punctured folks look at your every hunk of dangling metal as incontrovertible proof of your weakness and inability to resist whatever peer pressure or idiotic idea that caused you to mutilate your body that way. I know this may come hard, but you are not the creative and innovative individual you wish to be. You're just a simple sheep-minded follower willing to leap off the cliff of common sense in pursuit of whatever imprudent thought pattern is misguiding you through life.)

I suppose it's a dreadful consequence of modern society's permissive attitude. I blame a lot of it on Doctor Spock. That's right. That nice compassionate old dude who wrote the bible on rearing children, without allowing kids the opportunity to experience things like self-respect and personal responsibility. When parents no longer were permitted to discipline their children, and when those good-intentioned school administrators began leveling the educational playing fields, the inevitable result was generations of confused misdirected airheads. The unintended repercussion is that the kids end up in such a state of confusion they don't have enough willpower to avoid those edgy-looking piercing parlors, much less come in out of the rain.

It's a statement of truth and plain old good common sense that no one has to have a nose ring or a stud through *Their* tongue. *They* just do it because, for some inexplicable reason, *They* have an overwhelming desire to make themselves think *They* are unique. *They* want to be different. The reality is that *They* intentionally do disgusting things to *Their* body with the consequence being that *They* stumble through life making people immediately aware of the fact that *They* are dimwits. It sure as heck can't be because lugging around chunks of body metal is life-enhancing, much less sexually stimulating. It has to be the absolute worst possible example of peer pressure from the wannabes.

I have a theory that in almost all cases, there is a direct correlation between the number of holes one has in *Their* body and the number of drugs *They* consume which is in opposite proportion to the equivalence of *Their* IQ. Not to mention all the other laws of society that are broken and/or ignored by those who choose to dwell on the edge of being barely tolerable. If bad vibes count for anything in the grand scheme, because of *Their* lifestyle choices *They* will receive more than *They* could ever imagine.

Oh sure, most people will be polite and pretend not to mind or care that some drooling ghoul type walks around looking like a human pincushion. But if the pierced ones could read minds *They'd* get a whole new understanding of exactly what the ordinary person thinks of such freaks.

Their families and friends who don't compete in the "destroy your body race," realize how grossly ridiculous *They* are. *They* generally disgust sane and sober people. Small children are afraid of *Them*. Dogs and cats could care less, but then what do they know? (A side note for the ladies) *Honest to goodness girls, the creep factor of a lip ring is exponential to the utmost degree. You can't imagine how unattractive it is to the men who don't dig body mutilation.*

In the final analysis, there is no final analysis. The ear-splitting music is still playing and *They* just keep marching to *Their* different drummers. If *They* can stand to look at *Themselves* in the mirror, *They* are effectively proving that *They* are incapable of seeing their corporeal self. *They* may not know who or what *They* are, but the rest of us do. *They* may think *They* are sending a message of individuality, but *They* are affected by some intrinsic self-destructive gene.

I've got more bad news for *Them*. *These* self-mutilators will all be dead in a hundred years, just like the folks who manage to go through life without damaging their wonderful God-given bodies. The only difference is that while the rest of us are going right in, the metal detectors at the Golden Gates will gong loudly as they try to gain entrance and *They* will then be directed to that warmer clime where gross maiming and mutilation are considered fun play. At least that's my humble opinion.

UNCOMMON COURTESY

For several years I have been conducting a survey and I am now prepared to reveal the results—which are: when their hands are on the steering wheel of an automobile, men are generally more courteous than women.

Yes, ladies. It's true! I know you doubt, but hear me out before you throw your hands up in exasperation and write me off as another chauvinistic (albeit quite handsome) male pig. Believe me, I do not make such claims lightly. My theories on this vehicular dichotomy are irrefutable.

I realize you can regale me with countless anecdotal tales wherein women have displayed courteous driving behavior. However, I am not attempting to waltz through the criminal court where the accused must be found guilty beyond any shadow of a doubt. I am merely endeavoring to tap dance around in civil court where a preponderance of the evidence is sufficient.

It's very simple. You can verify it yourselves with just a little bit of clever observation. One of the easiest examples is to simply watch and see what happens when someone is stuck coming out of the driveway of a business onto a busy street with bumper-to-bumper traffic. Approximately nine out of ten men (give or take a few), upon seeing a fellow motorist stuck in traffic limbo will stop and allow that trapped car to proceed ahead of them. I maintain that this is due to two primary factors:

The man (generally better at math) immediately realizes that the individual who is being allowed to proceed will only be one car ahead of him, which is not a sufficient penalty of distance to become all excited about.

Males, tending to accept the inevitable more readily, are just more patient and tolerant when experiencing bumper-to-bumper traffic and take pleasure in pleasing another unknown driver.

Women (and we do love them) on the other hand, will seldom ever let someone go in front of them regardless of the situation. Again, I believe this is due to two primary factors

Women are almost always in a crisis mode of some sort (generally running late) and are only being themselves. The simple fact is: they are just not even aware that someone is stuck in a driveway exit.

Females generally tend to be oblivious when dealing with unknown people and instinctively do not give way to anyone. They are still getting even for being repressed for so long and therefore are continually trying to break through that *glass ceiling*. This is because they inherently fear not being treated as equals of men in some way, however insignificant and small it might be.

Don't take my word for it. Check it out yourself. Most men, upon recognizing that another driver is in distress due to being stuck in such a situation will immediately slow down and upon making eye contact with the stuck driver, give him a friendly "go ahead" gesture. I understand that this directly contradicts the occasional *road rage* situation that develops between men.

However, I believe that men demonstrate courtesy in inverse ratio to their speed. This remarkable trait is simply nature's way of compensating for the male tendency to go ballistic when other drivers commit some infuriating offense while driving at higher speeds.

The miracle does not end with the courteous driver's gesture, because in practically almost every case, if the driver who is being allowed to proceed is a male, he will invariably give the courteous driver a thanking return gesture, typically a two-fingered salute. This is accomplished in a friendly manner that is not to be confused with that other infamous one-finger salute often extended by men engaged in vehicular controversies.

If that driver is a woman she will generally proceed into the traffic as if it is her birthright, without any acknowledgment of the driver allowing her to proceed. There are not only no gestures shared, there is not even a sign of recognition of existence. Courteous drivers are invisible to women.

When I first discovered this phenomenon, I must admit that it sort of chapped my masculine buns. However, the more I observed this strange behavior, the more I began to marvel at these predictable, but highly unusual driver behavior patterns.

This led me to begin careful observation as to how men and women tend to behave in grocery stores, entrance doorways, elevators, and other places when courtesy may be called for. The following patterns have emerged:

Far more women than men will proceed through the "15 Items Only" checkout line with more than 15 items in their baskets. I know this for a fact because, on many occasions, I have been the person standing behind you, silently but assiduously counting your items. The inevitable deduction is that women either can't count or think that no one will notice and if they do that they won't have the gonads to say anything.

Many men with more items in their shopping cart will also thoughtfully allow another shopper with fewer items to proceed ahead of them. The possible exception for this is if the guy is on a beer run and there is a big game starting shortly. Surprisingly though, the women don't do too badly in this category and will sometimes allow someone to go ahead of them. More often than not, that someone is a good-looking and well-dressed man. It is seldom another woman, regardless of age, clothing, or degree of infirmity. Despite equal rights, modern women usually expect to be permitted to proceed through doorways and into and out of elevators first. Most women just assume the man will defer and will be surprised if that is not the case. They do not generally reciprocate and defer to other women, unless the woman is carrying a baby, is an elder, or is physically handicapped.

Women usually pretend that they do not see men in lonely underground garages and other isolated places when just the two of them are present. No one should blame them for this one. I suspect this may be some lingering instinct from cave-dwelling genes.

When alone in an elevator with a man, a woman will politely smile and pass the time of the day, but she will exit with a sigh of relief almost every time. Two men in an elevator alone will chat amiably.

Men do get into road rage situations much more easily and far more often than women, who seem to have enough common sense to realize that the several thousand pounds of metal she is in control of should never be utilized as a weapon. This can be substantiated by the following statistics, which I have cleverly fabricated:

76.4% of all road rage incidents involve two or more men.

21.9% of road rage incidents involve a man getting mad at a woman for cutting him off.

01.7% of road rage incidents occur between two women.

When inebriated, men and women are equally argumentative and likely to create an incident, but women tend to blubber or cry their way out of the situation while men will more often attempt to resolve their dilemma with shouting or brawls.

Some other peculiar idiosyncrasy I've noticed that men possess is that when there is a crowded intersection and the light turns yellow, men will carelessly advance across the yellow more often than women. Consequently, men tend to find themselves stuck in the middle of an intersection, blocking traffic. They get tickets for this. Men also get tickets for driving faster, drunker, and more dangerously. Perhaps that is why men cause twice as many traffic fatalities as women. On our behalf, we do drive much more than women.

For some unexplainable reason, men also seem to have worse telephone manners than women. They tend to be less patient, are prone to become angry quickly, and are generally less courteous on the phone than women.

I realize all of the foregoing is controversial, so feel free to argue it with your spouse.

In summation, I wish to emphatically state that we men are not the callus moronic boobs you ladies think we are. We have feelings too.

WHAT IT WAS LIKE

"What was it like down there?" I've been asked that question so many times, I long ago stopped telling people that I have spent years of my life underwater onboard nuclear submarines.

Now that the torpedo is out of the tube, I suppose I'll have to try and explain what it was like down there. But first, here is how it happened. In 1954, I was skinny and still wet behind the ears, a kid growing up in Waco, Texas where I was born. In January of that year, I saw a movie newsreel of the launching of the U.S.S. Nautilus, the world's first nuclear-powered submarine. I was stoked and thought how wonderful it would be as a crewmember on such a marvelous ship. Shortly thereafter, I began to suffer from a bad case of wanderlust. At the time, little could I have imagined, that the U.S. Navy and I would soon be joining forces. However, once I made a casual visit to our local Navy Recruiting Office, the sea began to call and I had to answer.

Boot camp in San Diego was arduous and exhausting, but I was inspired enough to work hard and consequently did well. It seemed like just about everyone wanted to go to submarine school. Out of the entire class, only two of us were lucky enough to be chosen. New London Connecticut was a long way from home, and if boot camp had been arduous, Submarine School was full of ups and downs (sorry I couldn't help and presented many demanding physical and mental challenges.

I studied assiduously, all the while dreaming of the possibility of getting assigned to a nuclear submarine. The problem was there were several hundred subs in the fleet but only 1 nuke. Somehow my Irish luck and hard-headed determination got me through, as again I persevered and was one of the two graduates in my class assigned to a brand new submarine still under construction. It was the U.S.S. SEAWOLF (SSN 575), the second nuclear-powered submarine and the only one ever built with a sodium-cooled reactor.

I was thrilled. My Mom's proud photo holding up a picture of me was on the front page of the Waco newspaper along with a "LOCAL BOY MAKES GOOD" story about my assignment to the SEAWOLF. That was my first submarine, although for some inexplicable reason just about everyone in my family still thinks I was initially stationed onboard the Nautilus.

When I first reported, the sub was still being assembled at the huge ship manufacturing facility of the Electric Boat Company in Groton, Connecticut. The crew had to subsist on a barge until the boat was completed. I should tell you that while submariners affectionately refer to them, as "boats" submarines are ships in every respect. The SEAWOLF was 338 feet long and 28 feet wide. It weighed 3,260 gross tons surfaced; 4,110 tons submerged and had a crew of 101. By the way, it's pronounced "new clee er" and not "nu-cue-lur."

I vividly recall the first time I went down the hatch into the SEAWOLF. Despite the countless hardhat shipyard workers scurrying around like busy bees, being inside the hull was visually and audibly overwhelming. It was an unbelievable cornucopia of gleaming stainless steel; a complicated maze of equipment crammed together into incredibly tight quarters, coupled with the noise of shipyard workers and machines of every type imaginable. Everywhere I looked was wires, cables, conduits, and pipes, connected to countless pieces of machinery, pumps, electrical, pneumatic, and hydraulic equipment, valves, levels, control panels, and switches. Each had a purpose, and from sub-school, it had already been instilled in my brain that in an emergency any crew member not knowing the function of every one of them, and not being able to respond correctly, might very well jeopardize the safety and lives of the entire crew.

Every submariner must be thoroughly familiar with all phases of the operation of the ship. While at sea a constant state of alertness must be maintained. There is a need for complete control, especially in an emergency. All crew members are trained to function smoothly with perfect teamwork and perfection in a calm manner as they go about their various duties. They are taught that fate of them all rests with every one of them. One mistimed flip of the wrist or a slight error in judgment can interfere with the intricately balanced anatomy of the entire submarine. All hands can be lost if just one man does not do his job correctly.

I was both fascinated and terrified at the same time. My mind was assailed by the continual whirring of various machinery, the myriad scents of oil, gas, rubber, plastic, and painted metal blended with the smells produced by the never-ending assembly process of getting the boat ready for the water. It was nothing like the submarines I'd been schooled and trained on during sub-school.

We had studied the old diesel-electric submarines, of which the fleet then consisted. They were often referred to as sewer pipes. I had been to sea on one of them during my training and they did tend to get pretty ripe. The odor of diesel fuel mingled poorly with the stench of the ever-present aromas emanating from the galley, as well as the pungent sanitary tanks, which held the human wastes until they could be pumped out of the sub. The sanitary tanks often became full and backed up, their foul contents overflowing into the berthing compartments.

Because there was a dire shortage of fresh water, crew members were only permitted limited showering and during deployments, they were unable to bathe or wash their clothes and linens for long periods. When sanitary tanks were discharged while submerged the putrid air in the tank had to be vented back into the sub. The sewer pipe name was fairly accurate.

Due to space limitations, subs are extremely confined and challenging for the crew. There is no tolerance for eccentricity or odd behavior. One must fit in or they will be quickly transferred. Some claim that a man has to be half-nuts just to volunteer for such duty. In any case, it is a challenging duty and crewmembers learn to live and deal with stress and danger. For that reason, they receive extra "hazardous duty" or "sub pay".

We all knew that we had to get along with one another. So we did. We shared a sense of propinquity, unlike no other group I've ever seen or been involved with since. We were not all goody two shoes, but it was well-known throughout the service that submariners stuck together. An unwritten rule was that if submariners, for any reason, became involved in a conflict while at sea, the argument would be quickly resolved with handshakes and apologies by all individuals involved, who would then immediately put it behind them and move on to more important ship's business.

I was still a teenager when I rode the SEAWOLF down the ways of the launching ramp at the Electric Boat Company in Groton, Connecticut. The first crew of any naval ship is forever referred to as "plank owners." Life as a plank owner wasn't easy. If I'd thought boot camp and sub school were hard, they'd been a walk in the park compared to qualifying onboard a submarine—much less a nuke.

To earn their dolphins, every submariner had to learn everything possible about their vessel, a time-honored procedure known as "Qualification." We had to be fully knowledgeable about every system and component to be able to properly respond to any emergency. The qualification system typically took about a year of full-time studying. We had to be thoroughly familiar with the multiple hydraulic, water, and air systems on board and there were dozens of each. We had to know how to operate every component from the smallest auxiliary pump to the largest piece of equipment. We had to learn all about the engines and nuclear reactor system, the weapons systems, the myriad tanks, and the methods for water transfer including blowing and venting of tanks, the huge battery bank system, and the multiple other ship's electrical systems. We had to be able to go through every compartment and identify and operate each piece of equipment blindfolded.

There is simply no analogy that will accurately describe the complexity of those first nuclear submarines except to say that they were comparable to an extremely intricate three-dimensional jigsaw puzzle comprised of thousands of different elaborate pieces made from a wide-ranging variety of materials that all amazingly fit together make up the functioning submarine.

Once I'd earned my 'dolphins' I found myself at sea serving as the battle station plainsman, which essentially meant the U.S. Navy trusted me, that young kid from Texas, to drive the world's most expensive machine built to that date. That was the beginning.

On September 26, 1957, Ike visited us and became the first U.S. President to ever go to sea on a nuclear submarine. The SEAWOLF later set a world-submerged endurance record of 60 days isolated from the earth's atmosphere from August 7th to October 6th of 1958.

The adventures were many, like venturing under the polar ice. After my four-year tour of duty on the SEAWOLF, I was assigned to the U.S.S. TRITON, at that time the 447' 6" submarine was the world's biggest and the first one to circumnavigate the earth completely underwater. Next, I went to the U.S.S. GEORGE WASHINGTON, the world's first Polaris missile-firing submarine. I was at the diving controls just off Cape Kennedy (then called Cape Canaveral) when we launched the first Polaris missile. There were several more nukes and plenty of adventures before I eventually retired as a Yeoman Chief Petty Officer. Now, that I have set the scene I will try to tell you what it was really like. A submarine is a long (think football field length as a minimum) watertight cigar-shaped cylinder. It has to provide adequate space for all the operating equipment, plus the crew and all the food, and other supplies they will need.

Submarines are famous for cramming more equipment into tight spaces than just about any other kind of vessel. It is all inside a "pressure hull", which is divided into several watertight compartments, separated by watertight doors that can be "dogged" or tightened shut. The inside of the pressure hull is always maintained at just about the same as the normal atmospheric pressure. The sea pressure outside is equivalent to whatever depth the submarine is operating at. For example, at 500 feet the sea pressure on one square inch of the hull is sixteen tons. In other words, the surface of your hand is about 20 square inches and if you could hold out your hand at 500 feet and support the pressure you would be holding approximately 10,000 pounds. You can see why the inside must be incredibly strong to bear that much sea pressure.

Outside the pressure-hull are huge tanks called ballast tanks. They are not built near as sturdily as the pressure hull because they always have sea pressure both inside and out and would not crush at extreme depths. They provide the "buoyancy" that enables the sub to go down and surface. They have air vents on the top and sea valves on the bottom. When both are opened the sea floods into the ballast tanks and makes the sub heavier so that it can submerge. If you could let in the exact amount of water to maintain perfectly neutral buoyancy, the sub could remain at any depth without any problem. Unfortunately, that is impossible, because only a gallon of too much water and the sub would eventually sink to the bottom. If that were to occur the submarine would eventually go too deep (assuming the ocean is deep enough at that spot) and it would collapse at the "crush depth", which is determined by the strength of the pressure hull. Steel is compressible but seawater is not.

The sinking is therefore stopped by shutting the top vents and admitting compressed air into the ballast tanks. Water is blown out or let in as required to achieve the desired depth. The depth is also maintained through the use of bow and stern planes that produce dynamic lift and hold the boat up much the same way that wings do on aircraft. When it submerges or dives, it admits just enough water to sink, and then the planes and the propulsion drive of the engines are used to maintain the desired depth. There are several other tanks such as "trim tanks" to maintain the fore and aft trim, "safety tanks" to cause the boat to surface in an emergency, "negative tanks" to cause the boat to sink in an emergency, and of course sanitary tanks to hold the waste of the crew.

Slightly forward of amidships, there is a structure called the Sail, which houses the various masts and antennae including the periscopes, radio and radar antennas, and the snorkel, (which can be used to bring outside air into the pressure hull when running on or just below the surface). The Sail contains the Bridge, where the controlling officer(s) and lookouts are stationed while the ship is surfaced. The Sail contains a smaller watertight compartment called the Conning Tower. It is part of the Pressure Hull and where Periscopes are manned when a sub is operating in an attack mode just below the surface.

When a submarine is on the surface it rolls a lot more than conventional ships because of the round-bottomed hull. So, when a sub is bobbing around on the surface there is naturally some queasiness and nausea, which causes mal de mar, upchucking, or if you prefer—puking your guts out. I have a very sensitive stomach and the ocean got to me a lot. It also bothered many other guys. There were a few with cast-iron stomachs, who could ride out anything, but I usually prayed for the time we would submerge; because when a submarine is underwater, unless they are maneuvering like crazy for some reason—everything tends to be smooth and peaceful.

There are, of course, up and down angles as the sub changes depths and side-to-side angles as it turns. But no rocking and rolling—just blessed calm. The first few years, there were times when I swore that if I ever got ashore, I was never going to sea again. But then, the time would come to cast off the lines and get underway and I was always on board. Eventually, I realized that I could tolerate occasional seasickness, and I began to consider it as just part of the job.

To understand what a voyage in a submarine was like back then, try to imagine the following. Stock up on lots of groceries and seal yourself in your house or apartment with about 100 of your closest male friends, closing all the doors and windows so no light can penetrate. Eliminate televisions, phones, computers, and all other contacts with the outside world for the next three months. You will live together and eat and sleep in closer proximity than you have ever experienced with other humans. Think about what you will learn about them in three months. That is essentially how it was for us.

Consequently, most submariners were gregarious and likable, with an easy-going demeanor and the ability to get along well with others. There was lots of joking and horseplay, but when it got to be time for seriousness, they instantly dropped the charade and became highly trained professionals.

Living in such close quarters for months at a time we got to know each other pretty well. After serving with a man for a couple of years, you not only knew where he was from but all about his family, personal life, and his dreams and aspirations for the future. There was an affable interface between the various ranks, which I believe included more trust and friendship between officers and enlisted than is typically found in any other area of the service.

Due to space limitations, berths on submarines were of necessity often crammed into tight little cubbyholes, among the torpedoes, or in other working areas. That was particularly true before the era of nuclear submarines, which were significantly larger. Even so, our sleeping accommodations were generally packed, and sometimes three men shared two bunks. This meant, that when one guy was on watch, another man was in his rack, which we called "hot bunking".

Most of our sleeping areas consisted of a small compartment with a dozen or so berths. When you were sleeping, men were continually coming and going at all hours. They opened and closed lockers with metal doors to get to their items, clothing, etc. Some guys snored. Some talked in their sleep or merely moaned and groaned. Lord only knows what they were dreaming of. All of them passed occasional gas. Suffice it to say, there was plenty of "strange". You simply learned to deal with it.

We became programmed to ignore certain sounds like the foregoing, while remaining alert for other noises like alarms, squishing water, leaks, and any dangerous situations. Because sound travels easily through water, some noises were fascinating—like the eerie songs of humpback whales endlessly singing, or other fish or unknown sea creature noises, which could be heard through the hull as you lay there, trying to get to sleep. Sometimes, if we were in close proximity, we heard the propeller and engine noises of other submarines or surface ships passing overhead.

There was always a wide array of reverberations, echoes, and resonances from something or other. Other internal sounds were more annoying—but we got used to them; like various machines whirring and humming—water being transferred about—air pressure being vented or blown as tanks were emptied or filled or water transferred for ballasting purposes—water slugs being fired from torpedo tubes to test equipment—the sound of men talking and laughing, a messenger waking up people for their watch or to notify them of problems with their equipment—shipboard communication phones ringing, announcing systems, etc.

Our berths were small, typically a little larger than a coffin, and generally closed in on three sides. The berths of some ranking petty officers and for the chiefs and officers had a few inches more breathing room, and a curtain that could be drawn across the open side for privacy. There was usually a small air vent that could be adjusted, much like those over airplane seats. Most bunks also had a small fluorescent light just above the head for reading. I found my bunk to be about the only place I could ever truly be alone, and even then there were other guys in their berths within mere inches from me.

While at sea we performed a wide variety of military tasks, some of which are probably still classified so I won't go into those kinds of details. But there was plenty to do. I was never bored. There were many moments of peaceful slow quiet running, and others of high-speed transit, or battle station maneuvering.

You have never really lived until you think you are going to die, and there were moments when I thought just that—in occasional instants of sheer terror. But, thanks to good fortune, incredible technology, and great shipmates, I managed to get through it all virtually unscathed. Perhaps my closest call occurred one windy day off Norfolk when I got swept overboard along with two other guys while we were on deck assisting in a helicopter transfer of a man from our sub to a nearby aircraft carrier. Thank goodness we were all secured and saved by the lifelines that constrained us to the sub. The water was extremely cold, and being fully clothed in heavy foul weather gear we all would have gone down like rocks and most likely have drowned but for those lifelines. They pulled us back on board and afterward, I lay shivering in my bunk for hours before coming out of the hypothermia.

Then there were the drills. To keep the crew in a state of readiness, there were continual drills. We grew to hate them but realized that they were a necessary evil. Without them, the crew might become stale and incapable of responding in as timely a manner as possible in the event of a real emergency.

There were fire drills, collision drills, flooding drills; toxic gas drills, equipment malfunctioning drills, and the most dreaded of all—radiation exposure drills. Anytime humans are living close to a nuclear reactor there is going to be a certain amount of anxiety about its containment.

There were real emergencies too of course. Interspersed in between hours of smooth undersea cruising, there were moments of real crisis. The only problem was that we usually didn't know if the alarm that just went off was for a drill or a real emergency. The Navy wanted us to react with the same sense of urgency for both possibilities, and so we did.

I can't begin to tell you all the emotions a submariner experiences. Submarine hulls are built to withstand great water pressure, but not punctures from a hard collision. Any penetration of the hull would cause flooding that might sink the submarine or force it below crush depth at which time everyone inside would be instantly killed by the hull imploding. For that reason, a submarine has many watertight compartments designed to maintain individual watertight integrity in the event of a breach of the hull or flooding for any reason. In an emergency, the watertight doors between the compartments, as well as any other pipes, vents, or pathways that might allow flooding to occur between the compartments had to be immediately secured.

Imagine that you are a submariner and the boat is running along quietly and smoothly, deep in the sea. As you lay in your coffin-sized bunk asleep at 0300 hours or 3 AM, the collision alarm goes off. You must leap out of your berth immediately and spring into action, closing and securing water-tight doors, certain valves, etc.—all the while not knowing if you are rapidly closing in on an uncharted undersea mountain (in which case everyone is going to die). Or perhaps sonar has detected an unidentified contact dead ahead that turns out to be a school of fish or some unknown biological phenomenon, which the sub passes right through.

Then just when you are about to go to sleep again and least expect it, the reactor alarm goes off and you must again leap out of your bunk and spring into an entirely different course of action. Many people couldn't stand that—but it was the way of life for us.

Things on a submarine have to be well secured for good reason. To give you an idea why just imagine you are asleep in your bed at night and suddenly the bottom is lifted into the air three feet. A few minutes later the head of your bed is lifted in the air three feet, and then one side is lifted a couple of feet. That's what a maneuvering submarine feels like while in your bunk. Sudden unexpected steep angles would often send pots and pans flying around in the ship's galley, sometimes loaded with hot food. That happened regularly. I once woke up with my head firmly lodged inside of a small locker at the end of my berth. Somehow the door had swung open and I had slid headfirst into the locker during a steeply angled depth change.

Submariners learn to be concerned about things like chlorine gas, created when saltwater makes contact with a battery. A submarine has huge battery banks, and any leak that allows water to get to them can be deadly since chlorine is odorless, colorless, and tasteless. Once, while submerged, the garbage disposal unit's inner door of our sub sprung a serious leak due to something becoming jammed in it, allowing a massive amount of saltwater to pour onto the deck of that compartment, which had a hatch directly over the battery banks. I was on mess cooking duty at the time, and fearing that saltwater would enter the battery space, I frantically dashed into the nearby Chief's Quarters or "Goat Locker" and grabbed several of their prized soft white blankets, which I promptly utilized to mop up the floodwater. I lost a ton of points with the Chiefs but was nevertheless commended by the Captain for my quick thinking. I think he had a smirk on his face at the time, but I was never sure.

There were leaks, fires, equipment failures, and unexpected encounters—and because of the sheer complexity of a nuclear sub, we regularly faced dangerous situations. The horrible thing was, we never knew where the next event was coming from.

Although there have been accidents wherein nuclear submarines and their entire crews were lost at sea, there is very little risk of significant radiation exposure. The most serious possibilities would arise from a collision or some type of equipment failure resulting in an explosion, which results in the leakage of radioactive waste. There is no possibility of an inadvertent firing of any submarine-based nuclear weapon due to the many built-in interlocks, safeguards, and complex procedures required to activate them.

We had compensation such as great camaraderie and wonderful food. The seemingly ever-present enticing aromas of chow being prepared in the galley made it everyone's favorite place to hang. When we were at sea a meal was served from 0700-0800, another from 1100-1200, a soup and sandwich call from 1530-1630, another meal from 1900-2000, and a midnight snack call. Some submariners had trouble with their weight.

Because space was a limitation in those days, we couldn't carry large supplies of produce. As a result, we quickly ran out of things like fresh milk and salad makings. Then it became "instant" time. We were besieged by companies wanting us to try out their various new instant products and seeking our endorsement and approval. Some were excellent, like the instant mashed potatoes, which were practically undetectable from real spuds. The powdered milk, which if served cold enough was almost as good as the real thing. Other products were iffy, and some were downright bad. I still cringe when recalling that horrible instant watermelon.

At that time, government funding approval for the construction of more nuclear submarines was critical to meeting the Navy's goals and was highly dependent on our performance. Therefore, we often found ourselves demonstrating our capabilities to various politicians. You can't imagine how many appropriation committee members and other officials felt a need to experience firsthand the remarkable sensations of a high-speed nuclear submarine diving deep and doing underwater maneuvers. Because I had some talent in that area I was often assigned to the diving planes during such maneuvers. Need I say—I enjoyed the thrill of controlling those huge metal behemoths. It felt like I was in control of a spaceship and I was proud of my ability to move it proficiently. I had the reputation of being able to park it on a dime.

One of the most exciting things we did was go to "Battle Stations". We constantly trained and often played mock war games with other subs, surface ships, helicopters, or aircraft. Depending on the situation and objective, we sometimes ran at flank speeds, with high-speed depth transits and fast maneuvering, while employing our active sonar detection equipment. Under those conditions, we could be easily detected by anyone listening as we made plenty of noise. Other times we lay still in the sea and ultra-quite, silently listening passively, with the crew barely moving and speaking in a whisper.

The daily routines might have become monotonous, except for the constant requirement of maintaining the boat. There are probably a million different parts or components on a nuclear submarine and things often broke, wore out, or just malfunction. In addition to military duties, each sailor, according to his rating, had his area of responsibility. For example, the torpedo men handled the torpedoes, the cooks cooked, the electronics technicians took care of the electronics, etcetera. Each different rating took care of its particular equipment by performing routine shipboard maintenance. All that state-of-the-art equipment required continual repairs, tweaking, and tune-ups.

In those early days of the harnessing of nuclear power, we were especially concerned about radiation, and wore clip-on film badges that would record any we might happen to receive. The Doctor and Hospital Corpsman regularly retrieved them and checked them for exposure. We also used cigar size radiation detecting scopes called dosimeters that we constantly wore clipped on our shirt pockets that revealed at a glance any possible contamination. If for any reason, someone received more than their allotted radiation tolerance, they were immediately sent ashore and monitored for a sufficient time to determine it was safe for them to return on board the ship. That rarely happened.

On the George Washington, (the first Polaris Missile submarine) there was a whole new set of radiation possibilities to be concerned about in the nuclear missiles we carried. You might think it was extremely intimidating to be living in such proximity to all that destructive power. Quite honestly, being young and naïve, I wasn't much concerned about a nuclear accident or thermo-nuclear exchange with the enemy. I just didn't allow myself to think about such things negatively. They (the nuclear weapons) were simply there. However, I also understood that if we ever had to fire them, it would probably mean the end of civilization, as we knew it, and possibly mankind's very existence.

During the Cold War period, the Soviet Union developed a formidable nuclear submarine fleet, and was our primary concern at all times. We constantly played underwater cat-and-mouse games with them, clandestinely tracking and observing their submarines while they in turn tried to do the same thing to us. Thanks to the brilliance of Admiral Hyman G. Rickover, the father of our nuclear submarine program, and his handpicked selection of top-notch officers and crews, along with America's premier engineering and scientific capabilities, our boats were technologically superior and enabled us to outperform noisier and less sophisticated Russian subs. With our ballistic missile subs on constant patrol, the Soviet Union dared not initiate a preemptive strike against us since our missile submarines would have always survived long enough to retaliate. Therefore it was a standoff, as both the Soviet Union and America could completely obliterate each other at a moment's notice. Looking back at how we lived on the edge for so many years, I can only thank God that somehow we came through it all without ever having an actual combat engagement between us.

The fact is, I now realize why at the time, I never gave the possibility of war its due. Much like the youthful members of the armed forces that serve us today, I was foolishly oblivious to the dangers we faced. I guess I now understand why the old ones who wage the wars send their young ones out to do battle. But I digress. I'll get back to what it was like down there in the deep dark.

At sea, most of the crew stood to watch for four hours and then had eight hours off. The off-time wasn't off, as that was when we studied for qualification, ate, slept, maintained equipment, and performed our regular duties.

There was no day or night inside the boat, except that during night hours, the control room lights were all switched to "rigged for red" (to not affect our vision in the event we had to surface for some reason). The temperatures were always kept the same at 68 degrees in working compartment areas and 62 degrees in berthing areas. We were fortunate in that on board nukes, we could distill our freshwater from the sea, so we were privileged with regular showers and clothes washing.

Diesel-electric submarines could only remain submerged as long as their battery charges lasted, which meant they had to come to the surface frequently because their diesel engines required an intake of air to operate and recharge their batteries. A nuclear-powered boat had no such demands and thus could operate deep down in the sea indefinitely, as long as the reactor had power and that was measured in years. Our limitations were only determined by other factors, a primary one being the food supply for the crew.

One thing that many people find hard to believe is that we never got bored. The closeness of 120 men onboard such a confined space meant that you were seldom ever alone. There was always plenty to do. If you weren't on watch countless matters required your attention. There was never-ending study, plenty of eating, coffee drinking, reading, reading, and more reading (I read countless hundreds of books).

Unless something military was going on, there was a movie shown in the crew's mess every afternoon at 1600 and another at 2000. If we went to sea for 60 days we usually took 60 movies. You haven't seen a movie at its maximum enjoyableness until you've watched one in tight quarters in the company of 30 or 40 satirically critiquing and constantly joking, shipmates.

I started at the low grade of seaman apprentice rank, and my first job was mess cooking. That was an eye-opening experience. It was the first task assigned to all young and inexperienced sailors and it was arguably the most difficult job onboard. Our function was to assist the cooks in any way possible. Our workday started at 5 AM and ended when the last dish was washed and put away sometime around midnight. There wasn't much time for sleeping. We mastered the art of washing dishes and peeling potatoes.

After my 90-day mess-cooking sentence was served I happily transited to the Seaman Gang. We did a lot of manual labor like loading stores, handling and caring for the docking lines, life jackets, etc. After mess cooking, the Seaman Gang was like paradise, except for all the scraping and painting when we were in port.

I seemed to have a pension for wackiness. One cold winter morning when we were going to get underway at 0800 I was assigned the 0400 to

0800 topside watch (which meant that I was all alone on the top deck until the maneuvering watch was stationed at around 0700). It was snowing like mad and one of my responsibilities was to keep the snow from accumulating on the top deck, which would have been a dangerous situation for the topside sailors who would have to walk around on it when we were getting underway. For reasons I could never explain, I decided to use the snow shovel I had to pile the snow up near the bow area where I used it to create a very substantial more-than-human-size snowman, which I intended to push off the sub before anyone could see it. Being from central Texas I'd never really built a snowman before.

Unfortunately for my plan, the temperature rose just enough to turn the falling snow into rain, which upon making contact with my huge snowman turned it into one big ice statute, whose base was securely wrapped around the slit openings of the walk deck. Time had gotten away from me and I suddenly found myself hacking away furiously at my huge and seemingly indestructible snowman to remove him. At that exact moment Admiral Rickover, who was riding with us that day, and loved a stealth approach, appeared at the gangway. Most Admirals travel with an entourage but not him. He wandered around alone and enjoyed sneaking up on those under his command. As the duty sentry, it was my prime responsibility to spot him and announce his arrival well enough in advance for the Captain and Officer of the Deck to welcome him at the gangway. Admiral Rickover was a feared tyrant known to devour anyone who gave him grief. He took one look at me hacking away at that snowman and disappeared into the conning tower hatch with a look of chagrin on his face.

A few seconds later, all hell broke loose as the Captain and Duty Officer appeared, having come on deck through the forward hatch. My problem was, the Admiral was standing down in the wardroom alone. I had announced far-too-late the Admiral's arrival. Within a few minutes, I had been relieved of my topside watch, the maneuvering watch had been stationed, and I was trying to be invisible while serving as the maneuvering watch lookout on the bridge, where Admiral Rickover, the Captain, and the Officer of the Deck stood watching several seamen trying to push my snowman over the side. Needless to say—they couldn't budge it, and we proceeded out the Thames River, and later on, submerged with that darn snowman still clinging to the bow. Although I never actually got into serious trouble over it, I never lived that incident down and the story of my snowman followed me throughout my career.

As a non-rate-designated Seaman, I was allowed to select whatever area of work I wanted to pursue and become a striker in that rating. That is, except for certain engineering specialists such as the reactor operators who had to attend special schools in their chosen field. I was heavily recruited by several senior petty officers seeking to expand their departments with the addition of one more warm body.

I considered becoming a cook, torpedo man, sonarman, medical corpsman, quartermaster, radioman, and even electronics technician. I briefly flirted with each of them as I sought out my chosen field. During boot camp and sub-school, we had been tested to determine our areas of aptitude. According to the experts, my best talents were in the electronics area and my lowest score had been in the clerical field. Believing that to be true, after much reflection, I decided to become a Fire Control Technician. They were responsible for handling the electronics related to weaponry. I studied hard and worked as a would-be Fire Control Technician for several months, but for some reason, my heart wasn't in it.

As luck would have it, a second-class yeoman who showed me the administrative ropes, so to speak, befriended me. I discovered that Yeomen were responsible for all administrative functions like pay, correspondence, etc. and consequently they had many special privileges and were everyone's friends. I had found my calling and the ship's office became my home.

At about the time my first four-year tour of duty ended, I passed the test for Third Class Yeoman Petty Officer. Naturally, I had to reenlist. After spending sufficient time in rank, I quickly made Second Class, at which time I did a tour of duty on board the only non-nuclear submarine I was ever stationed on. After a few trips at sea, I found out that I much preferred nukes and started looking for a new one to volunteer for.

Shortly after I was promoted to first-class First Class Petty Officer, I was transferred to the West Coast where I have stationed onboard a brand new fast attack submarine, at the time dry-docked at the Mare Island Naval Shipyard near San Francisco. We spent quite a lot of time near Seattle Washington and later were homeported in San Diego.

After that, I have stationed onboard a submarine tender where I was assigned as the yeoman for a submarine squadron. I then served my first tour of shore duty as the administrative assistant of the newly formed Submarine Base. We took over the old Fort Rosecrans Army Base on Point Loma in San Diego and established a new Submarine Support Facility there. Just before my eighth year of service, I made the "Hat" and became a Yeoman Chief Petty Officer.

Ask any submariner and they'll tell you that being a Chief was right below the Captain in importance. We were the backbone of the Navy and the safety net between the fantasy world of the wardroom where the officers dwelled and the real world where the crew made it happen. We kept everything on track and got the job done right and on Navy time. We provided the brains for the brawn that turned the wheels, which made everything go.

My responsibilities included supervising the ship's office where we handled the paperwork. My department prepared all correspondence, processed transfers of personnel, created the pay vouchers, and was responsible for such things as the mail, mail order courses, plan of the day, notices and instructions, filing of all paperwork, and handling all things administrative. As a yeoman, the typewriter became my best friend, and that is how I began writing.

One of the best things about my naval career was getting to travel and see much of the world. Early on, I was mostly stationed in the New London, Connecticut, area but I also got to spend some time at Cape Canaveral, Key West, and Norfolk.

My last nuclear submarine was homeported in Hawaii, where I spent several enjoyable years. I loved the foreign ports of call we made during our deployments. In retrospect, I must admit that I even enjoyed those long periods at sea, especially when we were submerged.

It's still hard for me to believe that this kid from Waco got to do all those wonderful things. It has been many years since I've been on a nuclear submarine, and I am sure today's technology makes those early submarines I served on obsolete. All of them have been decommissioned and relegated to the Navy's mothball fleet. When those subs and I were both young, I never dreamed that I would outlive those technological wonders. But I did.

My old dress blue chief's uniform hangs proudly in a spare closet protected by a plastic bag. It still fits, and most of the ladies are still ecstatic when they see the medals and all those gold stripes. I've worn it to a few formal occasions like weddings and ceremonies. The last time I wore it I was keeping a promise I'd made. It was at my mother's funeral.

These days I can only reminisce about those great adventures I had on nuclear submarines when the wonders of our great American technology were admired by the world, and the United States became a superpower. I am proud of those years I spent prowling the dark and forbidding oceans. They have become dreams I left in the past—another world and another lifetime ago.

So now you know. That's a rough idea of what it was really like. There were many more adventures than I could ever hope to relate to in one short essay. Perhaps someday I'll write a book about it.

'WATT' ENERGY CRISIS?

Though I do not claim to be an energy expert or any kind of transportation authority, I am a licensed automobile driver, which highly qualifies me to drill up some sardonic observations on the gooey side of the oil story. There are two sides to every controversy and this is the dipstick side of the energy mess.

Many people are wondering why gasoline pump prices tend to yo-yo. Drivers think it costs too much and pundits think we (mankind) need to get off oil—that to sustain our way of life we must become *energy impendent*. They rant about global warming and mine fields and wake-up calls and personal sacrifices that must be made. Mostly that is true—because we have become a too-fatted calf that must be weaned. The problem is that we must not let the solutions become more trouble than the problems.

Indeed there are some hard choices in our future. It has become obvious that despite political rhetoric and chest-thumping, oil prices march to their drummer. They go up and down in strange ways, particularly nowadays. But regardless of ups and downs, it is the magic elixir and we must have it, and we're about to pass the point of no return, where demand exceeds supply.

For a while President Donald Trump had us persuing energy without much regard for environmental problems. The United States was the number one energy producer in the world. That ended promptly when the Democrats seized control and reduced the production to manners that coincided with their ambitions and anti-global warming policies. I'm not taking sides here but rather admitting that alas, America alone cannot and does not control enough black gold to quench our thirst. We're no longer the only game in town. We are only 5% of the world's population, using about 17% of the world's oil. The most populated country in the world—China, with 1.3 billion people or four times the population of the United States—is already the number-two economy in the world and the number-two consumer of gasoline. They will, in the not-too-distant future, pass us like we're standing still.

India is coming on strong, as are many other industrialized and developing nations. As the world demands more and more oil, it will create inevitable price increases. The U.S. is already sending hundreds of billions of dollars out of the country annually—much more than the cost of the wars we had in Iraq and Afghanistan. This unprecedented massive transfer of many trillions of American dollars within the next decade spells doom for the economy, and if the damn hole is not plugged, will eventually undermine our country. President Trump opened up the pipelines so to speak, and allowed oil companies many more drilling opportunities. As soon as President Biden got into office, due to his global warming alarmist theories, he instituted policies of less production, closing down planned pipelines, and decreasing oil production and distribution. As the drilling options ceased and production slowed, gasolene prices began to climb and long lines at gas stations began to form. The media went nuts.

Those politicians demanding that "we" punish the *monopoly-exploiting* Big Oil companies for those *outrageous excess profits* they've been socking away are not being honest with the public. Rising prices in a free market economy are the consequence of either an increase in demand or a decrease in supply. The rollercoaster-ing of our recent price surges and declines can be primarily attributed to three things: (1) the highly leveraged oil futures contract speculators and (2) fluctuating demands and (3) antie energy production laws and regulations.

For example in 2008, U.S. oil demand started high (prices escalated) and the demand declined some 5.5% (resulting in lower prices) while China's increased by 6.5%. The average net profit for oil companies is a little over 7.5%, which is about 2% less than most manufacturers make. Gas station owners aren't socking it away either, making just pennies per gallon. Something else they (the would-be punishers of Big Oil) are not telling you is that we—the USA—are only contributing about 20 percent of those profits. At that time eighty percent was coming from somebody else. The U.S.-owned energy companies only accounted for 1.6% of the oil and gas we used. That picture changed when the Republican President loosened the controls, opened up drilling opportunities, and significantly increased the United States' oil production.

The big problem is that there are two separate and distinctive opinions on energy production. (1) Let it happen and (2) keep it under tight control in fear of global warming. Your position on these two options is a highly debatable subject. There is little doubt that carbon emissions are sending our Earth's temperatures high and higher. The alternative is that the Earth's temperature has always gotten hotter and cooler over the eons and that many of the alarmist theories are exaggerated. Your political inclinations probably dictate your opinions on these matters.

For example, the California governor has signed an Executive Order that there will be no more gasolene powered cars sold in California by 2035 which means that only electric cars can be sold. Currently, California car buyers purchase almost half of all EV cars sold. If one considers the reality of this mandatory plan, one will quickly realize that it is nigh on impossible. Just considering the infrastructure alone which will require charging access for all those vehicles creates a nearly impossible task. The dilemma will be: how is the government going to create enough charging stations to power all those vehicles and how on Earth is that power going to be generated? Will it be necessary to burn coal to create electricity to power vehicles equipped with very expensive batteries that have a pretty short shelf life and which cost a great deal to replace?

Call me an old fool, but what the hell are they thinking? Do they not realize that there are millions of 15 and 20-year-old gasoline-powered vehicles in use today? There will be just as many, if not more, in 2035. What's going to happen to them? The reality is people can't afford to throw away their only source of transportation and buy an expensive electric-powered vehicle.

Are all the excellent working gasolene powered vehicles going to be sold to third-world countries, crunched up in a huge scrap metal yard, or what? What good is it going to do if the entire rest of the world doesn't go along with the unrealistic mandates of our Sacramento bureaucrats?

In my humble opinion, the only way that electric-powered vehicles can replace gasolene powered vehicles is through technology that does not exist at this time. It's a foolish thing to think that anyone can order the population of a free country such as the United States to comply with the foolish whims of uninformed alarmists. It just ain't gonna happen.

Worldwide oil production had been falling since its peak in 2005 and is getting harder to find and more expensive to refine. Let's not forget that there are more than 500,000 uses for petroleum than gasoline, diesel, and fuel oil—such as the plastics in cars and planes, electronics, synthetic fabrics, detergents, and in some form of just about every consumer product.

Here is just a partial alphabetical list in case you are curious: anything plastic, ammonia, anti-histamines, antiseptics, artificial turf, asphalt, aspirin, balloons, bandages, boats, bottles, bras, bubble gum, butane, cameras, candles, car batteries, car bodies, carpet, cassette tapes, caulking, CDs, chewing gum, combs/brushes, computers, contacts, cortisone, crayons, cream, denture adhesives, deodorant, dishwashing liquids, dresses, dryers, electric blankets, electrician's tape, fertilizers, fishing rods, floor wax, footballs, glues, glycerin, golf balls, guitar strings, hair, hair coloring, hearing aids, heart valves, heating oil, house paint, ice chests, inks and toners, insect repellent, insulation, jet fuel, life jackets, linoleum, lip balm, lipstick, loudspeakers, medicines, mops, motorcycle helmets, movie film, nail polish, oil filters, paddles, paints and paint brushes, parachutes, paraffin, pens, perfumes, petroleum jelly, plywood adhesives, refrigerators, roofing paper, rubber bands/boots/cement, rubbish bags, running shoes, saccharine, seals, shoes, shoe polish, shower curtains, solvents, stereos, tape recorders, telephones, toilet seats, toners, toothpaste, transparent tape, trashbags, typewriter/computer ribbons, tires, umbrellas, upholstery, vaporizers, vitamin capsules, volleyballs, water skis, wax, wax paper.

Each of the above product manufacturers would be in big trouble if they could not obtain the oil. For example, just consider one of them; around 40% of a barrel of oil used to be turned into asphalt products. Refining techniques to maximize the output of profitable fuel has reduced availability to about 10%, meaning municipalities are unable to obtain sufficient quantities to make road repairs and fill potholes.

Then Donald Trump got elected President and policies changed dramatically. No longer was "fracking" which has become a big source of oil production restricted and/or disallowed by the government. No longer were areas of controversy such as drilling in areas that were designated as protected due to their beauty and/or "Not in my backyard" conservationists.

If we push the *Big Oil* sellers too hard we won't even be able to buy as much as we are now doing. They'll sell to the highest bidder. You might as well face it, folks! It's a seller's market and the avarice of sellers cannot be overcome. As the market gets squeezed ever tighter the temptation for rogue oil producers such as Iran, Russia, and Venezuela to bargain politically with their valuable commodity (by withholding it) is inevitable.

Meanwhile, our current oil-producing suppliers – Saudi Arabia, Kuwait, and the United Arab Emigrates - will continue to receive trillions of dollars in oil revenue. We are slowly but surely spending or driving (take your choice) ourselves into a very dark, oil-less corner. Ask yourself this: Would someone intentionally withhold a product merely to inflate its value and keep the price high? Ask yourself this - how does the De Beers diamond cartel—perhaps the only one with a reputation more fierce than the OPEC cartel—keep their prices up?

What is likely to be the ultimate cost of this? Think of it this way. The above countries are rapidly increasing their wealth and power by selling oil as the U.S. expends its capital and surrenders its power, buying oil from *them* in the largest transfer of wealth ever. Our money is being turned over to potentates and dictators who will use it to gain ever-firmer holds over their enslaved populaces. At the risk of stirring up a hornet's nest, I dare say that had we not provided the knowledge and technology to get the oil out of the ground, process, and refine it, they would only be using the oil to fuel lamps. This selling our soul for petrol will not only render us less capable of maintaining our national defense and crumbling infrastructure, but it could also prevent us from remaining the world's number one super power and keeper of peace. We are driving our super power status away—something that makes Earth a substantially more dangerous place.

Like it or not folks—energy is a weapon and desperate people are willing to do almost anything to get it. At this very moment a huge Saudi Arabian super tanker with three times the displacement of an aircraft carrier, the MV Sirus Star, carrying 100 million dollars worth of crude oil, has been seized by Somali pirates hundreds of miles off the coast of Kenya.

Every voter knows where we are not drilling and how many refineries we have not built in the last 20 years. Every time I hear some talking head astutely proclaim that "*we cannot drill our way out of the problem*" I want to throw up. What sheer brilliance. "Ah-ha!" they say. We therefore simply need to discover a clean-burning, non-polluting alternative source that provides unlimited amounts of energy. I have bad news for you. Most of the alternative energy aficionado's assertions are not much more than wishful thinking media pasteurized and well-adulterated 'BULLCHIPS!'

The oil and gas business is risky with many dry holes. It takes years and years of effort to explore for oil or natural gas—obtain the permits, drill and find it, pump it up and transport it to refineries, then store and transport it to end-users. I'm not by any means taking sides here, but they are being continually threatened, blocked, sued, and scorned by a wide variety of environmental extremists, not to mention every NIMBY who joins the frenetic dance of insanity.

Extracting that black goo from Mother Earth is a grimy, muddy, extremely dangerous, and seemingly impossible task. There are good reasons they call oil field workers *roughnecks*. I saw this happen up close and personal as a boy in Texas when they drilled for oil on my grandparent's farm. I watched in amazement as that purpose-driven hard-hatted workforce clanged, clunked, cursed, and bored their way down, inch-by-inch, into that hard Texas soil.

Much of U.S. oil production comes from the Gulf Of Mexico where companies are drilling 200 miles offshore in water 7500 feet deep with oil a mile below the ocean floor. Platforms cost billions of dollars to erect and it takes years to bring up any oil. The exploration risks, scientific knowledge, and engineering efforts required must be complex beyond imagination. How in the world they ever accomplish it is beyond me. But they do, when some interest group isn't blocking them. While protestors and self-serving politicians prevent offshore drilling, other countries are staking claims and drilling right off our coasts. While concerned road blockers debate the risk to our pristine coastlines, other countries are laying claim to our natural resources. For the last quarter-century, Congress has issued an annual directive barring the Interior Department from granting any leases for oil and gas drilling in federal water off both of our coasts. While we have been stymied by political haggling with anti-progressive environmental protectionist groups, other countries including China and Cuba are formulating plans to slant drill into our offshore oil deposits.

As previously mentioned, the oil business is risky. If we drill enough offshore wells there will inevitably be some problems. No decent person wants to see those hideous scenes of volunteers cleaning black sludge off seabirds and marine mammals. Not many people want to push their cars around either. But there are other options—aren't there?

Let's look at the miracle of biofuels for instance. We have all heard how Brazil has been *oh-so successful* with sugarcane biofuel. What they don't tell you is that Brazilians don't own near as many cars as we do. Major programs are underway everywhere and the biofuel race is on. In the U.S. alone production has exploded from 25 million gallons produced in 2004 to 500 million gallons or 20 times as much in 2007. China, desperate to find solutions to its 6 to 8 percent annual increase in energy consumption has set aside about 32 million acres (an area the size of Great Britain) to grow Jatropha, a wild species of African oilseed plant with highly toxic leaves and nuts requiring extreme caution in the handling. Cultivation is unreliably low and cost-efficient productivity has not yet been established.

America-grown corn is certainly not the answer either. If the United States committed 100 percent of our available cropland just to the production of ethanol, we would net some 2 to 3 million barrels of oil per day. America uses about 20 million barrels a day, which is down about a million barrels per day during 2008, due to soaring prices. Unfortunately, we would also have nothing to eat. Talk about escalating prices. Then there is the problem of those folks around the world we've been feeding. They might become a little irritated when they get really hungry. See the problem?

Other than the fact that the technology to produce ethanol is not yet that well dialed in, despite the four billion dollars a year in government incentives. It is mostly boondoggled, folks! It appears that it takes as much energy, if not more, to produce ethanol than the benefits it delivers, an effort requiring nearly as much fossil fuel as it replaces. Studies have shown that forests and grasslands plowed under to grow ethanol crops release massive amounts of carbon (greenhouse gases) into the atmosphere, requiring decades for the ethanol crop plants to recapture. Corn had remained steady at around $2 a bushel for many years. It recently jumped to $6 a bushel, so farmers, not being fools, are switching land planted in other crops such as wheat and soybeans to corn. This is escalating prices for those commodities and for the beef, poultry, and pork animals that consume the more expensive corn to sacrifice their lives for our tables. Fuel is competing with food and\

who are these whacko policies going to hurt the most? The masses—significantly those with lower incomes.

Another complicating issue is the increasing size of environmental dead zones being created in land-to-water boundary areas like the Gulf of Mexico. The culprit is agricultural runoff producing oxygen-starved patches that impact established marine life-disrupting their environment and life cycles. This is predominantly caused by the heavy-fertilization of crops in efforts to produce more ethanol.

Mass amounts of money are being invested by companies frantically trying to develop some kind of non-food-based biofuel from wood chips, green waste or algae, sorghum, camelina (flax), energy grasses like miscanthus or switch grass, and even municipal waste. Creating workable infrastructures for such products and bringing them online just can't happen that fast. As stated above, there are meetings to be held, political palms to be greased, environmental extremist protestors to be ignored, skeptics to be convinced, NIMBY crowds to be overcome and many necessary compromises to be fought tooth and blood over.

We are hearing a lot of talks these days about another amazing alternative fuel—Compressed Natural Gas or CNG, which consists mostly of methane. It is not new, having been around forever, and is one of the brightest lights on the energy horizon. It costs about half as much as gasoline, and we have an abundance of it. It is odorless, colorless and tasteless, and much less harmful to the environment since it has some 90% fewer emissions than gasoline. Sadly, the U.S. is lagging far behind the rest of the world with only 150 thousand out of the more than 8 million vehicles using CNG with many of these being commercial vehicle fleets.

We do not currently have enough CNG fueling stations and the costs to establish the infrastructure will be high. Present conversions average between 3 to 5-thousand dollars per automobile. Because the calorific value is much less than other fuels, CNG vehicles require more fuel space. The tanks are quite large and heavy, usually taking up the entire trunk area. In addition, the driving ranges are significantly less than comparable gasoline engines. There is also some concern about how to fight CNG fires. The prototypes we are just starting to see are merely the vanguard of CNG vehicles, which will undoubtedly be manufactured with safer components and lighter aluminum fuel tanks hung under the body leaving the trunk space free.

Well then you say—how about those flex-fuel vehicles? Aren't they going to seriously reduce the need for oil? Sure... and please allow me to tell you about this bridge I have for sale. There is hope, but it has not been widely revealed that E85 Ethanol currently ends up costing drivers more than gasoline. Why? The lower-compression automobile engines in use by the masses today are designed to operate on gasoline. Mixing ethanol into gasoline does not result in more *miles-per-gallon*—only a dilution of the gasoline. An ethanol-only (not a gas-ethanol hybrid) designed car would reduce dependency on imported oil but as with CNG, the infrastructure is still decades away from reality. On a positive note, the use of ethanol is more environmentally friendly (fewer emissions).

That brings us to the fuel cell and cars powered by hydrogen. There is much interesting research going on in this area. With only water as an emission, fuel cells are environmentally friendly and hold real promise. Who could find a fault in a system using the reaction of hydrogen and oxygen to produce electricity? While all auto manufacturers are wisely investing in creating hydrogen-based prototypes the ability to mass-produce hydrogen autos at a cost affordable to the driving public is many years away still.

Another significant problem to be addressed is the hydrogen-refueling infrastructure that will be required—more expensive than even politicians can imagine. While hydrogen atoms are 'everywhere' the ability to make them available as a source of energy is not easy. There are many economic and energy penalties associated with the packaging, distribution, storage, and transfer of hydrogen. Who is going to pay for all those many thousands of needed hydrogen refueling stations? Cars must be able to store enough of it to drive somewhere. So far, the calculated costs of the infrastructure are slightly less than astronomical to get such vehicles into the marketplace. I wouldn't hold my breath waiting.

Electric Cars? Hybrid cars. Sure thing. Except that when millions of them are plugged in every night recharging their large batteries draining those thousands of giga-watts of electricity required, the meters on our electrical grids are going to be begging for mercy. If you have owned one and enjoyed the thrill of replacing those very expensive batteries and still think it was a good idea, you probably still believe in Santa Claus. The battery systems of today are very heavy and do not provide long battery capacity; however, as the industry switches over to higher-capacity lithium-ion batteries things will dramatically improve. Lithium is the lightest metal and stores more energy with less volume than the standard nickel-metal hydride battery. It is the key to lightness and longer battery life. Even so, a hybrid lithium battery will weigh well over a hundred pounds.

Let me not be negatively charged here. I have no doubt, that in the not-too-distant future, we will be driving vehicles with a wide variety of alternative fuel technologies including gas/electric hybrids with electric fuel cells, lithium-ion batteries, hydrogen-powered fuel cells, rooftop solar panels with futuristic concepts beyond anything we can envision today. Shale oil liquefaction? No problem! Just tear down the Rocky Mountains. Who cares about them? Oh! That's right. I forgot about the hikers and mountain goats. Anyway, it has to be mined, crushed, and baked in massive quantities to extract the gooey prize. Vast amounts of water are necessary to cool and stabilize it. Once all that water has been located, piped to the quarry extraction areas, used, and contaminated, you can just pump it right back.... er... oh... never mind. Talk about carbon footprints. It is thought that the North American oil sand volume contains more oil than all the reserves in Saudi Arabia, but economic recovery is the problem. If the price goes high enough and remains there, it could be done.

Coal to liquid? Since it is technically a kind of solid petroleum it too can be converted using similar liquefaction presses. That is, once you get it out of the ground. Anything we can squeeze or process into killer watts should be on the table. Next-generation clean coal is an oxy-moron if I ever heard one. There isn't any such thing as clean coal. It's a dirty business and it always has been. Black lung disease. Mine collapses. Minors trapped. Enough said. Getting at those tar sands will result in equally great environmental damage due to the mining required.

Lest we not forget, other energy-starving countries could care less about such trivial matters as environmental pollution. China is currently building the equivalent of two 500-megawatt, coal-fired power plants per week even though there have been out-of-control underground coal fires burning there for centuries.

Wind power? An excellent idea. It proved very effective with that very first sailboat and is also excellent for kite flying. A ten-million-dollar grant was given to researchers to explore the flying of kites thousands of feet high to take advantage of stronger winds at higher elevations. Another innovative German shipping organization fabricated a huge kite, attached it to a freighter crossing the 12,000 miles Atlantic Ocean, and believe it or not, saved about 20 percent on fuel costs.

When used as an energy source wind does generate some interesting scenery—millions of huge (think football field size) towering wind turbines atop every hill and breezy pass, their huge rotor blades humming away as they whip the air converting mechanical energy into electrical energy, whacking the occasional dumb bird. Oceanfront homeowners do not like the look of offshore wind parks, so we mustn't think about putting them there, and wind turbines just wouldn't look well on top of cars. It's also pretty hard to store wind for later use.

Solar Power? The sun packs a lot of punch. There can be no doubt of that. We will more than likely have the mandate to install solar panels on the roof of every new building within a few years. Meanwhile, you can buy one for your home and get a small tax credit that will just about cover the beer consumed by the workmen who will be installing that huge contraption on top of your lovely future leaking roof. A residential installation can range upward from sixty to a hundred-grand today. They work fairly adequately too, when not in need of some kind of repair. You'll be able to recover the investment you made in about 20 to 25 years—which, with some good luck—is coincidentally—about the amount of time it will function before becoming obsolete, and you will have to tear it down and purchase another one. Proposed tax incentives and other innovative solutions will no doubt promote greater usage. Don't be too concerned about those high maintenance costs. Just think of how much money you will make selling your spare electricity back to the electric companies. Some brave dudes want to drill down into the earth to capture geothermal energy. Ooookaaay. You guys go right ahead. I'll just stand waaaaay back and watch. I've seen what Mt. St. Helen's volcano did. Just don't forget to have an appropriately sized cork handy. Perhaps we could arrange a free trip to the Big Island for these guys the next time Kilauea acts up. A nice hot glass of 2100 degrees F molten lava should calm them down.

Scientists are busy exploring ways to create hydroelectric power from the constant motion of surging waves, the forces of tides, or sea currents. Research is being conducted with floating devices that bob up and down and others suspended like swings under the water to generate electricity from rising and falling pressure as waves pass over. Others are trying to develop systems of anchoring huge turbines to the bottom of the seafloor in areas where steady currents would continually spin the turbines, generating electricity that would be carried ashore via underwater cables. Think corrosion, and how well electricity mixes with water.

In our never-ending quest to generate hydrodynamic power, we've already dammed up so many rivers that spawning fish can't penetrate the barriers. Politicians are investing (never call it spending) billion of bucks (that's a billion with a 'B') in putting salmon back into a nearly dry river. The chance of such a plan working is slim at best. However, the project would be deemed successful if only 500 salmon returned. That would mean spending 21 million on each fish. And you thought salmon was expensive the last time you bought it. This is no fish tale folks.

Do proponents ask what would be wrong with installing millions, if not billions, of assorted contraptions in our oceans? After all, the seas only cover 71% of the Earth's surface. And if you look at the ocean, it seems to be fairly placid, at least on the surface. So what if all the big fish are disappearing due to overfishing, the waters are becoming acidified, and pollution has temporarily closed, or put under advisory on almost every beach here in the United States? It's not too important that the algae and kelp forests in the oceans absorb carbon dioxide, which keeps the environment healthy. The fish are going to adapt. They always have.

Cutting-edge scientists are endeavoring to create power from all kinds of strange alternative sources such as geysers, old utility poles, garbage, algae and bacteria, and even cow manure. To manufacture chemicals for fuel cells, chemists have discovered how to imitate nature through artificial photosynthesis using solar power to split water into hydrogen and oxygen easier and less expensive than ever before.

One of the first things I learned when I went aboard my first nuclear-powered submarine was that it is the mother-of-all power source – nuclear energy. That energy is called fission and it is created by boiling water to create steam that spins a turbine. It's that simple and that complex. Interestingly, the first nuclear submarine I was assigned to, the USS SEAWOLF (SSN 575) was fired by a sodium-cooled reactor. At that same time, the first nuclear submarine launched in 1954, the USS NAUTILUS (SSN 571) was propelled by steam or a "water-cooled" reactor. That was the decision of the controversial 5 stars Admiral Hyman Rickover who developed the naval nuclear propulsion program and controlled its operation with his cast iron will for three decades after 63 years of service, making him the longest-serving naval officer.

After many trials and quite a few sodium leaks, it was decided that the water-to-steam reactors were the best choice to generate power, and all reactors since that time have been steam cooled. Amazingly, due to Rickover's diligent focus and my naturally charming Irish good luck, there was never a nuclear accident defined as the uncontrolled release of fission products due to damage to the reactor core on United States nuclear submarines. Our accident-free record is remarkable and stands in contrast to the Soviet Union which has experienced fourteen known reactor accidents.

The Three Mile Island Accident in 1979 with a radiation leak that allowed some of the reactor coolants to escape is the most serious nuclear accident in U.S. history. It caused increased security precautions and about a billion dollars to clean up. Although there were no deaths, that incident created a plethora of criticisms and complaints by anti-nuclear power forces and resulted in 82 million dollars in compensation to residents for "loss of business revenue", evacuation expenses, and detrimental health effects including 15 million dollars paid to parents claiming their children were born with birth defects. A class-action lawsuit against the operators was rejected by the courts. The movie "China Syndrome" did not serve the nuclear power industry well, and it remains a controversial subject despite the near trouble-free record of American Nuclear Power.

The United States is the world's largest producer of nuclear power, generating more than 30% of all worldwide nuclear generation of electricity.

However, much of this power is used by other countries. For instance, France obtains 71.6% of its power from nuclear sources.

There are currently about 440 nuclear reactors supplying about 10% of the world's electricity. Twenty-eight states currently have nuclear reactors helping power their needs. Illinois alone has 11 reactors, the most of any state. Nukes are the world's second-largest source of low-carbon power. The United States currently generates nearly 20% of its carbon-free energy from its nuclear power plants which are currently used more intensively than coal – or natural gas-fired power plants. In 2020 the United States generated 790 billion kilowatt-hours of electricity. There are now 94 reactors at work in the U. S. About a fifth of our power comes from these nuclear power plants while 60% of our energy comes from fossil fuels including coal, natural gas, petroleum, and other gases. One of the more interesting features of nuclear fuel is that it does not take up a lot of space like coal, oil, and other sources of power. All of the nuclear fuel produced by U.S. nuclear energy over the last 60 years would fit on a football field with a depth of fewer than 10 yards high.

Going nuclear is no walk in the park, however. Uranium-based nuclear power indeed provides practically unlimited sources of energy without leaving any of those nasty carbon prints. However, there are other significant drawbacks including containment (radiation leaks), terrorist attacks, and the dangerous disposal (storage) of spent enriched nuclear material. I spent years on nuclear submarines and am well-versed in the dangers of operating and containing nuclear power systems.

A nuclear reactor is kind of like having a pet rattlesnake; it is reasonably safe as long as you can keep it in its cage and be very careful when you feed it. Enriched uranium, which is more hazardous to humans and the environment than I can hope to define, has a shelf life of 4.5 billion years. Fortunately, nuclear reactor waste products, comprised primarily of spent fuel rods, but also of various pipes and structural components of the reactor, are not nearly as radioactive, and (thank goodness) it diminishes over time. It need only be kept isolated from all contact with man for hundreds of thousands of years. On the high plus side, the best thing about nuclear power is that it <u>does not</u> emit greenhouse gases while generating electricity.

However, you might be amazed to learn how much radioactive stuff is lying around. We're talking billions of tons. Most of it is now being dangerously stored in intrinsically insecure above-ground sites located within 75 miles of where more than 161 million Americans live. Proponents keep talking about big repositories—really deep caverns within the ground where it can be quietly tucked away until someone else is responsible. A few people want to impulsively dump it into the deep parts of the ocean. Opponents theorize that radioactivity could seep into underground water supplies and turn us all into bug-eyed crazed zombies. I'm not sure who is right. One thing is sure. In addition to generating plenty of power, nuclear reactors also generate plenty of controversies.

But do not be despondent. We are all being exposed to some radiation right this moment. Cosmic streams from space are shooting into us every second of our lives. We eat it in our food and breathe it in our air. Amazingly, it isn't killing us and we need not fear it, as long as it is properly contained. I've slept many a night only a few feet from nuclear reactors and atomic weapons and it never made me the slightest bit crazy, Tee Hee Hee. Stop that I say.

Lastly, speaking of nuclear, there is another race for the ultimate energy going on by cutting-edge scientists all over the world endeavoring to capture star shine creating plasma hotter than our sun. In theory, if this most difficult of all scientific quests can be resolved, enabling mankind to harness Fusion, it would provide an endless supply of unlimited power. Thus far, there have been some wild claims, but no actual breakthroughs. If such a miracle ever occurs our energy problems are over.

Certain Twilight Zone contemporaries and misguided political idealists may think that they can *make it all good* by simply insisting. They would set hard caps on carbon emissions, demanding high fuel mileage from automobile manufacturers, enforcing consumers to buy hybrid and flex-fuel vehicles with a minimum of 150 mile-per-gallon fuel economy. They fail to consider how many people will be killed in accidents involving lightweight kiddy cars instead of our big ole SUVs.

They would merely "REQUIRE" the vast energy sector to supply preset amounts, (which they, in great wisdom will determine) of energy from renewable sources. The most notable error in their miscalculations is that by

2050 there will be 420 million Americans— 40 million more households. Meeting such unrealistic hard caps would entail reducing per capita carbon emissions to levels below those of the colonial days when we only burned wood for fuel. In 2020 the United States used about 124 billion gallons of gasolene or nearly 3 billion barrels equalling over 8 million barrels per day.

Every time gas prices spike upward a bit, short-thinking fools demand that we relieve high prices by tapping our vital Strategic Petroleum Reserves to drive down the costs. Perhaps they think it is some vast unlimited storehouse for their political use. It is true we only paid an average of $28.42 per barrel for it, but there is presently only enough oil for 33 days at the 21 million barrels per day we are currently using. Unfortunately, or perhaps, fortunately, our withdrawal capability is only 4.4 million barrels per day, making it a 160-day supply. But then it would be gone, and we would either have to forget about that possible *rainy day* or replace it at the current higher prices, which makes it a bad idea all the way around.

I do realize that it's much easier to be a 'naysayer' than a doer. But I've been playing devil's advocate here and pointing out some of the reasons why there is no quick and easy fix to the energy problem. It is not surprising that about 60 billion dollars have been spent on research and development of clean energy technology by the U.S. Department of Energy in the last 3 decades. However, with the ultra-conservative-liberal Democrats currently in charge, anyone thinking the United States can obtain all of our energy from within our own country in the next few years is dreaming. By most estimates, we have only about 3 percent of the world's proven oil reserve and therefore energy independence can't and won't happen soon.

The universe runs on energy. It is everywhere. Anything that churns or burns, moves or grooves, heats or cools, bends, wends, or distends winks or blinks, flows, blows, splashes or crashes, shakes, quakes, or bakes, shivers or quivers, flops, drops or plops, slips, drips, or tips, jiggles, wiggles or squiggles, bumps or thumps, squirts or spurts, inflates, grates, evaporates or mutates, sprays, decays or emits rays or changes property in any way. Energy is a great wild horse (think horse power). We must harness it, saddle it up, and learn how to ride. We mustn't let it throw us. It is going to require using all the ingenuity and skill we've got—if we are to tame it.

That cannot be accomplished with panic. We must get real and face the fact that we are being left behind in the energy race. We need to stop the roadblocks by demanding that politicians cease fishing in the bottomless lake of our national debt. We must collectively shut down or find a way to ignore the *false promises, deluded thinkers, political opportunists, and paranoid environmental extremists*. It is high time we realize that the future is not nearly as bleak as the naysayer would have us think.

Galileo was imprisoned for the last 10 years of his life for theorizing that the sun was at the center of the universe. Columbus was doomed to failure, skeptics thought. Organ transplants were far too risky to work, naysayers said. History is replete with examples of egotistical road blockers who impeded the path of progress. Avoiding risk and playing it safe are natural human tendencies—especially for pundits and spin-doctors.

We need to provide incentives for our institutions of higher learning to turn out more engineers, scientists, and researchers and fewer fleets of hungry litigation attorneys, community activists, and anti-socialistic alarmists. We must not sell our souls to the 'devil' of environmental protectionism. We must unshackle the restraints imposed on America's energy producers.

However, we must not throw caution to the winds. What we obviously ought not to do is establish hasty and ill-conceived energy policies with devil-may-care drilling strategies likely to create significant environmental impact, or open up every exploration blockade, end-all deep ocean exploration prohibitions, and refinery development restrictions. We mustn't go hog-wild and just get rid of those unwieldy environmental regulations, and agricultural tariffs and begin to build, build, build—refineries, and processing plants for ethanol, methanol, bio-fuels, or liquid coal.

We need to establish the best possible protective and preventative measures to avoid problems, without forcing offshore drilling in shallow-water pristine areas where environmental impact consequences could be tragic. We don't need to demand at least (pick a number) of nuclear power plants by (pick a date). Neither should we allow political gridlock or create heavy taxation of those capitalistic fat cats Big Oil companies, which would likely prevent them from continuing to invest billions of dollars in research for alternative energy sources and the mythical ultra fuel-efficient car. Ultimately, profits are the best incentive.

Keeping all this in mind, we should proceed with caution at full speed pursuing every possibility. There should be no limitations and nothing held back. After all, if the energy-gobbling monster does annihilate us, it will be too late for this species to do it all over again. I sense what you are thinking. It's a hell of a lot easier to criticize than it is to do something about it. Do I only offer up criticism or do I have any real solutions? Sure I do. Here they are—for real!

1. Drive less, and if you can't...
2. Drive slower, and if you can't...
3. Get the smallest, most economical car you can to go where you need to go, and if you can't...
4. Telecommute (work at home) if possible, and if you can't...
5. Move as close to your job site as you can, and if you can't...
6. Carpool, and if you can't...
7. Keep your car tuned up, and if you can't...
8. Keep your car's tires properly inflated, (not over or under because both can be very bad). And if you can't even do that, you ought not to be driving a car. In which case I suggest you...
9. Take public transportation, and if you can't... or won't...

Walking is a very fuel-efficient means of transportation.

Lastly, America does have the willpower, the scientific/technical knowledge, and industrial know-how to resolve these myriad problems and will eventually do so. It can accomplish this goal even faster if the assorted road blockers mentioned above will just get out of the way. However, if you politicians feel you must do something—think incentives—tax breaks for energy-saving contributors, whoever they might be.

I'm tempted to lurch into the myths and realities of *global warming* because the activist movement (deluded or dishonest?) must not be allowed to force disproportionate restrictions to feather their nests or pad their resume. I have no trouble with America leading the fight against global warming, which is no doubt occurring, but not at the cost of our economic stability. We must not allow the irrational demonization of petroleum usage through the imposition of unnecessary expenditures such as increased taxes, more regulations, and those ridiculous (who gets the money?) carbon offsets. But I'll save that for another time.

WHAT IF?

It's hard to believe the Pony Express ever existed. But it did.

The first battery proving electricity could be generated was developed as a power source around 1800. It opened the door for many important scientific advances such as electric lights, motors, heaters, and eventually the telegraph and telephone allowing people to communicate long distances in a mere fraction of a second. My grandparents never had a telephone and my father was in his twenties before he ever saw a phone. The first gramophones appeared around 1900.

About that same time, mankind discovered invisible energy or electromagnetic waves, more commonly called radio waves. Wireless telegraphs. What would they think of next? Calculators. In 1939, the same year they released "Gone With the Wind" and "The Wizard of Oz" an amazing device filled with electronic tubes galore made the scene... the computer. But it wasn't until 1946 that the first fully electronic computer, containing over 18,000 tubes and using more electricity than a thousand 100-watt light bulbs, went online, changing our world forever. It was a tad bulky, requiring an entire building. But, only a year later, the much-needed missing ingredient, the transistor, was introduced. Transistors never got hot, required far less power than a tube, and gave us the ability to do anything vacuum tubes could do. They could also be made smaller than the point of a pencil. The electronic revolution had begun.

When I was hatched there were relatively few simple black-and-white televisions. When my first child sprang forth no space shuttle had ever flown. My first printing device was a crayon. I moved up to a pencil and then a pen. My first typewriter was a mechanical wonder with precise engineering. When my fingers touched the keys of my first IBM Selectric I was ecstatic. It wasn't too long after that when I acquired my first IBM computer. It had a small 10" green screen and enough memory to hold an entire chapter of a book.

My next computer had a 14-inch screen and enough memory to hold several books. It was quickly made obsolete by a computer with a 17-inch color display screen and enough memory to hold several sets of encyclopedias. The one I am currently typing this on has a 20-inch screen; plays movies and its hard drive can easily hold all the books in my local library. Although I've only had it a short time it's probably obsolete as there are machines out there right now with the capability of storing all the books in the Library of Congress.

My point is that science marches on logarithmically. It began to accelerate in 1945 with John Von Newmann's first written description of how an electronic computer should store and process information, a method, which is still in use today. Computer usage escalated with the advent of transistors as their much smaller power consumption replaced those old bulky vacuum tubes used to amplify electrical signals and switch electrical currents. Transistors were the building blocks of integrated circuits and the foundation of microprocessors, memory chips, and other kinds of semiconductor devices. Their usage enabled the brains of computers to grow exponentially providing nearly unlimited computing power.

Geeks know it's all about the bits and bytes, which are stored on memory chips. Personal computer memories quickly zipped from 8 to 16, 32 to 64, 128 to 512 megabytes – and higher, variously defined as RAM, SRAM, DRAM, BEDO DRAM, FRAM, DRAM, MDRAM, NVRAM, PRAM, SGRAM, WRAM, and the much-unloved *SPAM*.

If you've been at the keyboard a while you probably know a nano-second is .000000001 or a billionth of a second. You may also know that a byte is 8 bits and that a kilobyte is 1,024 bytes, a megabyte is 1,024 kilobytes, a gigabyte is 1,024 kilobytes and a terabyte is 1,024 gigabytes.

Moore's Law—an observation made by Intel co-founder Gordon E. Moore in 1965—postulates that the number of transistors that can be physically placed on an integrated circuit is increasing exponentially, doubling about every two years. This trend has been highly consistent; fomenting social change in almost every segment of the world economy through dramatically advanced digital electronics, increased speed, memories, and digital camera resolution.

One day all PCs will contain huge terabyte memories enabling us to move slowly away from a 'paper world' (save the trees). Theorists are now talking about the somewhat conceptive googolplex, which would be an amount of information greater than the number of elementary particles in the visible universe. A googol is 1 followed by a hundred zeros, but adding that *plex* and trying to describe it mathematically is almost beyond conception.

An amazing technology called *immersion lithography* is making possible a new generation of microscopic silicon-etched chips having a billion transistors squeezed onto a wafer chip the size of a fingernail.

I am quite certain that within a few hundred years, people will be able to own personal computers that can store all the knowledge currently available to mankind. It is obvious that the more we learn—the faster we learn and the faster we learn—the more we improve our technology. That brings me around to the reason for this discourse.

Perhaps due in some measure to the concepts of "The Matrix" films, some speculators on the frontiers of scientific borders have postulated the idea that we may be all only inhabitants of virtual reality or the 'VR' world created by advanced beings playing a computerized simulation game. At first thought, this would appear to be the ranting of deranged minds. But let's consider the hypothesis.

Perhaps you remember Pong—where you batted a little blip around. Then came Pacman where your little guy could eat his way around the game board. Space Invaders and Asteroids changed the orientation to avoid getting killed by reactions that prolonged your game life. Then came the shoot-em-up games with better graphics and motions. Battle Zone was the first game that created an environment approaching the then-unknown VR universe by allowing the player to control the war-world environment.

Today's games offer fully immersive 3-D displays, multiple player spectrums, and unbelievably high-quality graphics. Game designers apply extreme data compression using sophisticated software engineering. The cyber-world is expanding into the arenas of military and professional athletic training creating realistic simulations with three-dimensional designs, sounds, high-resolution graphics, and tactile feedback that challenge trainee-players both mentally and physically. Recent studies have determined that more than half of American adults, 80 percent of young adults, and over 95 percent of teenagers are playing video games. It's about a 20-billion dollar-a-year industry—roughly doubling the motion picture industry box office receipts. Today's gamers can not only shoot and dodge bullets—they can fly planes, drive ships, solve logic puzzles, go white water rafting, bowl, play golf, tennis, and baseball, dance and sing like they are heading a Broadway show, play musical instruments, live the life of a rock star, or immerse themselves in any of countless other exciting activities.

Enhanced proficiencies in areas such as quantum computing and optical switches will soon be utilized to extend technologies, which are accelerating and developing faster than ever. It is inexorable that ever-evolving expertise will ultimately enable us to create computer simulations far more multifarious than the currently existing virtual reality worlds some game players engross themselves in.

Without question, the future of VR has the potential to create games so realistically tactile they are beyond today's comprehension. Already, some VR games are pushing these *metaverse* reality concepts to the extent that they take over their players' lives rendering them completely absorbed by their VR world. The player's virtual telepresence becomes more valid than their reality. If you know someone into Virtual Reality, SimCity, or Second Life, you know what I mean. Vast sums of ***real money*** are already being expended to purchase digital clothing, home furnishings, hairstyles, and makeup on virtual world sites, by players too obsessed to realize they are merely buying cleverly marketed *thin air*. People are exchanging real coins for virtual world coins. For example, $10 buys an EverQuest player $30,000 worth of platinum coins to buy virtual goods and services. When you think about it, ever since we abandoned the gold standard all of our so-called *real money* is only virtual money. And you thought you got ripped off in Vegas.

It is not much of a stretch to believe the realism and resolution of the not-too-distant-future VR games will continue to be enhanced through a state of the art 3-D design technologies, tactile bio-feedback, incredible sound effects that fully immerse the player's vision, hearing, taste, smell, and touch to such a degree that they will collide with the real world. I am not merely talking about some pot-smoking *Dungeons and Dragons*-addicted college kids trying to escape boredom in an illusional alternative environment. The metamorphosis of future games could include vast amounts of data beyond our present intellectual capacity. Currently, state-of-the-art computers are exploring universe creation theories, mapping DNA sequences, and even our human brains. Computers are taking knowledge to places we never dreamed of a mere decade ago. Just look at the evolution of Hollywood special effects imagery to see how fast the VR world is expanding. It probably won't be long before they will have the ability to reincarnate long-deceased movie stars back to VR life to star in films.

Advances in the Internet, cell phones, and computer technology has given us the flexibility to work in virtual offices and conduct our business from home or just about any place else on the planet. Business trips are being set aside in favor of face-to-face teleconferences. Nowadays business phone call is likely to be answered by a virtual operator in India. The cubicles of brick-and-mortar offices are no longer required.

Astronauts will soon have a virtual computerized psychologist available during long space flights offering up understanding guidance and therapy as needed. Researchers in the field of genetic biology aim to soon create living entities by using bits of lifeless chemically treated DNA to build genes by inserting them into an empty cell, thus giving life to a new organism. Other scientists are close to developing materials that will render people and objects invisible. Only Heaven knows what the secretive military complexes are working on. Assuming mankind does not manage to find justification to use the vast storehouses of nuclear weapons, technology will soon permit players to create super-realistic actual images of themselves, literally inserting that cloned image double into computer-generated worlds. With better human-machine interfacing, these virtual clones will be able to play games to the abilities of their controlling creator as easily as we watch a movie, or play out our lives. This sense of presence will inevitably evolve far beyond today's understanding as networks expand and technology matures.

Einstein said, "In the case of skew symmetry the components with two equal indices vanish, and the components with equal indices are equal and opposite in pairs. What does that mean? I haven't the faintest idea, but the point is: the well of knowledge seems deeper than our imagination. Who among us understands the magical mystery of our existence? Mathematicians recently discovered a 13 million-digit prime number on a network of 75 computers verified by a second computer system running a different algorithm. Exactly where does our conscious awareness spring from? Science can't say for sure that it comes from somewhere within our brain because as of yet, no specific neural regions can be identified. We just don't know whom or what may be controlling or moderating our intentions, to which we have no conscious access.

Human consciousness may one day be shocked to discover its egotistical belief of self-importance is epiphenomenal and that our consciousness could simply be a paradox beyond our perceptions. Our every action and behavior may be controlled by forces beyond our awareness. How do you think you control your decision-making impulses, thoughts, and feelings? What motivates you?

There are some excellent plausibilities of proof in our very existence. This is an extremely intricate universe that science struggles continuously to understand—and despite all our knowledge, scientific laws simply cannot account for non-living objects coming to life. Consider the evolution theory for example. Biology just does not fully support the evolution theory, because only living things can give life to other living things. There is no proof that molecules can increase in complexity without a cellular originator. One cannot assume proteins without the DNA that codes them. Who or whatever created all of those unbelievably complex DNA sequences had to be a heck of a lot smarter (I state this meaning no effrontery toward my brilliant son-in-law) than any humans I have ever met—much less heard about. Fossils? Ever hear of Red Herrings?

Why not an unseen, unexplainable creator? Could the Great Operating Director (GOD) be our unseen controller? If GOD is real, then we can only be as real as he wishes us to be. Maybe. Then again, maybe nothing is real. Maybe this is all only "**your**" dream.

Tilt.

TWENTY EXTREMELY VALUABLE LESSONS

1. When someone says "of course it's safe" or "you can trust me on this" be very dubious.
2. Never accept as Gospel anything someone claims that God told *them* to tell you to do.
3. If a repairman tells you he will figure out how much it costs after he completes the job, get another repairman.
4. If you don't think you can make it and someone tells you that they know you can—be pretty darn skeptical.
5. If you find yourself on the short end of the stick, don't expect to come out on the long end of things.
6. If a person is truly innocent they will take a lie detector test, take the witness stand, and won't try to make a plea bargain agreement before the trial.
7. If your exterminator has managed to kill every cockroach but two and they are a breeding pair, he hasn't accomplished very much of anything.
8. The mere fact that someone has the exact opposite opinion of yours doesn't necessarily make that person wrong—or right.
9. Never sign any contract longer than you are willing to read.
10. Where there is a will ... do it their way.
11. Don't borrow money from anybody who tells you they'll fill out the paperwork later.
12. Never tell yourself "this passing stranger looks so darn clean and upright that just this once—I'm sure it will be okay not to use protection."
13. Never try to socialize with any animal you meet in the wild.
14. The free lunch is never really free. The customer always pays for it, one way or another.
15. If someone says to you "money is not the issue" it probably is.
16. If you have to fight some big brute and a friend tells you that the pen is mightier than the sword, take a sword anyway.

17. A penny saved may be a penny earned but never stop to pick one up in a busy intersection.

18. Whenever anyone tells you that "rules are made to be broken" let them go first.

19. In many cases, it is far more prudent to not brag about how, why, or when you did it.

20. The absolute truth is that there are no absolute truths.

MORE MACKSIMS

Every rock is destined to ultimately become a grain of sand.

Thoughts, like radio waves, journey out into the forever of eternity.

Don't spread yourself too thin for the bread you are going on.

Rattlesnakes don't heckle well.

The only limitation to acquiring knowledge is time.

Proof doesn't prove anything unless someone wants to believe it.

A helping hand has no business being in your pocket.

Kleptomania can steal your reputation.

Beware of sheep wearing wolves' clothing too.

Intuition is what you want to think.

Love, like children, should be observed and not loudly heard.

It is not impossible to win an argument based on illogic.

God keeps the longest hours.

When a politician says, "I speak for the people" they are generally speaking for their ego.

Forgotten memories cloud the mind.

Cajoling is much better than steamrolling.

Bad judgment seeks out its punishment.

The more unlikely the statement—the more likely it is unlikely.

A good rationalization can justify just about anything.

The shadow of our awareness casts itself across our conscious nature, allowing us to comprehend our abstract thoughts.

In life, almost everything is in color. There are few blacks and whites.

A spiritual awakening can leave one sleep-deprived.

Today's mistake becomes tomorrow's wisdom.

The top dog shouldn't be surprised when some other dog is nipping at his heels.

The daylight dreams of stars and the nighttime dreams of blue skies.

When you think about it, it doesn't matter all that much if the chicken or the egg came first as they are both delicious.

Perception is severely handicapped by any unwillingness to see.

Real faith will never let you down and real doubt can never lift you.

Fulfillment is an ongoing process.

Whenever you hear someone drunk yell "Get a rope!" leave!

Lies seek out fools for support.

Déjà vu repeats on you.

There is no season and you don't need a reason for huggin' and squeezing'.

Beware of wolves wearing Greek clothing.

There is nothing more pathetic than a bulimic King.

If you don't believe in God, just pray that he believes in you.

Three-point shots are easy if you ignore the rim.

Stupidity makes good bait.

Save your reminiscing until tomorrow.

It's hard to float with a hole in your boat.

The bigger they are the more they weigh.

Ignorance is mostly a state of mind.

God already knows what you want before your prayer, but remind him anyway.

If you fish in another man's pond, you may end up being the one who gets caught.

In real life kissing frogs does not make princes, but it may give you tongue warts.

Destiny doesn't negotiate.

Having God in your corner is good. What better ally could one hope to have than the creator of everything?

If you park your car on a runway don't be surprised if a plane hits it.

You can't outwit an invisible monster.

Desperation is a great motivator.

Sometimes hard choices are the easiest things to do.

There is no such thing as a cross-eyed zombie.

You will never get upriver by going with the flow.

Sometimes we must learn to see in the dark to break into the light.

Everybody has personal baggage. Some of us just pack it better.

The best-helping hand is your own.

Most men would sooner get a nooner than come home late and have to spoon her.

The best compass always points toward heaven.

A good failure is usually better than giving up without trying.

True love is the best medicine of all.

UFOs are merely optical delusions.

Never play poker with sweaty palms.

The difference between heroes and cowards is that cowards never act out of control while heroes often act foolhardy for brief periods.

Anything good is enjoyed more by occasional abstinence

It's often easier to accomplish something than to try to undo it.

You can't conquer your fears until you learn to rule them.

Sometimes it's better to have a big problem than a small one. A big problem will force you to take action, while you may be able to endure and ignore the little one.

A man should only drink as much as he can hold.

If one has an impossible task to perform, procrastination works.

Fear has a way of scaring the heck out of you.

Ordinary men can achieve extraordinary things if they put their minds to it.

Never call anybody a kumquat.

Riding a wild rage is a lot like trying to blow out a tornado.

Triggers equalize strength.

You can't cross a bridge until somebody builds it.

You can't deny what you won't admit.

Sunshine on your skin warms your heart.

Birth is a once-in-a-lifetime event.

Never play darts in a pub with a one-eyed stranger.

A penny saved takes up a dime's worth of room.

If you are going to fly dangerously—take a parachute.

The fourth place in a horse race isn't in the money.

Nothing can give you that warm feeling like transcendental cremation.

Never hitchhike on a railroad track.

You can't be what you can't imagine.

Black roots often reveal blonde ambition.

War is not a sport.

The sky won't bleed.

The root of all money is evil.

People smoking grass in houses may get stoned.

The dark knows things the daylight never sees.

The Devil floats his boat on a lake made from the tears of lost souls.

Wishing is the quicksand of achievement.

A small crack in the wrong place is likely to become a large fissure.

There are few successful pessimistic optimists.

Stillwaters slowly infused turn into fast whiskey.

Dogs know things.

Nature could care less about men's time.

Never get so busy getting ready that you never get started.

Unless it is a curriculum specifically directed toward your chosen career path, furthering your education is only a way of putting off having to go out into the world.

If you are thinking you can't do it, you probably can't.

A fair price is always a bargain.

The closer to perfect—the harder to maintain.

Morality is the hip boots one wears when wading through the cesspool of life.

There is no good use for a bad excuse.

The brain knows, even as the mind betrays.

Every fool wins an occasional poker hand, but few fools ever win a game of chess.

Lies are like quicksand.

People who have bestowed titles as "the most beautiful" aren't really.

A person ought to be his or her own best friend.

The longevity of an opossum is inversely proportional to the number of times it crosses the interstate.

The biggest mystery of our life is our life itself.

A man can only be as rich as his soul is pure.

Business is much better when the buyers have money.

If you want an interesting autobiography, you will need to do some remarkable living.

Poetry is the key to unlocking the emotional universe within.

No matter how good a story is—it isn't a tale until somebody tells it.

Where a smile is planted, a tree of laughter will grow.

Nobody likes a pushy broad.

An opera is an entertainment that is enjoyable to miss.

Assertiveness is only an asset when it is tactfully applied.

Running shoes don't make one a jogger.

Lightning doesn't care how important you are.

Everything for sale is always "on-sale".

A wise man never begins his reply to a serious question until he knows the answer.

Being self-centered often puts you in the middle of trouble.

Pack leaders can't run in the middle.

It's hard to appreciate a sunset while crying.

A sharp spaded tongue often digs an early grave.

Kind words are the building blocks of strong friendships.

An experienced cowboy never gets off his horse until it stops.

Human nature is consistently unpredictable.

Wicked intentions often result in unintended consequences.

No one wants to get drunk more than a sober alcoholic.

The loudest speaker seldom wins the debate.

If you can't face it, fake it.

A little danger is nothing to worry about, except little dangers, which tend to grow bigger in time.

A fine parachute isn't worth a dang if that cheap ripcord doesn't work.

The low-calorie donut is a myth.

Stray bullets are nobody's friends.

An untrained pit bull can either maim someone innocent or prevent a mugging.

The desirability of a diamond is in its ... karativity.

Almost everyone enjoys someone else's misery.

No brakes are a bad break.

You can hear a lot better when your mouth is shut.

People will like you if you have an I.Q.

Today will be yesterday tomorrow.

There can be no answer ... until there's a question.

You can't fake altitude.

The people with the most ruthless religion will be the ultimate winners.

Everybody who is anybody was nobody at some time.

Love doesn't care how it treats you. The choice is up to you.

Revenge usually tastes bitter.

SIDEWALK KARMA

It's a beautiful day. The sun is shining. The sky is blue. The birds are chirping. You feel like a million dollars. You recently received a nice promotion at work and purchased a brand new car as a self-reward, which during your lunch break you have just picked up from the dealership. On the way back to work you decide to run a couple of errands. The parking lot of the dry cleaners is jammed, so in consideration of your new wheels, you opt to park a block away.

You are casually strolling toward the cleaners, when you suddenly spot a wild-eyed homeless transient, or "wretch" if you prefer, right in your path blocking the sidewalk. He is between you and the cleaners and you'll have to go around him. He's wildly jerking his shopping cart around and having one of *those moments*, arguing rather vociferously with some invisible foe. Your only options are to walk past him or turn around and go back to where you came from. But you are a taxpayer and that sidewalk belongs to you as much as it does to him.

So you brace yourself and try to look non-threatening. He reeks of alcohol and tobacco and other stenches you're glad you can't identify. As you are passing him he shouts something about *chickens in Bethlehem* and makes eye contact with you. You smile politely and avert your eyes as you go by him. You almost make it, but out of his shopping cart, he produces a four-foot segment of two-inch plumbing pipe, acquired from God knows where and cracks you hard in the head with a whack that renders you immediately unconscious.

You fade into brief consciousness in the intensive care ward with the world spinning around like crazy. As you drift in and out of consciousness you gradually become aware that there are all sorts of tubes and wires running into and out of your body—your head is haloed by one of those circular framing contraptions that freeze it in place with screws penetrating your skull. It feels like there are a thousand woodpeckers with jackhammers trying to work their way out and there is a constant ringing in your ears.

When you regain enough awareness, a weary doctor solemnly explains that you have experienced a severe brain concussion and that the top of your

114

skull had to be removed to accommodate the swelling and repair some of the damages. But your prognosis is good. That cheers you up dreadfully. A week later the fog starts to lift and you begin to piece it all together in your shattered mind, realizing that you were attacked for absolutely no reason by a demented guy, wielding a pipe, who you unexpectedly encountered on that sidewalk. You can even recall how he smelled.

Your expensive medical insurance covers a lot of, but not all the medical bills. It does not cover the ambulance bill, which cleaned out your checking account all by itself. You have been granted a leave of absence from your place of employment and friends and family and one or two ex-fellow employees have visited and/or sent cards and flowers. As you lay there wondering how the heck you got into such a situation, a police detective visits to take your statement. He shows you a photo ID book with several different pictures of down-on-their-luck homeless types. It's easy for you to pick out the deranged thug who did you in, and so you identify him.

He's the nut who was seen whacking you by several other citizens and the police know him too. He's a familiar 5150 by police radio code, a mental case—a victim of personal demons unseen by the normal world. Fortunately, he is currently in custody and being housed in the mental ward of the local jail where he gets three 'hots' and a cot and whatever free drugs his taxpayer-paid doctors prescribe, all courtesy of the taxpayers. There will of course be a trial. Since your attacker has already been diagnosed as a paranoid schizophrenic everything should precede through the court without any problems.

With your head ring, neck brace, and skull wrapped like a mummy, you are quite a sight when they wheel you out the hospital door to where your relatives wait. Ignoring your protestations to go back to your apartment, they take you back to your parent's house to convalesce. The doctors have said it will be at least two and more likely three or more months before you can even think about returning to work. Since you are no longer earning a salary, and won't be able to afford it, it has been decided for you that your apartment will have to go. You are depressed about losing your job and sulk. Your best friend volunteers to go over and get your things and turn in your keys.

At the preliminary hearing for your attacker, you discover that he has been in and out of the government system for years. It seems that in compliance with a 40-year-old civil rights movement, hundreds of thousands of mentally ill patients were freed or released from hospitals in the sixties and seventies and many of them have been roaming the streets ever since. They were supposed to be treated in their communities but because of the screwed-up legal system and our broken social health care system, in many cases, it never happened.

According to the National Institute of Mental Health, about 6% of U.S. adults have a serious mental illness. While 1% of the adult population has been diagnosed with schizophrenia, about 3% have some form of bipolar disorder or severe depression, and nearly half of all of them do not receive any help. That's primarily because mental patients are free to refuse help and many do. They are also free to loiter in the parks or wander the streets attacking passers-by.

Of course, their families want them to get help, but the overloaded systems often fail and the treatment strategies are woefully inadequate. Your attacker's parents had even sought out help for him, but were on welfare themselves and had no way to assist in his care facilities. What with food stamps, subsidized housing, and SSI disability payments they barely got by themselves.

Some of the lucky ones are sent to live in residential facilities, but they provide only housing and little medical supervision. Even if a patient desires to take proper medication, they might not have the personal resources to acquire them. Others are out of the loop due to budget cutbacks, and a plethora of overly bureaucratized state and federal regulations.

You have learned more about your attacker. He has hurt people before. The voices in his head made him, and the marijuana and alcohol he continually abuses helped. His biggest problem however is that he is highly addicted and especially fond of methamphetamine. Common street names for this widely-used drug include: 'crystal', 'speed', 'crank', 'tina', 'ice', 'snappy', and 'glass'. He will gladly take it in pill form, inhale or smoke, or inject it into his bloodstream depending on what type he acquires. The street form is easily cooked up in a small lab-made from about 15 substances which are mostly pseudoephedrine (a cold remedy), red phosphorous, and iodine. It also includes delicacies like ether, ammonia; paint thinner, Drano and lithium from batteries. The reason it's so widespread and popular is that it is so easy to make. Instructions can be readily found on the Internet. Practically anyone can set up a lab where for a hundred and fifty bucks and a little mixing they will get a yield of about $10,000 worth of drugs. Big profits. It's prevalent everywhere on the street and your attacker scores regularly.

Your attacker has been treated and released at least 20 times for his long-time drug addiction and mental illness. Over the years it became increasingly difficult to differentiate between the effects of his drug use and mental illness. Each time he was institutionalized, he was ultimately kicked back out on the streets for lack of funds. The beds had to be freed up for the continual influx of newly arriving patients. He subsequently attacked seven other people and has been incarcerated quite a few times. He has had numerous social caseworkers diagnose him as a potentially violent offender and recommend permanent institutionalizing—but that wasn't done—mostly because the funds were not available. It seems society just doesn't have the will or the wallet to force such individuals into appropriate mental health facilities. Besides, that old civil rights law keeps popping up.

Over the years he has been prescribed a variety of different anti-depressant, anxiety-controlling psychotropic drugs by several different psychiatrists, and some of them proved to be effective in managing his erratic mood swings and violent behavior patterns. However, he dislikes his authorized medications and will not take them consistently unless they are given to him while he is under supervision in a treatment facility.

He does however receive permanent disability assistance and gets a monthly stipend from the government (meaning taxpayers), which would normally be adequate to cover his rent and necessities, except that he spends it mostly on street drugs, alcohol, and cigarettes. He spends little on food, choosing to eat out of dumpsters and paying nothing for rent, preferring to sleep in any cardboard box he can find. He sometimes uses shelters when the weather turns cold, but disdains them because he is too controlled there and he doesn't like to be told what to do.

Your attacker's trial starts and is held in public court facilities, paid for by the taxpayers. The state has provided him with two public defenders that are paid by the taxpayers. The judge, also paid by the taxpayers has a staff of police officers, bailiffs, and clerks, also paid for by the taxpayers. The prosecution has several competent district attorneys handling the case.

They will use expert witnesses including your attacker's social caseworkers, court-appointed psychiatrists, and various other experts and witnesses as necessary. The taxpayers pay for them all. Of course, the Public Defenders have their contra-witnesses of similar ilk that will also all be paid for by the taxpayers. A trial jury is selected after much hullabaloo and expense. Taxpayers pay the jury expenses too.

Your attacker appears in court as a different man. He is cleaned up with a shave and normal haircut and wearing a taxpayer-purchased suit. He sits there silently with a blank look on his face while his two public defenders and their various assistants represent him. He never says a word during the trial.

The D.A., who represents the *people,* (you) informs the jury how your attacker acted in a criminal way committing an assault with a deadly weapon on your person and that he ought to go to prison. His public defenders emphatically state that he was temporarily insane and needs to be sent to a treatment facility. Their positions are argued back and forth for several days with you attending every day. Finally, they call you up and permit you exactly one hundred and five words of testimony, and you are excused without anyone even so much as asking you if your head still hurts. The trial ends and after several hours of deliberation, it's a hung jury.

You go home to resume life, but you have no job, your car has been repossessed. Your savings are depleted and your credit is shot. You start looking in the help wanted ads and trying to rebuild your life. Then you get the call that they are retrying him. It all starts over. Another six weeks out of your life. By this time you've gotten rid of your crown, and some of your hair has grown back in to help cover the scars.

You sit patiently through the second trial, with all the same stuff as before. You can't help but notice how friendly the various lawyers, court officials, and legal persons have become. You realize it's just a job to them. It's like one big happy family because they are all getting their paychecks regularly. Even your attacker looks perfectly sane these days because he is getting plenty of free drugs to keep him mellow.

You, however, are experiencing frequent headaches and you can't get any medication because they've canceled your medical insurance due to too many claims. You owe the hospital over thirty-seven thousand dollars in uncovered bills. You are thinking about filing a medical bankruptcy. You would sue your attacker, but he has no money. You are told you can apply for victim's aid, but even if your request were granted, the award you could receive would be relatively small and it would take over a year to get it. Your life is changed forever.

The jury finds your attacker guilty in the second trial and you breathe a sigh of relief. At least the nut won't be attacking anyone else for a period of ten to fifteen years, which is the sentence he receives.

You have had a couple of tide-you-over employments, but are still having trouble finding a decent job when the state appeals court throws out the verdict of your attacker's last trial because of technicalities. It seems that during his trial your attacker was a little too docile and compliant because he was mellowed out on prescriptive psychiatric medications, given to him while he was incarcerated. The high doses of mind-altering drugs had impaired his memory and cognition, thus making him indifferent to his surroundings and negating his ability to understand his trial and contribute to his defense.

You sigh a lot and cry some and prepare yourself to go into a third trial when your attacker, in a moment of fleeting dumbness suddenly cops a plea bargain offer of simple bodily assault and is finally sent off to the funny farm for a few months rest, courtesy of the taxpayers.

Meanwhile, everybody's (including yours) taxes are being increased as more and more money is being appropriated by the socially concerned to take care of the mentally ill. When you add up the costs of all the police efforts, the judicial expenses, the costs for the prosecution, the public defenders, the jury, the expert witnesses, the cost of your attacker's incarceration and treatment, your paid and unpaid medical bills, and all of the time wasted in this matter, you have to ask yourself one question.

Wouldn't it have been prudent to make an about-face on that sidewalk and walk clear around the block instead of trying to walk past that maniac? If God forbid, it ever happens to you again, please remember our recommendation and comply. The taxpayers would certainly appreciate it.

RANDOMLY THUNK THOUGHTS

In the great scheme of things, we are practically nothing. If you consider the size of a human being in relationship to the vastness of the cosmos we would be almost invisible. A good analogy would be comparing the size of an electron inside of an atom to a human. Bear in mind that no one has ever seen an electron, much less an atom. We can only theorize that they exist. That is how proportionally significant we would be to God.

I recently read that many scientists think that there are more living creatures inside a cup of typical garden soil than there are living human beings on Earth. We may not be able to see them because they are too small, but they are probably there. There could be trillions of unknown worlds smaller than a trillionth of a quark, spiraling about within every hair of our bodies, existing on a physical scale impossible for us to recognize. There is no way for us to know.

We cannot grasp the infinite or imagine the endlessness of possibilities. We cannot envision the footprint of the fourth dimension, the color of the soul, the inconstancy of our virtual reality, or the essence of an interstellar psyche. That is the realm of the creator of all.

It is sad to realize that our marvelous brains are merely captive passengers forced to stand by as casual observers while our bodies race through their temporal paradigm like runaway trains. The question is: are we the only creature aware of this?

So, now that you have thought about time and concluded that It is all there is—what are you going to do about it?

The estimated measure of the speed of thought is inversely proportional to the gap of intuition. Consider it.

Who counts the wishes and prayers passing each other in cosmic flight? And where are they ultimately cataloged and stored? Surely they must be—or else why would they exist?

The resolution in a bottle is a myth.

Could there exist a sanctuary in an invisible sea where unlived passion accumulates and waves of love roll longingly onto a desperate shore?

If "faith" was bricks and "hope" was mortar, could we build a stairway to the great beyond?

After a great deal of reflection and many years of deep thinking, I have decided that 'life" is the primary cause of stress.

If you find yourself awake late at night, all alone when everyone else in the house is asleep, just sitting there and thinking deep thoughts and contemplating things you do not understand, it would be a very good idea for you to go to bed.

There are a few things that one should be concerned about and then there are other things that one ought not to be concerned about. How to tell them apart is the hardest thing and something you really ought to be concerned about.

It is very impolite to turn down a slice of homemade pie, or ala' mode if offered.

Nearly everything in the Bible happened in an area about 400 miles long and 80 miles wide. Isn't that miraculous?

Poverty is like quicksand. The more a person struggles, the deeper they sink.

We exist in a sensitive universe of light and time. A shadow is as real as a moonbeam and every breath we exhale will travel through the cosmos until it reaches eternity. Every infinitesimal particle will eventually merge with every other piece of matter that exists until everything is the same. The past, the future, and the present are the same except for our perception.

Could it be that we humans are, in the grand scheme of things, about as insignificant as a wee ant we discover scouting our kitchen countertop and that we can be taken out of the grand scheme as easily as we might dispatch that invading ant?

The secrets of enjoying a long and happy life are 50% good luck, 30% good genes, 15% good attitude, and 5% good lifestyle.

The best possible gift for your children is your choice of the right spouse.

With all our scientific accumulated knowledge, mankind has no idea at all how to bring a grain of sand to life, and we probably never will. Life is God's purview.

Somebody has got to help the one who helps out.

Have you ever noticed that wherever you are at any given moment that spot becomes the exact center of the universe?

To see most clearly look with your brain. To see most fairly look with your conscience. To see most compassionately look with your heart.

It is an indisputable fact that once the last song has been written it will be the end of our existence on Earth.

There was no "before the beginning".

Short-term memory is...

The "big picture" requires a screen larger than our eyes can see and more colorful than our minds can conceive.

THE UNIVERSAL MIND

I believe that there is an inimitable universal mind to which I am somehow fortunately coupled. When I was younger, I used to struggle with accepting it, but it has now become a collaborator on whom I know I can rely upon. I believe this preternatural connection is precisely the instigating font of literary creativity. While I aspire to share the perplexing secret of how you too can get connected, I'm vexed because I have no idea. I don't even know how I got coupled. It's just there. If you can't sense it and don't believe it exists, perhaps you are not meant to be a writer.

I know some erudite individuals suffer from occasional writer's block. That has never been my problem. By the time my fingers access the keys hundreds of thoughts skirmish to burst through into words. My problem has been evicting the mind-numbing ones.

I never struggle with trying to craft anecdotal ideas. They flood into my too-crowded mind at such a pace that I must persistently reject thoughts to avoid rambling. Even now, as I type this there are a thousand tangential directions I could digress toward. Hopefully, I won't, as I do have a summit in mind, which is simply to offer up a few starter lines to anyone who would like to seize them and run.

Therefore, I shall now plant a few thought seeds for any fertile writer's mind—mere ideas anyone can use as the zygote for an article, book, opus, or whatever. There are innumerable corridors each one may take, according to your esoteric intellect, to demonstrate that every human brain has the option of being directly connected to the limitless universal cerebrum. Since I have no preconceived thoughts in my head, I'll endeavor to do this extempore conjuring up gist seeds as I roll along applying no great amount of fertilizer—tossing them out randomly as they flood in.

The well is deep—and because I'll never get around to using them, feel free to plagiarize at will. I pledge no litigation if I happen to see them in your great tome. However, if any prospective publisher chances to observe them and implores me to expand a particular idea to fruition, please don't hesitate to contact me at any time with your offer of an appropriate advance. Bear in mind, I don't work cheaply.

FREE PRETERNATURAL THOUGHTS

It isn't every day that you see a dwarf, completely nude except for a huge cowboy hat, riding an enormous silver-saddled Rottweiler down the center island of a busy city freeway during drive time rush hour. Yet there he was, casually loping along while smoking that immense cigar, seemingly oblivious to the problem he was creating with rubberneckers. I couldn't wait to hear his story so I hit the siren and pulled up alongside him.

—-

There is no more despair than to be dying without heirs and yet—that is exactly the position that (name) found himself in. He struggled to raise his head to better see the first rays of dawn breaching the blinds of his sixth-floor hospital room. From somewhere outside he could hear the unmistakable drone of a buffing machine polishing the floor. He looked at the slowly dripping IV bottle hanging above his bed and his eyes followed the tube down to his wrist. Bright sunlight stabbed in through the blinds laying slat shadows across his bed. He ripped the tape off the IV needle and carefully pulled it out of his hand. It was going to be a hell of a day.

—-

His sprinting heart synched with the panting of his steed and he badly wanted to rub away the sweat scuttling into his eyes but dared not let go of the reigns. His darting eyes nervously traversed the barren plain and he thought for an instant he could see a town ahead. The wind began to surge and a dirt devil raced across the distant emptiness. He had some important things to do and hoped he could make it there in time for the hanging.

The blood made the small cutting shears slippery as (name) lopped off another finger, casually tossing it onto the pile of body parts. He licked some sulfur-tasting blood off his fingers and took a robust swig from the bottle of Bailey's Irish Cream. He smiled. It was going to be a long night...

—-

She could smell wildflowers all about her as she fixed her eyes upon the drifting clouds sky-scraping above. She could almost see the face of her father in one of them. It took her mind back to that day she last saw him—that morning he'd kissed her on the forehead and said, "Don't worry babe, I'll be back before the start of your summer vacation." That was thirty-seven years ago. She wondered if he still had those same beautiful eyes. Soon she would know. She reached up toward the cloud image, but he was no longer there. Tears came into her eyes...

—-

The blast was violent, and the shockwave hammered him like a bus striking a careless jaywalker. He could feel trickles of blood oozing out where fragments had penetrated his body. "Sarge" he called out, but there was no response. He didn't know it, but he was the only one left alive and he was on his own. He tried to move his right arm, but there was something massive pinning it down. "Sarge!" he cried out again." "Sarge!"

—-

I know every prisoner claims to be innocent. But a short-timer on the row ought to be making his peace with the Man. He should be able to cope with his crime and admit that he deserved to be there. It's a time to beg forgiveness for sins. The only trouble is, I was innocent, and there is no way I'm going to be forgiven by anyone. The death-clock is ticking short. My incompetent PDs have exhausted my appeals and nobody believes me. Shoot, my momma despises me. There is only one thing to do...

—-

It was time. Forty-six generations had transpired since Earth Exodus, and now he was fortunate to be one of those to commence the actual colonization. He felt epic anxiety. All the expedition knew was that this new planet had been well probed and scientifically determined to be life sustainable. Supposedly it had similar habitability parameters to the home planet. But he had not been born on Earth, and there was no way of knowing. The transport ship was all he'd ever experienced. He had doubts.

—-

Bunkie the Chipmunk had a toothache. "Boy! This is some tough nut," he thought, spitting out the shining round thing he'd been chewing on. It rolled across the dirt floor and came to rest in front of Bunky's mother, who was curled up in some leaves and seemed to be happy and deep in sleep. Bunky was restless, having a strong urge to leave the snug bower and go out to explore the day. The bright sunlight splashing into the burrow entrance seemed to tug at him. He could smell the excitement and hear the haunting musical medley of blended nature sounds. Out there were robins, wrens, sparrows, lizards, frogs, butterflies, babbling brooks, green grassy meadows, wonderful trees, rustling leaves, dew-wet flowers, and a million things to explore. His heart was so full of anticipation that he thought it might burst if he couldn't get out there soon...

—-

There are some things that neither the cops nor the criminals want you to know—hard stuff, like the fact that the most likely weapon you will ever be murdered with is a knife taken from that butcher's block in your kitchen. That's the first place I'll head after breaking into your house. If I need a gun, I'll just take that one stashed in your nightstand. It's already loaded. But first, while I'm in your kitchen, I'll check the freezer for that stash you've got hidden in there. It'll be wrapped in tinfoil and camouflaged as meat, but it'll be cold cash, and you thought you were being so clever to think of storing it there. I've got expenses too you know. And regardless of what you hear, crime does pay very well. I should also tell you that most crimes are never solved.

—-

The fifth richest man in the world widened his deep-set blue eyes in amazement and leaned well-back in his brown leather office chair." Are you positive?"

"Yes sir," answered his Chief of Microbiological Research and Development." We've isolated it—there is no doubt."

"So—what you are telling me—is that we now possess an incurable and highly infectious airborne virus contagion that seeks out and overrides the dendritic cell function that alerts immunity warriors; replicating itself at such astonishing speed that within twenty-four hours, ten viruses become trillions.

The fifth richest man in the world bobbed his head. "Am I understanding you correctly that this means our multi-rotavirus/hantavirus cocktail etiology can now be programmed to disproportionately affect the specific DNA of any targeted- race, spreading airborne human-to-human and killing everyone who gets it within 72 hours?

The scientist nodded, "Yes sir, that's exactly what I am telling you."

The fifth richest man in the world clasped his hands behind his head and smiled...

—-

Almost all serial killers are indeed men. But there are exceptions. This then is the story of an exception. She was born in a single-wide trailer in a seedy park on the outskirts of Oklahoma City. Her mother was a heroin-addicted prostitute who worked the truck stops and her father was a passing unidentified speed demon long-haul driver who never knew she existed. To say that she'd started life off on the wrong side of the tracks would be an understatement of the worst kind. She was born addicted to fetal alcohol poisoning. She...

—-

It was as big as 1500 football fields and weighed less than 3 grams. It was a drifter riding the cosmic winds with no power to direct its motion. It was no more visible than the heavy ions that continually shoot through the earth, but it was more deadly than all the combined weapons ever possessed by mankind. For want of a better name, let's just call it a Space Jellyfish. It...

—-

Evil sometimes wears an excellent disguise. In this particular case, it wore priestly vestments. His prey was joyful and young. He'd been watching her for months and knew his quarry well. She took the same route to her first-grade class each morning, always dressed in her sexy little Catholic schoolgirl outfit, her blonde pigtails dancing in the sunlight as she provocatively skipped along. He would have her soon.

—-

The inevitableness. That's the problem. We know it's coming—that final curtain. Oh sure, when we are young it's not a priority. But then time goes on and sooner or later we realize that time is an hourglass and the sand is running out. It occurred to me on a Tuesday as I was waiting for the subway in Times Square. That was the first time I saw him. He was eating something he'd dug out of a trash receptacle, and looked right through me. I...

—-

A dark shadow awakens and slips from its dank sepulcher in a spasmodic shudder. It knows not of mercy or grace, consolation or religion, only realizing its mission and purpose. It sees through deep-set blood-veined eyes that survey the surroundings to get its bearing. It has been assigned a task, and now it arises to pursue its unsuspecting prey. It sets a course and floats lightly above the dew-wet ground, off to perform its sacred rite...

—-

(Name) gazed casually out over the busy street where cars, buses, and all sorts of motorized vehicles streamed by in the never-ending parade. Through sheer willpower, she had learned to ignore the honking horns and screeching brakes, the shouts and profane rants of those thousand of strangers passing beneath her window daily. She smiled and tilted the small green watering can, allowing a stream of fertilized water to pour onto the potted geranium carefully placed on the sill of her tenement window. My great day has finally come she thought, and...

—-

Have you ever been making love in the middle of a great dream and been jarred unexpectedly awake at four o'clock in the morning by an annoying telephone ringing loudly in your ear? Well, that's exactly what happened. I grabbed it before it could ring twice and wouldn't you know there had been a murder. Naturally, they needed me there immediately if not sooner. "Don't even take time for a piss," was how the Captain had so succinctly phrased it. To hell with him. I rolled out of bed and took both a number one and two, grabbed my badge and gat, and went to see what the big deal was. It was only another murder, or so I thought.

—-

"I'm telling you upfront—there is no need-to-know basis for what I'm about to reveal—our little group and that's all. You all know that there is only one effective way to confront them, and that is to be more ruthless. I'm not talking about any eye-for-an-eye crap. I'm talking a thousand pairs of eyes for an eye. Maybe even a million. I'm talking extreme brute force and no holds barred. That's how Saddam did it.

"I figure we'll start with a five-megaton in Pyongyang. The suitcase will go in crated as Russian food aid. That ought to get that little bastard's attention. We'll follow that up within a few days with another fiver in Tehran. They want to play terrorists—we'll play far better than they can. It won't take long to convince them that de-escalation and friendly relations are the better way to go. They want Stone Age; we'll give it to 'em. Questions?"

—-

I live with it day and night. In the daytime, I think about it and at night it haunts my dreams; that unforgettable sound of the screeching tires and my screams as my car plunged off that 90-foot cliff. I clearly remember going through the guardrail and that feeling like I was on a roller coaster when my stomach leaps up into my throat. I forget the landing, but I know it was bad. Then I woke up peering through one eye into the bright light of that intensive care ward. There were lots of wires and tubes and bandages. When that kind of young doctor told me what body parts I'd lost I fainted.

—-

He came in loud. And drunk. She could hear him cursing as his key fumbled in the front door lock. She imagined how fowl his breath would be and knew she would be in for another beating. She pointed the 38 at the bedroom door and pulled back the hammer. Her hands trembled. She knew it didn't take any more effort to pull a trigger than it does to swat a fly. Suddenly the door flew open...

—-

How vividly I remember that night when my husband (name) and I lay in the tall weeds behind that rusted iron fence in the shadows of the darkened moon with our little son (name) and the others. There were twenty-two of us in all, not counting our coyote. We wore sweaters and wool hats because we were told it was going to be very cold. Even so, I perspired heavily and my heart beat so fast I thought it would burst. My backpack was stuffed with what little clothes we could take, as well as some bottled water, three cans of soup, a single loaf of bread, an old photograph of my mother and father when they were young, and my little icon of the Virgin of Guadalupe. That was all we were bringing to the United States of America...

—-

Once you pass the feed and grain store, take your first right till you see a rickety red and yellow barn and make the next right onto the gravel road and keep on goin' over that wooden bridge and on through the cottonwoods. About a half-mile down you'll see an old white farmhouse with piles of farm equipment. It ain't no palace, but it's where I live. It's a strange and pretty-near worthless little slice of nowhere but I call it home. It ain't even on no map, and there sure as heck ain't no convenience stores nearby. But if you got a hankering to be left alone, it's the perfect spot. Why, I even got my little graveyard, outback where I put em' when I'm done with em'...

—-

The great womb contracted and something began to crown. It was not exactly ahead—more of an appendage. A "thing" if you prefer. Slowly it began to maneuver out as the labor convulsions found their rhythm. Then eyes appeared— lots of them. Some were closed and some were open. It was going to be a strange birth...

—-

I struggled up the mountain of garbage, gagging my way to where she lay. There must have been a million flies swarming around the body. Birds had pecked both eyes out and a huge greasy-looking rat was enthusiastically gnawing away at what was left of her nose. There were no arms or legs attached to the torso, which appeared to be riddled with bullet holes and stab wounds. It had also been doused with gasoline and set on fire.

Frankly, I'd seen prettier death scenes, even in a city dump." It's a perfect place to kill," I said to my young partner, as I unpinned the note attached to a charred flab of skin that had once been her left earlobe...

—-

Her idea of a perfect man was someone she could siphon all the money and blood out of. She'd leave you high and dry quicker than a drop of water could dance off a hot griddle. She was a she-devil in a speedboat and she'd leave you in her wake like a minnow flopping around in the middle of a burning desert. She made the word painfully seem mild. She was a one-way alley of muggers waiting for a victim to come along. So why did I fall for her? I'll tell you...

—-

Impossible! It couldn't be. There was no way. And yet, there it was. There could be no doubt. I had to believe my own eyes. I never expected it. I never even thought it possible. Yet, it had happened. I had to face it. It was one of those impossibilities that destiny has a way of providing. Sort of like a miracle, or having a winning lottery ticket. Okay. Now, what would I do? I...

—-

Most people think a hitman has no feelings. They're right. We don't. It's one of the main job requirements. Being a hitman is after all—just a job—a way to make a dishonest living. Let's face it—it's easier than construction work. Pays better too. Just think of me as being employed in the first stage of the undertaking, involved in pre-arranging the transportation of passengers for the ferry that crosses the River Styx...

—-

She wobbled into my office late Friday night on pins that would have made Betty Grable spin in her grave. She was precariously balanced on bright red stilts and matching lycra capris. Her shoulder-length hair was the color of a ripe banana and her Madonna's face had been crafted by Aphrodite. She looked like she would be as comfortable as a well-worn pair of sneakers. Unless I missed my guess Lilac Champagne by Revlon enveloped those Botoxed lips.

Her double-B-cup topside deck was loudly accentuated in a bumblebee yellow designer silk see-through with headlights shining on bright. She was packing a pair of perfectly pyramided 44 Magnum C-cups that made me involuntarily drool as my mind flashed back to infancy and the ecstasy of breastfeeding. She was so hot the temperature in my pants immediately shot up 15 degrees. My brain boggled. My eyes erupted. My tongue tingled. My loins lusted.

She blew out a slow hiss of invisible smoke she got from someplace and ran a small wedge of the perfect pink tongue over her lips. Then, in a voice that would melt Kryptonite said, "Are you a Private Dick?"

—-

Happy writing.

MY PRESIDENTS

It was an election year, and I was as oblivious to politics as a camel is to the Antarctic. All I cared about was selling Waco newspapers to the gathered crowd. When the speech-making part was over I started hustling. There was a line and I was going down it, wearing my earnest "buy a paper from me please" smile. I suddenly realized this loud-talking man was coming toward me, distracting my potential customers by shaking their hands and joking with them. I stopped in my tracks, wondering if I ought to be on the other side of that darn rope when the big guy stopped right in front of me.

He looked huge and glared down at me like he was deciding if he was going to eat me or not. Then he grinned and spit out some Texas drawl. "Cain I rub yore haid fer luck red?"

I looked up at him awkwardly, having only a vague idea of what he had said when he grabbed my shoulder with his left hand and stuck out his huge right hand, and gave my natural curly red hair a thorough tossing. Ordinarily, that would have been cause for a fast fistfight, but he was way too big and I was way too stunned to react. I was dumbfounded. Having rubbed off all the luck my hair had, he moved quickly past me, pumping any outstretched hands and kissing any babies he could get at. I recall hearing someone in the crowd remark (behind his back of course) that Lyndon would have a good future in politics if he was not so damn crooked. That brief contact with LBJ was my first Presidential meeting, so to speak.

Since that time, life has had a funny way of playing the "meet the President" game with me. I don't know if it could be passed off as just dumb Irish luck, or strange providence. I'll tell you about it and you decide.

The next President I met was not in office either. He was a composed and unassuming young nuclear submarine officer stationed in New London Connecticut. I just happened to be a nuclear submariner stationed there at the same time. Although we were not assigned to the same submarine, I did attend some of his lectures and see him around regularly, which meant that he had to salute me. Well, technically since I was the enlisted man, I had to salute him, but President Carter-to-be did have to return every one of my salutes.

My next Presidential Meeting was more dignified since Ike was already in office. He came to see me on board the U.S.S. SEAWOLF, which made him the first U.S. President to ever go to sea on a nuclear submarine. I ate lunch with him. Yes, at the same table and seated adjacent to the President. I got there on account of hailing from Texas (Ike was originally from Abilene) and also being the youngest sailor on board. Later, when we were at sea, I was standing right behind him in the conning tower as he peered through the periscope. Unfortunately—only the top of my white hat made the cover of Time magazine with him.

I briefly met JFK, or President Kennedy as I called him; when he came to observe the U.S.S. PERMIT, another nuclear submarine, perform. But I don't count it as one of my official presidential meetings because I didn't get to shake his hand or anything. I just stood at attention and saluted as he passed.

Not long after I got out of the Navy, I found myself in the recreational boat business in southern California. One day, a charming and personable rather fast-talking young fellow came to inquire about a position as a yacht salesman. It was Michael Reagan and we gladly brought him on board. He and I became close friends and worked together at several dealerships. We've been friends ever since.

Thanks to Mike and his lovely wife Colleen, I spent lots of 'black-tie' time at political affairs and consequently, had long personal and meaningful discussions with Governor and later on President Reagan, to whom I gave lots of advice on world affairs. I wish. But I did meet him. Without a doubt—President Reagan was one of the most impressive, kind, and dignified gentlemen I've ever met.

I've also met an ex-president. In the 1970s, after Richard Nixon had resigned his office, I was involved in the marketing of a new type of ultra-sonic baby monitor and in that capacity, I traveled to Washington D.C. to make a speech to parents of babies who had died of the sudden infant death syndrome or SIDS. Wouldn't you know that Dick would be traveling by common carrier and be on my return flight. Unfortunately, he was in first class and I was in, shall we say, the back of the 'bus'.

My attractive traveling companion, having no fear of rejection, name-dropping, or self-pandering, casually strolled up there and managed to take a seat next to him long enough to secure his promise to make a speech at her ladies club, which of course he later on never did.

The hard pill for me to swallow though—was when she insisted on dragging me up to first-class for a heartfelt introduction. Didn't the woman know I already knew enough Presidents? I shook hands with RN and we briefly chatted. I then skulked back to the cattle car while my worse-half enjoyed a cocktail with the defrocked Ex-President, who was slightly lacking friends at that time.

The epilog for this particular tale has to be the most ironic thing of all. I'm from Waco, and George "W" Bush's ranch was located only a short distance from my little sister and brother-in-law's ranch. By Texas standards, it's a fairly small and low-populated rural area, and most folk there-bouts know most o' thar' neighbors. And yet—even though I've hung out a bit in Crawford—and driven right by his spread—I never even met the man. Of course, neither has my sister. Since then, my sister has moved back to California. But President Bush has a home not very far from my other sister's house in the Big "D"—so I still have hope.

Speaking of hope—as for President Obama... well... I've lived in Hawaii and been to Chicago several times. Does that count for anything? Is my Karma fading or what?

VIVA LA DIFFERENCE

I must admit I have never read that book about men and women and Mars and Venus. Nevertheless, since I am approximately one-half of the man/woman equation, Therefore, I feel half qualified to comment on a few of our idiosyncrasies. I shall endeavor to elucidate some of our more obvious contrasts. None are cast in iron of course, as there are exceptions to every rule. One thing is for sure; it's a lot more complicated than merely declaring that most men are tall and most women are short.

When it comes down to poking your head up out of a foxhole, some men will fearlessly and without question do it, while most women have enough sense not to. Perchance they have more common sense.

Strength and dumbness count in many things. Being a retired military man I can state with some degree of confidence that most professional military men will readily admit to believing (but generally not out-loud in mixed company) that women have no place in up-close combat. Bullets and bombs are not their forte' and never will be.

In WWII, or the Big One if you prefer, out of the 400,000 American military deaths there were about 500 females and most of them expired from accidents or disease. Only about a dozen bit the bullet so to speak. Amazingly, of the 47,400 American military personnel killed in action in the Viet Nam war, only one female nurse lost her life in a rocket attack. In the Persian Gulf War, although there were some 40 thousand military women deployed, only 15 female deaths occurred.

Most women serving in War Zones until recently were in positions such as truck drivers and helicopter pilots. They are now being permitted to serve in combat with some 220,000 women who have already gone to the wars in Iraq and Afghanistan. With about 15% of all troops being female, they have thus far contributed only about 2% of the causalities.

I'm not saying that women are not fearless, but the reality of it is—war is a man thing—which we men ought not to be proud of. Men need to blow things up and participate in battles. We even excel at looting and pillaging. If there were only women there would be no wars.

Let's apply just a little inane logic and consider the effectiveness of women in the Fire department. A 120-pound woman, no matter how determined, due to physical limitations, simply cannot tote a 200-pound unconscious person on her back down a ladder from a burning building as easily as a burly fire "man". Note the *as easily*.

This also applies to police work. Whether they will admit it or not, *most* male police officials are of the general opinion that *most* female officers tend to get in the way in truly dangerous life-threatening situations requiring strength and physical dexterity. Before you hunt me down and bloody my nose please recall that I did not say all.

You may also be aware that I haven't even mentioned pregnancy. On the other hand, if you are looking for someone perceptive—seek out a feminine mind. Did you ever wonder why there are very few male fortunetellers? Women are naturally intuitive, and wily. I think this may be because they are also naturally suspicious. Perhaps it is due to eons of co-habiting with cheating males.

Men play it close to the vest, keeping their private stash of important secrets internalized. Women tend to tell their closest friends, who in turn tell their closest friends, ad infinitum.

Care for a few more chauvinistic observations? Men are the more madcap; women are the more manipulating. Men get angry; women get their feelings hurt. Men cuss; women use profanity. Men pass out; women faint.

Women charge; men pay. Women befriend; men bond. Women compromise; men negotiate. Women bitch; men grumble. Women are perky; men are studly. Women picket; men riot. Women understand; men get it. Women shoplift; men steal. Women try it on, envision the possibilities, and attempt to make a purchasing decision. Men see it, note the size, and if it sort of fits—they buy it.

Women tend to be more patient. Men hunt; women gather. Men fish; women knit. Men saw; women sew.

Men may be Players. Women may be loose. Unfaithful husbands "cheat" on their wives, while unfaithful wives "run-around" on their husbands.

Women are more easily hurt. Men are more easily teed off. A woman will pout. A man will shout.

Men do not cry; women weep. Step on a woman's toes and she will say I'm sorry. Step on a man and he will push you out of the way and possibly deck you. Male voices while occasionally (especially when intoxicated) being loud and booming, are generally more mellow and calming, while female voices (especially when intoxicated) tend to be high-pitched and irritating. Testosterone distribution I expect.

Men can hold their liquor better. Give a woman a few drinks and she lets her hair down. Give a man a whole bunch of drinks and he will yank her hair down and give her what he thinks she needs. When women become inebriated they may up-chuck. A man gets drunk and pukes.

If a woman finds a wayward twenty in a gutter, she carefully picks it up with a Kleenex, wraps it cautiously, and tucks it away in her purse while looking around guiltily. A man smiles, grabs it, and stuffs it into his pocket thinking how lucky he was.

A man stands up and absently mindedly does a number one while a woman sits and worries about whether or not the toilet seat is clean. A woman passes gas quietly while a man loudly farts.

A man proudly puts on his jockstrap while a woman squeezes subtly into her girdle. Women tease and toss their hair; men may or may not comb theirs—if they have any.

A male throws a baseball as hard as he can and slam-dunks a basketball. A female will underhand a softball gingerly and lob a basketball into the net. Men play football. Women don't. A male golfer drives his ball as hard as he can for distance. A female golfer hits hers as straight as she can for accuracy.

Males like movies with lots of explosions and exploitation. Gals like films with lots of explanations and exposition. Men enjoy sports; women like soap operas.

Give a man an inch and he will take a mile. Give a woman a mile and she will ask for another inch, but only if you can spare it. Ask a male friend to do you a favor and he'll reluctantly agree. Ask a female friend to do you a favor and she'll be thrilled.

Send a woman some roses and she will be overjoyed. Send a man a gift of flowers and he'll wonder what you want.

Ask a man to risk his life and he will be honored. Ask a woman to take that same risk and she will demand (see War stuff above) to know the reason why.

If a man shoots a wild animal he will usually skin and clean it. If a woman accidentally kills a creature of nature she will bury it and say a prayer. If a man kills an insect he will flick it away or wipe it off on his pants. If a woman conquers one, she will wrap it appropriately and release it outside, or if it's dead, honor it with a burial at sea by flushing it down the toilet.

A gentleman opens the door for a lady. A lady thanks him. A rude and crude male ignoramus pushes to the head of the line. An ungentle woman impolitely cuts in front of the line.

A deeply depressed man buys a sports car and/or has an affair. A deeply depressed woman commits suicide or kills her husband and/or kids.

Men belch; woman burp. Men argue; women discuss. Men scream; women mew. Men fight; women quarrel. Men destroy; women disassemble.

Men are erotic

Women are neurotic

Women are demure

Men are cocksure

Men are ambitious

Women are malicious

Men are obsessive

Women are expressive

Men are lascivious

Women are oblivious

Men are grateful

Women are hateful

Men are into sports

Women are into resorts

Men tend to derange

Women just get strange

Women are emasculating and exasperating. Men are complicated and emasculated.

Men are better at math. Women are better at spelling.

Men are better at architecture—women at spelling.

Men are better at science—women are better at spelling.

Men are better at cooking—women at spelling. Okay! Okay! Just kidding ladies.

There are as many differences as there are *us*. Men are the yin and women are the yangs. Men are the yew and women are the yaw. Men are the creeps; women are the angels (this makes up for those spelling cracks).

We do balance out one another. Thank God!

ON A LEG AND A PRAYER

It was mid-August, and hotter than Hades. The circulation of high pressure was causing stifling Santa Ana winds to descend out of the high desert north of Los Angeles and surge through the mountain passes pushing dry desert-heated air onto the California coastal plain. The local fire departments were all standing by in anticipation of the inevitable fires that would result. I was sipping a tall glass of ice tea in the blessed shade of my covered patio when I heard the front doorbell ring.

I reluctantly left my shady spot and went to see what manner of being would be roaming around in that midday heat. I opened the door fully prepared to defend my territory against any Jehovah's Witnesses or traveling salesman and say no to anything. But, I was unprepared to see the one-legged man standing there, perspiration spouting off him like he had sprung a thousand leaks.

His right leg was missing from the thigh down, and he was about five-eight and street thin. He wore sweated-out khakis and I could tell he was a man who used to earn his living the hard way. He sprouted about two days of beard stubble and had deep blue eyes set well back in a thin face that had seen its share of troubles. He smiled politely showing lots of missing teeth.

In a slightly raspy voice, he said he was sorry to bother me and wished me a good day. I immediately felt sorry for him and bid good day back to him. As he stood there dripping and balancing himself on an old crutch with a well-worn pad, he nervously explained that he was building a wheelchair ramp for my neighbor Caroline and he had been trying to cut a piece of plywood. But she only had a handsaw. He said he was having a really hard time trying to see through the plywood and with lowered eyes, he sheepishly inquired if I possibly had a power saw he might borrow.

My heart went out to this hard-working handicapped man, and I naturally sprang to his aid. I told him to meet me at my garage and watched as he one-legged it toward the garage door. I peeked through the mail slot to make sure he was clear and hit the button to raise the door. While he pre-thanked me exuberantly, I began to look for my jigsaw, knowing approximately where it was buried among my shelves of seldom-used tools and equipment.

I pawed through the assortment and within a few minutes sited the saw. I inquired if he knew how to use it, and he replied that he surely did, almost making me feel bad I'd even questioned his knowledge of that workingman's equipment. Before he left, even though I'd only used the saw a couple of times, I was resolute in replacing the old blade with a new one I'd never used that was still in the box, even as he insisted on doing it with the old blade. I wanted him to be able to cut his piece of wood as easily as possible.

As he profusely thanked me, I handed him the box and wished him well. I told him to take his time as I was in no hurry. He assured me that he would certainly be able to cut the plywood with my saw with no difficulty, and said he would return it as soon as he was through.

I went back to my ice tea and tried not to feel guilty about him, over at Caroline's working in the sweltering heat, probably for only a few bucks. My wife came home from a shopping trip and I proudly told her of my good deed. She gave me a funny look and inquired as to where Caroline resided. I wasn't sure.

Several hours later I began to wonder exactly where Caroline, who needed that wheelchair ramp, did dwell and so I went next door and asked another neighbor who had lived on the block for over thirty years. She didn't know Caroline either. Around dusk, I began to ask myself questions I didn't want to hear the answers to.

I will admit that I was reluctant to phone the police the next day, but my wife, who was making great sport of my apparent stupidity, insisted. I procrastinated on making the call as long as I could, hoping that the one-legged man might have taken longer than he had anticipated constructing that wheel-chair ramp. I just knew he would return my saw at any moment. I finally gave up around noon.

The desk sergeant on duty laughed when I explained what had happened. It was painful to my ears as the policeman proceeded to gleefully inform me that the guy had scored about 40 borrowed saws, power drills, and various other good size tools and equipment as he worked his way through our neighborhood. He stated they had an all-points bulletin out on him and that they would notify me if he was apprehended—but not to hold my breath.

Of course, the one-legged crook was long gone, and I never heard of him again. I suppose he is out there right now, hustling his way through another neighborhood, borrowing something from some other kind-hearted stranger. But he did teach me a valuable lesson, and for that I am grateful. What you hear knocking at your door is not always an opportunity.

THE NEXT TO THE LAST MACKSIMS

Everybody can't be in the parade. Someone has to stand on the curb and cheer as it passes by.

Laborers use their hands. Scientists use their brain and their hands. Artists use their brains, hands, soul, and heart.

Very few authors can live what they write.

America was born in revolt and raised on dissent but it could die in apathy.

One of the difficulties with becoming a senior citizen is finding someone older to mentor you.

Time wrinkles your skin, but a lack of enthusiasm wrinkles your soul.

Sometimes a tactful retreat is the only way to advance your cause.

What Mother Nature gives Father Time steals.

Never use a sledgehammer to kill a cockroach.

The more you know—the less you crow.

A posthumous anything isn't worth it.

If you smell a rat break out the cheese.

About the time a person learns how to make the most of their life, most of their life is already gone.

A good general knows to never send an airplane to do a submarine's job.

Before you decide to live your life in the fast lane make sure you can afford the gas.

Religion is an invisible cloak that protects us from the storms of life.

Many tasty trout have been caught with catfish bait.

No matter what it is, just ignore it long enough and Father Time will take care of it.

Always clean your gun before the showdown.

It isn't how old you are, but how you are old that matters most.

A bad meal is a tasteless thing to serve.

We are each the God of our small universe.

It's better to give—before somebody takes it away from you.

Love drinks from a fountain fed by the waters of trust.

There is no point in having a dull knife.

It is possible to be larger than life but no smaller than death.

Cleaning up the Earth starts in your backyard.

The secret of a long life is not dying.

You are not required to love the whole world, just whatever part of it you happen to touch.

There are many ways to fly a plane, but only one way to crash.

There are no innocent crimes.

Getting there is only the beginning of arriving.

A bad joke is no laughing matter.

An honest politician is a proverbial oxymoron.

Never lick a gift horse in the mouth.

A snake with legs has probably been to law school.

Never make an incision without precision.

A pardon never helps the victims.

Spoils must remember they belong to the victors.

If your burdens are not too heavy, help a laden friend carry theirs.

Power depends on trust.

It is the reader who makes a book worthwhile.

You will never be what you are not.

True wisdom means more courage than strength.

Accept what you cannot avoid and avoid what you cannot accept.

A well-lived face is never a disgrace.

Sing only as loud as ears can hear.

Belief begets hope.

Try not to get too famous until you are willing to sign autographs.

Being famous with a complete lack of talent is a talent in itself.

Too much rust can ruin an engine and too much trust can break a bank.

We all finish our last race lying down.

To have never truly loved is to have never truly lived.

God is where ever you want him to be.

Most people are poor because of a lack of common sense—not money.

A bad memory is hard to forget.

Punishment after the fact never stopped a crime.

Old age is the price of life.

We generally learn courtesy from a discourteous person.

Nothing good comes from good for nothing.

The closer you watch a good magician the less you see.

Hard labor is a good habit to break.

No matter how much sugar you use, rotten fruit makes a bad pie.

Only a fool gives foolish advice.

Keep your business out of other people's faces.

The easiest things to give your children are money and position. The best thing to give them is our love and understanding.

If you want to climb the ladder you mustn't be afraid of heights.

The biggest unexplored area is within the human mind.

Truth is the only constant.

Religion must have faith to exist.

Smallness and immenseness are only perceptions.

Praise is only genuine when given without conditions.

Honor cannot be bought—it must be earned and bestowed.

Indetermination is highly contagious.

Generals cannot aim rifles or pull triggers. Those who carry them must do that.

A little boy may grow into a big man but when he goes to sleep, he will always become that little boy.

Grief comes to us all eventually, even the lucky ones.

Self-pity is a poor excuse for failure.

Without imagination, there would be no greatness.

The shadows of time are vague.

There is no such thing as too perfect.

It is better to be with someone unhappy than to be alone and unhappy.

Be thankful for small troubles, for they can easily be replaced by big troubles.

A man cannot move a mountain and he might as well face it.

Too much profanity is insanity.

A wry "thank you for the excellent service" is the best tip for a rude waiter.

Good music not only soothes the soul, but it also tunes up the brain.

Like it or not, we are all passengers on the same spaceship.

The most effective criticism is couched in tactful encouragement.

Too much motivation can be a bad thing for a soldier.

If you can find a job you truly enjoy, you'll never grow tired of working.

A good joke has opened many closed doors.

Any meal is a dog's best friend.

There would be no rainbows without wetness.

It's better to face the truth and pay the consequences than deny it and face the consequences.

Temptation is a wicked mistress.

Bad customs make unhappy traditions.

In the end, lots of desperate lies will not overcome one small truth.

You should believe in a cause because.

Desire justifies.

To keep it interesting, one should say "you don't say" every so often.

Facing danger doesn't take much courage if you don't realize how dangerous it is.

If a thing appears to be unbelievable, you are not required to believe it.

While stopping to smell the flowers beware of working bees.

If you are going to waste your time wishing for something, you might as well wish for some more wishes.

Before plunging into the pool of life, learn how to swim.

Depravity has no bottom and virtue has no peak.

If you can't ride a horse don't volunteer for the posse.

A short streak of luck can quickly surpass a long-suffering talent.

God knows all about science. He invented it.

Setbacks are mere stepping-stones to stimulate determination.

You can't be a conservative until you have something to lose.

Even the simplest microbe is an extremely complex life form.

One man's adventure is another man's nightmare.

The degree that matters most is the degree to which you are willing to work.

Accomplished chefs do not need to brag about their cooking.

If you opt to play poker at a table of idiots and someone pulls out a gun you have no one to blame but yourself.

A happy person is usually poor enough to want something and rich enough not to need it.

What committees mostly do is put obstacles in the way of people who want to do things.

Eighty percent of what you think of as recreation, others consider "work" and the other twenty percent comes under the category of "sitting".

A good stiff wind makes a better sailboat.

A good way to make a child unhappy is to give in to all their demands.

If you want to be well known—find yourself a real small town to live in.

Fools coerce. Leaders inspire.

Stars don't fall. They implode. Eventually.

Don't expect to have a miracle hunt you down. Go out and seek it.

Everyone has a certain amount of control over the future, but only God can rearrange the past.

The stars belong to astronomers, astronauts, navigators, and lovers.

A seldom-used brain becomes atrophied.

A king without a kingdom has little need for a throne.

The simpler the theory, the more people will believe it.

Controversy promotes interest.

You may not know God, but He surely knows you.

All things fail, eventually.

Every frog kissed by a beautiful girl hopes to turn into a handsome prince.

When term limits fail, try hanging.

A good jump shot is great, but it takes a magnificent jump shot to become a pro.

Time is irretrievable. Even a millisecond, once lost, can never be recovered.

You have to learn how to teach before you can teach how to learn.

A rock can't.

Nobody knows what the fly on the wall knows.

There is no such thing as a bad cookie.

Fervor is seldom ever a panacea.

The triumph of politics is the dichotomy of minds.

Stasis is usually the best solution.

Time and rust work hand in hand.

Never give a dog a name with more than two syllables.

SOME SUGGESTIONS FOR GOD

It's a nice universe, God! You've done a miraculous job. Truly impressive! Although, I do think perhaps I would have liked to see a few things done differently. Like what you say? What am I talking about?

If you will indulge me, with your kind permission I'll explain. Yes, sir, I realize that I am out of line. Yes, Lord, I promise to get right to the point.

Basically what I am talking about is... Life—and the way we go through it. How about changing the way life works? I've always thought you might have gotten it backward. But please don't be alarmed. It's just an idea.

I can tell you are concerned. Let me explain. I'm not saying it's for sure, but maybe you got us going the wrong way in life. It's certainly a confusing journey. I think you will admit that. Just consider the possibility that maybe we are doing it backward. You aren't dyslexic by any chance, are you? I didn't think so Lord, but just hear me out.

Just consider the "what if?" Let's say that in a little dark spot, six feet under a particular piece of earth things started to stir. You know, molecules and stuff like that joining together and creating the miracle. It could develop slowly over time, until eventually the outline of a human was formed, and then in an amazing transformation, the dust would begin to come together and slowly evolve into a life form. The being would be all wrinkled and grizzled, and completely inert and lifeless. It would be cold and unaware of its existence inside that container. But someway (I am sure you could figure out how) people would know it was there and come and dig it up. There would be a service and people would pray for it to become a human.

It would be taken to a hospital or some other appropriate place where it would slowly come alive and gain strength. The newly created person would be very decrepit—but wise and all-knowing and eventually, they would get out of their bed and begin to walk and talk and develop an appetite. They would get strong and better looking by the day until within a year or so they would be able to walk nearly normally and enjoy their existence.

As time went on they would grow stronger, their vision would become better, hair would begin to grow on bald places, and new teeth would form in their mouths. They would begin to take an interest in sex and eventually find an appropriate mate of a similar age to grow young with.

Things would get better every year and soon they would take a job of their liking as a senior employee or manager, and begin to work regularly making a nice income. They would get younger and better looking by the day and go on vacations and take up sporting activities. As they required more time to devote to such activities they could be demoted to less responsible positions and of course, receive less pay. They would enter their prime getting healthier and younger, enjoying an active lifestyle.

There would be a long period of such activities until they become a young adult, at which time they part ways with their spouse. Soon they would start forgetting some of the things they knew, so they would have to go to college, where they would party all the time until they become a teenager, as they grow dumber and less concerned about the world.

About this time, As they grew increasingly more incompetent, they would need to be assigned to a nice family and move in with them. They would be happy because they didn't have to work anymore, but they would have to go to High School. They would begin to enjoy playing games more and get increasingly more unaware of responsibility until finally progressing through grade school and finally kindergarten, requiring a babysitter to take care of them.

Then they would forget how to walk and have to crawl or be carried everywhere. One day they would develop a great fondness for breast milk and forget how to go to the bathroom on their own. Eventually one day they would grow so weak and incapable that they would be compelled to crawl feet first into their mother's large warm vag...."

What? Did you get the point? You don't like it? Where would procreation come in? Well, I know there are a few kinks but... to tell you the truth Lord, I haven't worked that part out yet—but I'm sure that if...

I see. Well then, I have other ideas, Lord. How about giving us the ability to read one another's minds? Think how nice that would be with no more deception. We would have to be honest with each other. Just imagine. We'd have to tell the truth when we are asked a question. If someone says, "I love you" they'd have to mean it.

The way I see it—that would make things considerably easier for us all. Why, it would practically eliminate the need for the police, not to mention the requirements for background or security checks. A simple question would do the job. I can see how mind-reading would work great. What do you mean to give an example?

Okay, let's just say that a guy comes home after being gone for an interminably very long time and his wife asks, "Where the hell (pardon my pun) were you?"

The man then proceeds to explain that he had been on the way home from work on a Friday afternoon when he was carjacked at a red light, during which time he was struck in the head with a gun by the carjacker, left unconscious in the street, and subsequently taken to the hospital by a helpful passing stranger for treatment. He had been treated for his head wound and released from the hospital and was taking a cab home, but the cab had been involved in a serious accident and he had been once again injured and taken back to the very same hospital by ambulance, where they treated him for a concussion. Then somehow, while in a trance, he had managed to remove the IV, get dressed in some clothes he found in a locker, and escape from his room. He had stumbled out of the hospital in an amnesia-induced daze and mysteriously took a plane to Oklahoma, where he became a chicken farmer for the last twenty years until he was struck by lightning during a ferocious rainstorm, after which he remembered who he was and promptly came home. His wife could look him in the eye and know he was telling the absolute truth.

What? You are not impressed? You don't think so? Well, it was just an idea. What do you mean people would be getting their lights punched out all the time? Are you saying that no one would ever stay married and that practically everybody would have to spend his or her life alone? More bar fights? There would be more wars? No one could go to church and worship you?

Wow! I guess I never looked at it that way. Okay. I was just trying to be helpful. I guess when you put it like that—maybe your way is better. I've got lots of other ideas that I'd like to get your opinion on sometimes if you would be so kind. Is there any possibility we could do lunch one day next week? Oh.

Okay? Well... if you ever do have the time... you know where to find me. It'll be on me.

SOME BIG MISTAKES

I suppose this hit piece could also be entitled "It seemed like a good idea at the time." I have an overpowering urge to play devil's advocate on behalf of Joe Citizen. I am referring to some of those things politicians and other well-intentioned leaders tend to do to taxpayers when they think with our pocketbooks instead of their brains—stupid things that should gripe you as much as they do me. In all fairness, I probably ought to point out that one could also make a reasonable argument for each if one were a well-greased lobbyist standing on the other side of the fence.

Number one on my hit list has to be PORK. No, I'm not talking about pork belly futures in the commodities market. I am protesting the avarice of already bloated pigs greedily slopping at the public trough. My lament is PORK as in "bringing home the bacon." PORK as in "surplus fat." PORK as in "grease." PORK as in the old "pork barrel." PORK as in "political largesse" is directly correlated to political seniority. PORK as in "Politically Originated Reward Kickbacks." PORK as in "Power Obtained and Righteously Kept." PORK as in "Partisan Optionally Requisitioned Keepsakes." PORK as in "Payola Oligopoly Replenishing Kitties" or as in "Price Of Representative Kookiness." I could go on, but I'm sure you get the idea. Politicians who rob the public till to pay for outlandish, unjustified, and normally unnecessary projects in their districts just because they can; ought to be ripped from their cozy beds at night by vigilante gangs of roving taxpayers, taken into the nearest woods, stripped buck naked and thoroughly humiliated, then painstakingly tarred and feathered.

One thing that got my goat is when they started letting lawyers advertise. I figured it would turn into a can of worms the minute they did it, but excuse me worms, for lowering your standards that much. Nowadays a plethora of daytime ads (coinciding with the period *when those to whom the ads are directed* are not plying a trade) on television is from some ambulance-chasing scofflaw firm scouring the under-brushes of society for anyone willing to sue any organization, person, or entity with deep pockets.

The incessant ads went from hyping personal injury claims to insidious attacks against anyone trying to market a product or service. Any manufacturer whose product hits a bump in the road is in for a litigation tornado, the likes of which drive many businesses out of business. The vulture-like attorneys gorging on their bloated carcasses appear to have similar table manners to a carnivorous grizzly freshly woken from hibernation and rapaciously searching for a meal as they file one annoying baseless suit after another. All ethics are off the table and its open season for anyone who can pay. It doesn't matter who gets hurt, as long as those outrageous legal fees are collected. When some fair-minded politicians tried to effect "loser pays" laws the legal profession descended 'en masse upon the legislature and managed to defeat it.

I'm sure those well-meaning politicians had nothing but the best intentions when they imposed their world-changing welfare policies. I wonder if they had known what devastating consequences their generous intentions of charitable fairness would bring if they would still opt to affect them. We all know the parable about teaching a man how to fish instead of giving him a fish. It couldn't be any truer. If you dare to go there, just take a quick tour around your nearest inner-city housing project or the *other side of the tracks* of just about any large urban area. There is a heck of a lot of folks that would rather subsist on very little and live on small government-supplied handouts than go out and work for a living to secure a better life for themselves and their families.

Don't think I'm knocking on all social programs. There are practical reasons why some are necessary—when they help those in need rise out of poverty and become productive citizens, benefiting society as a whole while keeping crime in check and preventing us from becoming a *3rd World Country*. I also wish to point out that there is a great big difference between *charity* and *welfare*. The charity helps those who cannot help themselves. Welfare, regardless of how well-intended, fosters communities of indolent sloth who refuse to help themselves merely because they don't have to. Welfare cultivates laziness and corruption, followed by contempt and anger if someone threatens to take it away once the benefit has been given.

Freedom of Religion. Hold your horses. I'm not talking about the freedom to practice your religion of choice, but rather the freedom to operate a business under the guise of religion. There are many so-called "religions" that are operating under the *right-to-worship laws* that are profit-generating businesses that ought to be paying their fair share of taxes. Politicians know who they are. Religions that are used as a cover should not be allowed a free pass on the taxes bus. In that same vein, harmful cults should not be allowed to escape the clutches of the law under the guise of being a religion. Our *go-along-to-get-along* leaders ought to have applied a little common sense to determine and clearly define the differences between religions and cults a long time ago—and then outlawed cults.

I don't have any trouble with the moral premise of Affirmative Action. But the reality is that it does not work some of the time. It may in some cases backfire instead of helping serve to prevent ethnic minorities from competing fairly in the job market. When stretched too thinly it only weakens *the cause* and creates incompetent employees who lower productivity and perhaps, more importantly, place citizens in danger when someone is incapable of properly functioning in jobs such as police or firefighters. It stands to reason that the ability to properly perform any job should be the first prerequisite applied before giving anyone that job. People should never be hired based on their gender, race, religion, ethnicity, or sexual orientation. No person could feel all that terrific about themselves if they need to be given special treatment and an inordinate overlooking or ignoring of the rules, simply because they are considered to be incapable of competing fairly in the amazing American job market.

Our *cultural fairness* thing is another dogma that fuels the fires that burn at the core of progress. How on earth can any thinking person rationalize that teaching the children of our immigrants in their native language is going to serve them better in the long run? Children are capable of learning new language skills much faster than adults. Delaying their integration only holds them back and forestalls their ability to succeed. Society is not doing them any favors by pretending young children are powerless to learn how to speak, read and write the language of this country. Hiring foreign language teachers predictably delays the children of immigrants from assimilating and is a waste of taxpayer money. It is also draining the educational system of much-needed funds that could be better utilized elsewhere. The more this sort of over-protectionism occurs, the more our ethnic separation and the more we will have isolated walled-off enclaves of impoverished non-English speaking third-world cultures scattered throughout America, which can't be a good thing.

Lest you think these are the ramblings of a crotchety old codger, let me remind you that it's your hard-earned money those *good intentions* are pissing away—not mine. I'm out of the rat race personally—and getting my social security check regularly. I ... guess that's enough for now. I'm sure glad I got that off my chest.

GAMES OF CHANCE

As a young street-hawking newspaper boy in Waco, I did lots of business in beer taverns, domino parlors, and pool halls. So did my Dad. I was looking for customers—he was there for entertainment and winnings. He was a serious and skillful gambler. I'd often run into him as I plied my trade in places a boy ought not really to have been hanging out. However, a boy had to do what a boy had to do, and besides, the tips were better where the patrons weren't. Alcohol played a serious role.

I used to observe my Dad with conflicted feelings of disdain and admiration that left me somewhat confused about my inclinations toward games of chance. Dad was good. He held his cue as tenderly as his longnecks and treated them both with loving care. He played cards and dominos with purpose and as far as I could tell, he seldom ever lost. I couldn't help but wonder—was I going to take after him someday? Would I ever be able to stand in his brilliant gambler's shadow?

And so my voice changed and I discovered a hankering for handling a cue myself. I shot minor-league pool and was a few notches better than okay. I beat most average players but never packed enough lead in my pencil to be a hustler. I watched guys go wild-eyed and gun-pulling mad-shooting craps. Then I rolled a few bones and realized that dice weren't my forte'. From time to time I'd visit Vegas and turn my hands green at the slots. Each time I'd ask myself why anyone who dared to think of them-self as any kind of serious gambler, would rather have intimate contact with an inanimate machine than perform intellectual combat with real live gamblers.

I'd occasionally make a few wagers at a Blackjack table, but card counting seemed like way too much trouble. The House owned the cards and the odds worked for them. In my way of thinking, blackjack is to poker like checkers is to chess. Bluffing didn't work and there didn't seem to be a real exchange between the gamblers. I liked looking into their eyes and betting against players and not the house.

And so I considered poker. There was something about that round table of green felt that tweaked my hot button. It was sort of comparable to Robert Duvall's great "I love the smell of Napalm in the morning" line in

"Apocalypse Now." The smell and feel of green felt touched my gambler's soul. I realized that what I was longing for was the interface with others in a game of skill, where one might also experience an occasional dance with Lady Luck. Poker was calling.

I'd played quite a bit in the Navy, so I knew the rules and the odds. I understood the advantages of playing like a rock. I could also bluff with the best of them. The only problem was—I was busy pursuing a career, raising a family, and trying to pay the monthly bills. Poker simply took too much sitting at the table kind of time, which I never had a surplus of. So I just dreamt about it—allowed the urge to lurk in the dark recesses of my mind. Do you know that old saying about being careful what you wish for? Well, it happened to me.

At last one day there I was—kids are grown and gone. No wife to rein me in—plenty of free time with no one to account to—and a little spending money that could be flushed down the toilet if I wanted. I also knew there were several card casinos a short drive away in Gardena. So I slapped myself around a bit to get psyched up and was ready to test the generosity of the gambling gods. Yee Ha!

That first time I walked through the doors and saw those hundreds of bizarre-looking characters sitting around the green felt tables pushing around plastic chips my knees were shaking so bad I must have looked spastic. Excuse my crude metaphor, but that's exactly how it seemed. I had to get myself psyched up to persevere. I stood around nervously watching the table action and observed and plotted, calculating the skill levels of the various tables. One could play at a table where the antes were only a dollar, and the raises small. Or one could play at tables where the ante was a thousand dollars and you could lose your house and/or inheritance in one night. It became apparent to me that in most cases the skill levels corresponded to the amount of money being wagered. So I naturally sat down to play at the dollar table.

My fellow gamblers were an odd lot, coming from all walks of life. The only thing we had in common was an urge to dance with Lady Luck. In many cases, it was an uncontrollable addition. Some of them played with as much and in a few cases more skill than I did, employing instantly conceived mathematical calculations to gauge the odds for each draw of the cards and wagering accordingly. Those types usually won. So I tried to avoid butting heads with them. Other players were not nearly so skillful or careful, depending entirely on madam fortune to see them through. They usually lost. I decided I'd fit in best being one of the winners.

It wasn't really difficult. I just bode my time, waiting for the rights hands, when one of the luck-depending types was in a betting mood, or better yet when they were running a bluff and I knew it. I seldom ever drew to shorts. I never showed or used emotion at the table. I made every conscious effort to display no "tells" and utilized the best psychology I could to "buy" an occasional hand.

I also concentrated hard on reading tells of other players. Even at that level, it was difficult, since proverbial poker faces were worn by everyone except the genuine fools and drunks, of which there were only a few. Some would display body language, or easily read emotions to reveal their hands. Some tried to fake tells to set traps for other players. The constant psychological warfare made it fun. Now and then I'd get fortunate and have one of the better players beat on the board and I'd pour it on. Most of them quickly caught on and tried to avoid butting heads. I'd reciprocate. It took a couple of weeks before I was a regular, and by then I also had a justly earned reputation as a winner.

It became more than a hobby. I'd often spend 24 or even 36 hours sitting there, playing like a rock, and slowly building up my winnings. Eventually, sleep deprivation and/or frozen buns would demand that I end the episode. I discovered the most profitable time to indulge was Friday nights. When the bars were let out, the casinos would be flooded with inebriated gambling-crazed individuals possessing a strong need to give what remained of their paycheck away. They had just closed up the bar someplace and were ready to make some well-thought-out mathematical equation judgments on odds in an unpredictable assortment of poker hands. In most cases, they'd wake up in the morning and blame Lady luck for all their bad decisions. It was easy pickings. There was a visceral thrill in beating them. I rationalized that it was fate and that somebody had to take the money.

Those gambling-addicted little old ladies who were playing on their social security checks or welfare funds were not quite so easy—but they could be taken if one had the patience and determination. But I never quite felt comfortable doing it. If I had one beat on the board and knew it, I found myself taking it easy, and not making them pay the piper. Although I knew that if the situation were reversed, they'd be happy to skin me alive. I realized that showing mercy wasn't an advisable skill set or a good trait for a gambler.

Nevertheless, I still managed to consistently win. Generally, after a long session, I'd be up a hundred or two. A few times I won as much as four to five hundred and once I even staggered out with three days of beard some twenty-five hundred ahead. On bad luck days, I would lose a few bucks. But mostly I won.

I had mastered the dollar table. I was ready to move up in the gambling world. Making my move to the five-dollar table was the next step. I quickly found out that one could win, or lose five times as much, and even though I still played like a rock, I was apt to find myself sitting there with a bunch of other players also playing like rocks. It was a rock-fest and much more boring, and no longer as much fun. It was more like work—only I lost more.

Slowly it dawned on me that gambling was something a person could make a hobby of if they could handle it, but not a very decent way of life. It tended to devour you. It ate up your personal life and took you out of circulation. Those long hard hours simply took more patience than I was willing to give. I had come to realize that unless one became completely obsessed and committed, they could acquire more money easier by simply working than they ever could by playing poker So I left that place where time was the enemy to those who had no other use for it, and went back to the real world.

Decades later Texas 'hold-em burst on the scene and poker became the rage. Nowadays it's on television practically all the time. I will watch it for a few moments and remember when. Then I change the channel.

My best advice to *want-to-be* professional gamblers: Don't learn the hard way, like I did, that it's a hard way to make a bad living. Don't risk more money than you can afford to lose. Do it for fun, and quit when you know you should. It's a fact that the gambler who has lost his entire poke thinks that the next hand would have been the one where his luck would have changed for the better. It's also a fact that the gambler who quits while ahead think that the next hand would have been the one where his luck turned sour. It's also a fact that only one of the two could have found out the truth. Be that one—if you are going to gamble and as the Kenny Rogers song says know when to fold 'em.

THE ROOT OF ALL EVIL

We are living in tough economic times; vast economic tides have been ebbing and surging wildly in response to the multifarious complexities of countless factors. The sub-prime loan debacle has severely tapped the housing market, crashing home prices. Massive amounts of money were pumped into exotic homeownership schemes through the financial machinations of Fannie May and Freddy Mac to finance homes for those who could not pay for them. The bad wallpaper for these risky loans was hung on Wall Street creating a cataclysmic financial tsunami of hitherto unimagined magnitude. The bursting real estate bubble coupled with other risky practices such as overleveraging, toxic securities, ridiculous pork-barrel spending, and the high costs of the war against terrorism have got the dollar on life support. It is truly a *grizzly bear market*.

Let me guess. Your 401K has been downgraded to a *101 No Pay*. "Why you ask?" As Sherlock might say, "it is elementary dear taxpayer". The bedraggled U.S. economy is beginning to melt away like a stick of butter left out in the Sahara sun. Most investments have sunk to abysmal levels and the economic outlook is as bleak as the prospects of an apprentice blacksmith at the North Pole. The politicians are incontrovertibly proving, one cannot spend their way to solvency or borrow their way out of a hole. Your assets have been set upon their ass and your nest egg has cracks bigger than the San Andreas Fault. Don't feel pregnant, because you are not alone.

Congratulations are in order. You have experienced the worst economic collapse since the Great Depression and you are still standing. The country suffers from a downward spiral of fear from seemingly unexplainable increases in gasoline prices, growing unemployment, and a weakening economy. The Federal budget deficit continues to grow and the American Dream is withering on the vine. In this unexpected, protracted period of global economic malaise, as governments, financial institutions and industries struggle to survive; financial stress levels do not make for pleasant jest. Yet I must, for though the doldrums of depression beset us, I feel compelled to provide some perspective. If your bottom line is bleak and you don't know a derivative from a hedge fund, do not despair, for I, an uncertified investment "guru," shall help you analyze your future financial postures to begin the healing process and fashion your innovative strategies to face the challenges. You need not read the scores of survival tomes on how to acquire your fortune.

As an inherent part of my commitment to help you to establish a disciplined but opportunistic income stream, and create dynamic personal net worth, I shall herein endeavor to examine the reliable and relevant principles of developing a sound economic policy and viable asset allocation strategy. I will advise you on the methods for employing long-term investment and withdrawal principles designed to generate healthy and quantitatively significant but durably sustainable financial growth.

You will be able to meet defined goals and accomplish primary objectives through a comprehensive analytical and sound periodical review of your chosen economic diversification according to the assessment of monetary market expectations. We shall explore avenues to mitigate risk while maximizing potential, including tax incentives and implementation of accounting practices for all fiscal and pecuniary policies. By identifying the markets we will implement an honest and forthright geopolitically well-conceived risk assessment plan that embraces compelling investment opportunities for economic development in a global free-market economy.

Okay. I've had my fun and I'll cut to the chase. You mean those impressive words didn't give you a sense of confidence and make you want to turn over all your money to me so I can look after it for you? How cynical and suspicious you have become. Someone must have done you wrong—some sagacious appearing investor-type individual who spoke in vague generalities using a plethora of multi-syllable words to convince you to trust them with your hard-earned dough. I wouldn't do that.

The most important piece of advice I can give you about money is that money alone will/can not make you happy. If that were the case all wealthy people would be content, and we know that is not so. Many of them lead lives of despair, always wanting something else, continually searching for the elusive self-satisfaction and true contentment of being comfortable in their shoes. True happiness can be found/achieved only by taking responsibility for your finances and learning to live within the boundaries of your limitations. Never let money become an elusive Devil that haunts you or the God you worship.

Instead, think of money as a tool to be used in securing comfort and making your life easier. The power of money cannot and should not be ignored. It can make your life easier, as long as you handle it with care. You need to develop the proper respect for the security money can provide and understand how it can make the difference between the way you want to live and how you can live. Most people who get in trouble with money do so because they rationalize that they deserve rewards that they cannot afford. They justify their bad financial management because of the stress and strain of their everyday lives. Your life will be a heck of a lot easier if you have a sufficient supply of money. The objective is to acquire enough of it and learn how to make the most of it. You must learn to save it, budget it, and use it wisely.

Now, let us discuss some differences between wealth and money. Money is the object/product used to get you to a state of wealth, which is the goal. The crucial thing you've got to know about becoming wealthy is that you can't depend on winning the lottery or finding a pirate treasure. That being the case, let's begin this primer with a close look at the product to which we are referring—to wit: money. I'm sure your three primary questions are as follows:

What is it?

Where is it?

And how does one get their hands on massive quantities of it?

First, perhaps I ought to say that nobody can explain exactly what it is because "money" is not that simple. On the other hand, "money" isn't all that complicated either. If that sounds contradictory—it is. That is because money itself is contradictory. It's mostly just paper, that's been churned out by some authoritative entity as a symbol of value. All U.S. paper money is the same size, which is 6.125" wide by 2.625" tall. The primary difference between a one-dollar bill and a hundred-dollar bill is what is printed on the paper.

Everyone knows that a small piece of old scrunched up, badly worn, often folded, paper with any amount printed on it is in itself worth little or nothing. Its only true value is the solidness of the organization behind it.

To prove this, merely ask yourself the following question. Would you rather have a million U.S. Dollars or ten million genuine Confederate Dollars? Or perhaps you would rather have some seashells, beads, or any of the other stuff that some cultures have used as money over the eons.

So we can agree that money itself is not the objective. It is the actual products or goods that the money would buy that create the value. What one wants to do is be able to get their hands on enough money to acquire those things one wishes to have. That being the case, let us assume that the mere acquisition of a large quantity of U.S. dollars will suffice. Let's say that you somehow manage to win, inherit, or earn a million dollars. That's 10,000 hundred dollar bills or a hundred packets of a hundred. It would weigh about twenty pounds and fit into a very large briefcase, or a small suitcase—just perfect for taking on the plane as carry-on luggage assuming you can get it past security. But what should you do with it? That's the real question.

Let's assume you are ready to start spending it like the millionaire you have become. What will it be? You could buy yourself a seat at a Baccarat table in Vegas and walk out penniless after a few minutes of high roller fun, or you could invest in a lovely diamond for an engagement ring for your wife-to-be, or perhaps pay cash for a modest half a million-dollar home and invest the other half-million in no-load mutual funds. Or, you could use it as seed money to start your own business and hopefully turn it into a hundred million in five years. The possibilities are endless. First, you must be able to determine the true value of things.

Look at it this way. In your left hand, you hold a flawless VS1 diamond appraised at 1.5 million, which you will cleverly be able to buy for only a million. In your right hand is the knob that opens the front door of a 2600 square foot home that is just perfect for you to raise a family in, with a half-million dollars in mutual funds to help you through those rainy-day rough spots. It's your choice. Left-hand or right?

I think the above example illustrates perfectly well the point I wish to make, which is that what you do with the money you do get, is the most important aspect of fiduciary prosperity. There are a thousand ways to throw money away for every single way there is to use it wisely. I'll elaborate on a few of them. I'm no Ben Franklin, but I do think that this may just be the best financial advice anyone will ever give you in such a short narrative.

Here are some huge financial errors that many people make and ways that they throw large sums of money into the wind, and how they can avoid it.

<u>Choosing the wrong spouse.</u> This is probably the most costly mistake one can make in life. Your lifemate must be someone with similar goals and aspirations. Many successful people have been turned into soup line standers because their significant other either stole their nest egg and departed or spent them in the poorhouse. Before you hitch your star to someone, make sure they share your financial ambitions and will help you achieve them.

<u>Big weddings.</u> The average American wedding these days runs almost thirty thousand bucks. If you are looking for a foolish investment; nothing can top a good extravagant wedding. That's not merely "splurging". It's submerging your ship of state before it even gets away from the pier. For goodness sake, it's only one day. Look at it as a business transaction. Set a budget and stick to it. Instead of blowing a big wad of cash unnecessarily, you need to consider all the years you will spend together. If your "special day" is going to cost a ton of money you don't have to throw away, perhaps you ought to do the smart and reasonable thing and settle for a small intimate affair with just close family and friends in attendance. Better yet, elope! Get a Justice of the Peace or a man of the cloth to marry you in front of a couple of witnesses someplace and consider it done. It will be just as legal and you won't have to put up with troublesome relatives getting drunk and ruining your wedding. Have a nice little honeymoon if you must, but for heaven's sake, use all that money you saved on that big wedding as a down payment on a house, or for other important expenses that new couples incur. The odds are only fifty-fifty that you two will stay together anyway. At least with a house, you'll have some equity to split and manage to walk away with something. Believe me, walking away with your memories of that impressive big wedding blowout won't be nearly as comforting.

<u>Piling up credit card debts.</u> The little-publicized but very real truth about credit cards is that they should never be used by anyone who has to use them. Credit Cards in the wrong hands are just plain **Evil!** Everyone knows by now or should know unless they've been in a coma for the last few decades, that the interest paid on credit cards is excessive beyond all reasonableness. If the interest you can earn on a savings account is only 1 or 2 percent, how could

one possibly justify paying 18 to 20 percent on something they ate last week? Don't understand that? Okay. How about this? If you owe... let's say a measly two grand and you pay only the minimum payments at 18% interest—it will take you 18 years and cost you $4615.00 And that's with no late charges or additional spending. Credit cards should be used for convenience only. The only time one should use a credit card is if they will be paying the amount charged in full by the time the monthly bill becomes due. That cost is zero. If you really and truly want to become the master of your bottom line, you must never fall into the bottomless pit of owing money on credit cards. And whatever you do with credit cards—never fall into that loser's game of paying off one that's due with another new one and then when it's due getting another new one to pay the one you used to pay the last one off with, etc. That's a Ponzi-bankruptcy scheme of fiduciary suicide.

Financing anything. The general rule is: don't do it. If you can't pay cash for it, you don't need it that bad. This applies to everything from furniture to breast augmentation. Never finance anything (except real estate). But, you scream, we must have furniture. And she needs those breast implants to cheer her up. I don't agree. You can completely furnish a house or apartment for only a few hundred dollars by shopping estate sales, thrift stores, and the personal ads in your local paper. As for those breast implants, I feel quite certain that surveys have proved that babies are happier nursing on small real breasts than large plastic ones that taste like rubber.

Buying new cars. Many people finance their wheels because they want to experience that brand-new car smell. As they drive it over the curb it loses a quarter of its value. A year later it may be down to half of the initial value. Two years later only one-third of the original value remains. My suggestion: save up that one-third and use it to buy a low mileage, two-year-old car in good condition and pay cash for it. It may not have that new car aroma, but if that bothers you, there are some scent sprays available for about ten bucks that will give it that new car smell. That way, you'll have just as enjoyable a ride, and imagine how much you'll save without finance charges. And oh yeah—leasing a car is Dumb with a capital D. If you buy a car and keep it until a few years after it's paid for, all the money you would have been spending on monthly lease payments can be applied to your next set of wheels. That requires proper maintenance, but it's by far the least expensive way to accomplish automotive transportation.

Renting your housing. Sure, real estate has been through some rough times lately. It is easy to be afraid of a housing investment—but you must live somewhere. Let's consider it. In the past, the quickest way for the average person to acquire any significant amount of personal net worth has traditionally been through real estate. Many fortunes have been accumulated through real estate investments, and still may be. However, with all that has been happening in the housing market, I can understand anyone having hesitancy in this area. But with prices low, as well as interest rates, opportunities are abounding. This may well be the best time to make the jump.

The sooner you own your own home the better. The stock market will come and go, but equity in a home is the best hedge fund available. As the cost of housing increases, which it pretty much always has over the long haul, (the recent collapse of the sub-prime loan market notwithstanding) it will increase your net worth while the interest deductions provide tremendous tax breaks. Also, it's just a comforting feeling knowing that your largest asset is a place to live.

No down payment you say. So what? Save one up as fast as you can. Also, every day people are finding creative paths to homeownership. Find a good real estate salesperson and see if they can help get you into a home. There are many ways but beware of the high-risk marketplace wherein home buyers get trapped into any number of higher-interest doomsday loans that they can't handle. However, if you can afford the payment, you needn't be averse to other arrangements such as second mortgages, joint ownership, rent-to-own deals, etc. Just make it happen. But, I repeat, keep it affordable, so you don't lose it to foreclosure.

Because it will probably be the largest single purchase you will ever make, my best advice on home buying is to do your due diligence and become a shopaholic before making any commitment to a house. Look, look, and then look some more. I have a personal rule of comparing a minimum of fifty homes before making any home-buying decision. When you do spot the right house you will know, especially if you've done your research well and comped a whole bunch of similarly priced homes in that area. You not only want to know the fair price, but the neighborhood reputation, property value trends, tax laws, etc. Have your financing arrangements in order before shopping. Know what you can afford and how you are going to pay for it. Have the desire to know at least as much as the seller, and the real estate agents involved, and then drive your best bargain. Make a lowball offer and see what happens. The worst that can happen is a counteroffer. Don't be afraid to get your best deal possible. Once it's done, it's done and you can call yourself a homeowner.

Excessive food costs. Many people have no idea how much their food costs. Constantly eating out, or dining on take-out food is very expensive when compared to the cost of cooking at home. If you don't know how to cook, learn. Get a cookbook. Also learn to shop for food wisely. Buy what is on sale at the supermarkets and use coupons whenever practicable. It will ultimately save you a fortune. Each week the grocery stores run specials on certain items. That is what you should be eating that week. Another tip. Get a freezer and use it. When something is on sale, you can cook enough for several meals and freeze some for easily prepared meals later on. And last but certainly not least, avoid take-out food and junk food as much as you can. It's expensive and generally not good for you.

Going uninsured. Failing to have proper insurance can cost you a bundle if you get unlucky. This is true with medical care, as well as automobile insurance. Most bankruptcies are because of unpaid medical bills. If you are buying a home or car, insurance is mandatory.

Risky behavior. It is really simple. Don't do it. There are many facets to this category. I'll just mention five, so you'll catch my drift.

A DUI charge can ruin your life for a good long while. No buzz is worth taking that risk.

Surfing, snowboarding, or mountain climbing. If it is your calling do it, but for Heaven's sake, learn how to do it properly. Many healthy young adults become lifelong paraplegics because of a slight or bad misjudgment.

Street drag racing has ended many careers. So has road rage. Treat your car with respect and drive safely. You will be driving many years longer.

Unnecessary violence. Bar fights are so dumb. So are eye dissing, chest banging, and all those other macho things that males do when their testosterone is raging. Learn to control your temper and avoid confrontations.

Looking for trouble. Hanging out on a dark street corner in the wrong part of town late at night is like attempting slow suicide. Don't run with any group that will use peer pressure to get you to do something you know is stupid.

Maintaining expensive hobbies. It's real simple. Don't bite off more than you can chew. Sure, we'd all like to collect classic cars, but that costs heaps of dough and requires a big garage and tons of funds to maintain them. Perhaps a few model cars would suffice. No matter what your downtime entertainment will consist of, keep it reasonable until your big shipload of money comes in. No bigger sinkhole will suck a bank account dry like the hobby of some fanatical collector of rare and expensive whatever. Few people ever make a profit from their hobby.

Dropping out of school. If you are determined and your life's ambition is to be a plumber's helper and/or you have someone (like perhaps a relative) offering to make you a paid apprentice, and you hate school because you are failing most classes, and your girlfriend is expecting twins, and you need to pay for her medical bills—you may want to consider dropping out of high school to enter into the public workforce. But everybody else, please remain in school until you get the job done. Leaving early will mean you will not be able to get as good a job as those who finish their education. (See below) This is no big secret. Everyone knows it. But many choose to ignore it and suffer lifelong consequences.

Working at a job you don't like. This is a guaranteed way to be unsuccessful and miserable your whole life. Show me a person who enjoys his or her work and I'll show you someone who will be successful. They will be promoted earlier, and advance farther and faster than those who feel trapped in a dead-end job. It's not complicated at all. A happy employee performs better and consequently continues to be happier and happier as they move up the career ladder in their chosen field.

Stupid things you can invest in. There are some purchases one ought to avoid, no matter how skillful the salesperson, is or how enticing the offer is. Here are a few of them:

Time Shares—an industry noted for high-pressure sales tactics, exorbitant prices, and ridiculous fees. Most people who buy them end up stuck in regret city. Learn to look at the negative sides of an issue as well as the positive. For example, let's examine the downside of Time Shares. Here are some of the expenses that a typical Time-Share purchase doesn't include:

Cost of travel to the location.

Cost of food while on vacation there.

Cost of entertainment while there.

Cost of a car rental while there (if one is needed).

The annual maintenance fee. By the way, this can be adjusted upwards to whatever amount the Time Share Management folks decide on, with no input from you.

The depreciation of the Time Share buildings and facilities.

The high interest on the money they loan you to purchase "their" Time Share.

Here are some other examples:

Expensive Pets. They can eat you out of house and home, not to mention costing a small fortune to maintain. If you are serious about acquiring a pet, make sure you can handle it both emotionally and financially. I'm talking dogs and cats here, but this applies to all creatures of the wild. I once knew a guy who thought he owned a male lion, but actually, that lion owned him. You would not believe what he went through to keep that beast. Animal lover or not, I suggest thoroughly investigating the dining and mating behavior as well as the emotional needs of any animal before you bring it home to poop on your Persian rugs and eat your furniture. Otherwise, keep it simple and get a goldfish.

Recreational toys: airplanes, boats, racehorses, motorcycles, ATVs, etc. These should be obvious, but many people sink themselves financially and/ or literally in their new boat, or crash and burn in their what-cha-ma-call-it. These kinds of possessions are usually rationalized and justified as hobbies. Their initial cost may not be all that great, but give them time and they tend to evolve into obsessions that clean out your bank account and take over your life.

Jewelry. A $50 watch tells time as accurately as that $10,000 diamond-crusted European timepiece. Diamonds are not a girl's best friend.

If the diamond cartels were to release their vast stockpiles into the marketplace, their per-karat value would fall to just a little above costume jewelry. If you just have to impress someone you would be well advised to consider man-made. Modern science, through some amazing technology, has developed wonderful counterfeits that sell at a mere fraction of the price, which even professional jewelers have trouble differentiating from the real thing.

Expensive vacations. If you must, take your vacation, but keep it local and cheap. Look around. There are a thousand things to do right near your home, and you'll feel so much better knowing how much money you are saving.

Collectible artwork. Most art doesn't increase in value nearly as much as the highest commissioned salesperson will tell you. It is a risky investment and the kind that is best left to the experts. The same goes for stamps, coins, rare wines, antique furniture, Beanie Babies, and whatever the fad of the week happens to be.

Health care costs are often the biggest and most unexpected expenses encountered in life. If you want to have a long and prosperous life—try to stay healthy. You know the rules. Don't smoke, drink, or do drugs. Eat well. Get enough sleep. Use protection if you must escapade. Do moderate exercise regularly. Maintain a healthy lifestyle and see a doctor when necessary. And for goodness sake, always make sure you have the best health care plan you can afford. Establish a good working relationship with the necessary doctors and get the appropriate vaccinations, including an annual flu shot. And oh yes-take care of your teeth!

A healthy mind is as important as a healthy body. Start and maintain a reasonable hobby. Write, paint, do crossword puzzles, and read books, newspapers, and periodicals to keep your mind active.

This tip is mostly for younger readers. You've been with me for a while now and I like you. So I'm going to reveal one of the most useful financial tips you will ever receive. If you heed this you will be able to retire at least a couple of years earlier, and your life will be significantly more enjoyable. I am going to spill the beans about something that has been the curse of humankind ever since the advent of the automobile. That's right—I'm talking about driving.

You will save yourself a veritable fortune if you will do the following. Simply pretend that you have a delicious fresh pie sitting on the back seat of your automobile as you drive. Or if you prefer, a carton of eggs will also work. Wherever you go, remember it's there and drive accordingly. Start by accelerating slowly and give yourself adequate room behind the car in front of you to have sufficient time to slow down and come to a smooth and gentle stop. Do not speed up and slow down at stoplights or burn rubber trying to impress someone in another car. Never swerve and pass others recklessly. Drive so your pie doesn't fall off the seat.

If you drive like this throughout your driving lifetime it may save you more money than any savings account. You will save money on tires, brakes, clutches, and engine repairs. You will save money on gas, speeding tickets, and car insurance. It may even spare you the high costs of attorney fees in defending yourself in court and prevent bankruptcy for medical reasons due to injuries incurred in accidents.

Perhaps the singular most common obstruction to wealth accumulation and the thing that keeps people down the most is the proverbial divorce war. You simply wouldn't believe how much the typical well-fought prolonged splitting-of-the-sheets can cost in today's litigious loving society. If you don't believe me, just check out the mansions, play toys, and lifestyles of some divorce attorneys. If you do find yourself in a situation where the parting of ways is necessary, for goodness sake, be reasonable. Sit down at the negotiating table with that special someone whom you once loved, but can no longer stand, and talk it out! Don't be too greedy and whatever it takes—part as friends.

That's about it. Those are my "can't miss" basic rules guaranteed to bring you a slow but steady wealth accumulation and help you establish a sound bottom line. I assure you that if you follow this sagacious advice you will be successful and happy.

What? I didn't say anything specifically about investments or saving money. Okay... if you insist.

All investments have a certain degree of risk. The more diversified your asset allocation is, the less potential there will be for loss. As a general rule, the greater the possible reward, the higher the risk potential. The longer you have before you will need the investment funds, the higher the risks can be. The amount of time you have for the investment should always be the determining factor in the amount of risk tolerance. The willingness to take risks should always be based on the amount of time before the target date for requiring the money.

I guess I ought to briefly explain compound interest. It means don't wait until it's too late to start saving. If you leave the money invested for a long time it will create a whole lot more money. For example, if your grandparents had invested $4000 for you when you were the age of five, in a nice conservative mutual fund and it averaged 8% (which it would have until the recent Wall Street implosion) with a provision that none of the principal or earnings therefrom could be touched until you were 45, which is tomorrow, that investment would have grown to $1,124,000.00. And that ain't pesos my friend. That's dollars, which of course would have less purchasing power because of 40 years of inflation, but it would still represent a big return on a small investment. And you would be in a fat city. That's what time and compound interest do.

Is compound interest still a little vague? Okay. Suppose you don't have a generous grandparent. Let's assume the market is going to stabilize at some future time and return to normal. If you invest $10 a week in a stock market mutual fund for 35 years and earn an average of 8 percent interest you will have close to 100,000. If you left it in a saving account paying 2 percent, you would only have about $27,000. If you begin putting away $858 a month in some ultra-conservative 4% investment when you are 25 years old, by the time you are 65 you'll have a million bucks. If you're a late starter and wait until 35 to begin saving, you need to increase the monthly savings amount by 70% and invest $1,455 a month to acquire that same million. If you still don't believe in compound interest and spend all your money on booze and high living, waiting until you are 45 to begin your million-dollar retirement quest, you'll have to increase the monthly savings amount by 219% socking away $2739 a month. You don't even want to know the figures for waiting until you are 50 to begin filling your treasure chest. But you can see how *time* makes more than a little difference, huh? That's compound savings.

I'd like you to just consider how much money you would save annually by not paying 10 % interest on a new car loan, 20% interest on $10,000 in credit card debt, and the $5 a day you spend on your morning latte. I'm sure there are many other items you could add to this list. I'm not near enough of a mathematician to figure out how much money it would all be, but let's just agree that it would be a lot. I might also point out that every penny of it you save is like an additional penny of tax-free income that you could invest.

Create a good credit record by paying all your bills on time. Build up a healthy nest egg for rainy days. Establish a healthy balance between saving and spending, using the previously discussed principles and investing your savings for long-term growth in sound real estate and the stock market. As you acquire investment capital purchase a wide spectrum of no-load mutual funds with low expenses. Never buy from a broker as their commission alone can run up to 5.75%. I assume that by now you realize this is the slow but sure method. Quite honestly, if you want to get rich quickly, you'll have to become some kind of entrepreneur and find a way to make a whole bunch of money fast.

Oh yeah, one last thing—unless you want to live under a bridge and eat dumpster food, don't count on social security or the government to take care of you after retirement.

MY GOD

It's late at night—time to conceive—when my sails appear to catch a creative wind—enabling me to write. It's when I can make contact with that level of my mind where imagination and inspiration live. I have no idea why I can dive more deeply into the cerebral sea at this hour. Perhaps I'm just a night diver. I only know that this is when the keyboard sings as thoughts come flooding in and I am besieged with the muse. The colors are more vivid. The ideas are more visual and thoughts emerge from infinity. My mind begins to wander and I begin to wonder.

Am "I" real or merely a thought of someone who is thinking me into existence? Is this life a dream or is this dream real life? Is my perception skewed or are these thoughts coming from the ultimate source of all knowledge? Am I who I think I am, or someone who thinks he is I? Are you reading this, or am I only imagining you reading this? Is space infinite? How can that be? What about time? Will I be a child forever? Is this all as tangible as it seems, or does it all merely seem so in my bemused unempirical mind?

I am alone with my psyche—communing with the forces of the universe. It is when I stand on the precipice of confusion and gaze into the realm of possibilities. It is when the source of existence accepts me, and allows me into the normally inaccessible zone of awareness. I transit from the subjective nowhere to the joyful bliss of intuitive consciousness. There are no interruptions, and nothing to forget. The day has been spent, and now I turn the cerebral mechanisms over to the imperceptible intellect; the amazing brain that guides me through these soul-searching moments.

A seed of spirituality springs forth. I have no idea what causes such all-encompassing enlightenment to come into my head. I only know that my fingers cannot keep up with the myriad of ideas that flood the well of thought processes. I think—no make that known—that my source is God. Yes, "IT" is God talking to me. The sheer brilliance of this human thought is all the proof I require. God is the mirror of my soul. He is the guide of the spiritual labyrinth through which I wander. He is my all-pervading conduit to eternity. There is no other reasonable explanation. He has always been there, and He always will be.

Scoff if you must, but I feel a personal connection with the Creator of this Universe. His perspective effortlessly flows into my mind. I am not, however, trying to establish myself in any way as His messenger or spokesman. Nor, have I ever required a middleman to interpret his messages to me. I am no visionary. I do not have any great revelations to proclaim, except perhaps that there is certain enlightenment that comes with belief. I sense this unity with God and know intuitively how He wants me to live my life. I am but a lone sailor of my small boat, navigating the waters of divine inspiration according to whatever winds and seas He wills that I encounter.

I humbly acknowledge and accept his supremacy. As the scriptures say: "He" is the Beginning and the End. He is the longing fulfilled. He is the giver and taker of all existence and poses questions that cannot be answered. He claims my thoughts. He owns my soul. He is the light of power that illuminates the truth. He is the light of being and the center of everything—the master of the infinite.

I am not conflicted or on some spiritual quest, but have always been curious about the phenomenon of faith, and the purpose of life. I have only concluded that life is a lesson and a journey, granted to us by God. To that end, I have explored a myriad of convictions. I am aware of man's many ways of worship. I can truthfully state that I have tested the religious waters, and believe me, they are deep and plentiful. The World Christian Encyclopedia states that there are over 34,000 different Christian denominations alone and over 10,000 distinct religions.

I got my commencement by being born into, baptismally sprinkled, and confirmed a Lutheran Protestant in the fundamentalist concave of Waco, Texas. Later in life, I was re-born and fully dunked in baptism in the Church of Christ. I have also been saved in the Baptist church. Once upon a faith, I attended the Church of Christian Science in Hollywood. I have been substantially indoctrinated through marriage to Catholicism in that all-embracing religion and have attended Mass. I have witnessed services at the Crystal Cathedral, which is essentially non-denominational, although loosely affiliated with the Dutch Reform Church.

I know about the teachings of Muhammad and the Dead Sea scrolls found at Qumran. I'm a bit familiar with Jewish History and its wonderful traditions. I've read about Hinduism, Jainism, Sikhism, Buddhism, Taoism,

Confucianism, and various types of folk religions. In weakened moments I have permitted Mormons, Jehovah's Witnesses, and Seven-Day Adventists into my home and patiently outlasted them all as I allowed them to take their best shot. I've spent some pleasant hours in Christian Science reading rooms and once listened politely while a very determined Scientologist endeavored to convert me. I have read the Dali Lama's books and the inspired writings of Deepak Chopra. I listened to an entire series of lectures by the great Maharishi Mahesh Yogi and for a while practiced transcendental meditation.

I enthusiastically watched each of Joseph Campbell's "Power of Myths" lectures. Being part Native American I even gave wise old Chief Seattle a read. I have attended a few stadium revivals, and thoroughly enjoyed a few Tent Revivals and Holy Roller services. Fortunately, I haven't been in a church of acid-drinking poison snake handlers. Thanks for the invite, but no thanks.

My searching and quest for knowledge have charily guided the evolution of my faith into monotheism. I have not received a definitive revelation from God, but have decided that God's oneness is simply because—to my way of thinking—that is the most comprehensible and probable possibility. However, I do not condemn those who choose to believe otherwise.

After all my searching and exploration, I have come to realize God does not need religion—man does. Although most folks my age are locked into one belief or religion, Is there only one pathway to Heaven, through belief in Jesus Christ? The Bible says so, yet I am not God and do not care to debate if a child born in the wilds of Africa and never exposed to Christianity can go to heaven or not when it dies. I hope it can. I know that God is slow to anger and displays love, kindness, tolerance, conscience, morality, faith, and hope. My God-given mind tells me there might be different ways to get there, and that's good enough for me.

At this point, I take peace of mind and do not profess to be of any particular religious denomination. Instead, I believe in the brotherhood of humankind, regardless of race, ethnicity, or religion. I see God everywhere I look and accept as true that He dwells within each of us, and will give us a spiritual compass if we will merely accept His guidance. I concede that I am but one insignificant mortal being whose soul is spiritual. I acknowledge God as the one who supplies my conscious brain with these very thoughts.

He (and I use the masculine "He" only because of tradition) is all-knowing, all-being, and always "there" for me. He is great and He is good and He alone knows the mystery of creation.

He crafts the sunrises and the sunsets. He made animals and people and all life forms. He is nature. He is science. He is the Bible and the One. He is the essence of indescribable. He is the all-embracing consummate God of Moses, Jesus Christ, Buda, Muhammad, and all the other Gods and prophets mankind has adored and worshiped over the eons.

I assure you I am not Bible-thumping here. I have no desire to debate anyone about the Bible being allegorical or discuss where I think all those fossils came from, even if evolution remains mostly theory after all the years since Darwin; with no irrefutable fossilized evidence of transitional life forms. Nor do I wish to ask anyone to give up all joys and pleasures and ignore the seven or more decades of their earthly life to concentrate only on the salvation of attaining eventual eternal spiritual bliss. I am certain God wishes us to attain as much happiness as possible during our time in this world.

I know God because of the miracle of being a human being, capable of developing complex theories to explain ourselves. We see a flower, or butterfly, or witness a sunset and comprehend the true beauty therein. We probe the deepest regions of the cosmos and contemplate the very meaning of our existence—something no animal can do.

With mankind's continually improving intellectual and technological knowledge, our capabilities to look deeper into the sub-microscopic world of life, and see farther out into space, we are just beginning to understand how vast and complex a structure the cosmos is, requiring incredibly intricate precision and awesome composition, which cannot be rationalized away as mere chance. We did not spring from nothingness. Something or somebody (God) HAD TO BE THERE before matter existed. The universe is too complex, regulated, and well-organized to be created merely by chance. There has to be a Controlling Intelligence. You may refer to It by any name you choose such as Lady Luck or Father Fate but I call this the Almighty God.

I think God reveals His existence in the intelligent design of the universe and the unlimited wonders of nature. Nothing explains it all except God.

More importantly, perhaps is His gift of human intellect and our ability to reason and allow Him into our thoughts. It is only logical then, that God leaves it up to each of us to ultimately decide to believe in Him or not.

If He chooses to be invisible to us, it does not prove He is not there. The wind and electricity are invisible, but they are real. He knows his absolute nature and infinite existence are far beyond the limited capacity of mankind's facility to fully comprehend. His reality exists beyond human perception. However, I find it comforting to believe that He does extend spiritual insight to those who search for it. Therefore, if we seek Him out faithfully, he permits us to find and journey through life on the absolute one true path that we must follow.

I find it interesting the ways a religion will always remain enigmatic. For one thing, even though God is all-powerful, He chooses not to give us free to direct our day-to-day lives. I am not disturbed by that fact, because it makes a lot of sense. I do not think He is unable to communicate with us if He desires, and therefore needs to use other humans as conduits. Some are called to the ministry, Does this mean He selects certain people to talk with, informing them of what to tell His followers? Possibly, but God doesn't personally need lots of money.

One alarming thing is that religion and aggression in some cases seem to be synonymous. It's a sad fact that religion as an idiom attracts extremism that is sometimes not good. But it's understandable. It's all a matter of control. Extremists want it and seek to acquire it through the auspices of religion. Control can be achieved by several methods. The most common is through *dominance* or *fear*. Another is by *repetitious memorizing* of doctrines and rules or *brainwashing*. Still, another is by offering compliers some sort of ridiculous *quasi-materialistic or financial reward* for a subsequent spiritual existence. Such tactics are commonly employed by those seeking control but are not conducive to true religion. They should be identified, ousted, and eliminated wherever and whenever possible by any means necessary.

Political opportunists and warp-envisioned extremists can find justification for any cause or act by selective interpretation of the scriptures of any religion. Through twisting the teachings and misdirecting the moral compass any faith—no matter how benevolent—can be used as a tool to gain control over the masses. Mixing politics with religion concocts an evil brew.

That is when it can become a dangerous mania. The most basic precepts of religion are abrogated whenever theocratic fascism is employed to impose that religion on others. If a particular religion is successful, it will always be voluntarily practiced by its believers. No bona fide religion would ever be forced on anyone.

For example, look at the current violent world condition. We all know that Islam is not a religion exclusively for terrorists. But, through their unconscionable actions, the small faction of radical jihadists that are attempting to hijack the Muslim faith are distorting the face of Islam, making it appear—too much of the world—as they face of terror and death. That small group is no more representative of Islam than those extreme folks who murder abortion doctors in the name of Jesus and call themselves Christians.

Or consider the time when religion ruled the world in the bloodiest period of all, known as the Dark Ages. Remember the gory Crusades that spread Christianity by the power of the sword? Look at the horrors of the Inquisition, the burning of witches, the enslavement of Africa, and more recently, think about the killing of hundreds of thousands of Eastern Christians and Muslims and the Catholic-Protestant pogrom cycle in Europe. I find it ironic that by leaving the "s" off the sword we have the "word." Religious wars have always been with us and still rage today. The *honest-to-God* truth is that God transcends religion and therefore, religions survive despite themselves.

One might therefore deduce that God is callous. The point could be made that only a disinterested God would allow us to stumble around making the mistakes we humans make. I don't think God particularly enjoys or condones watching us wage war, kill, main, rape, torture, and do the evil and stupid things we humans do to each other. That is another entity called evil with a D, which must also exist. But I digress, as evil is not the subject of this essay.

So God must have other things to do. I'd like to think that He's just very busy. Perhaps He has other time-consuming obligations, hobbies, or other universes to oversee, the very nature of which we can't even begin to imagine, much less fathom. War is our choice—not God's. I think any thinking person should realize that deep down in their heart.

So, I believe God allows us to live as we see fit. He tends to be a "free will" proponent, allowing us to be compliant with His will ... or to screw things up on our own. We seem to do a pretty effective job of it. That's why we need forgiveness for our sins.

I also don't believe He is particularly amused by our incompetence and failure. Nor do I think He is disinterested. I feel like He is merely being resolute in His decision to remain distant and allow us to fail or succeed, much like a swimming teacher might choose to allow a hesitant student to sink or swim on their own, knowing they could always jump in and save them if necessary.

Now comes the big question. Is there an afterlife? I think so, but God's truth is—that being an optimist, all I can do is <u>believe</u> there is. I recognize that the Bible proclaims Isaiah, Peter, Paul, and Jesus through the power of God brought people back from the dead ... including Jesus' resurrection after being crucified. None of us know when the end of time will come, or when it comes for ourselves, much less for all of mankind. All I know about it is what Jesus told us and believe His promise to all who believe.

Preachers proclaim the promise of an afterlife, as does the Bible. But it's impossible to know while we are still flesh and blood. That question will only be answered when our body gives up our spirit ... the dark veil of death is pulled back to reveal what comes next.

Everything that "is" will in some distant eternity "no longer be." Everything dies or wears out in time. God's universe depends on that. I'm afraid that the hard cold reality is that life itself is but a fleeting moment of eternity, while death is every other possible second of forever.

Please don't think I am telling you—or in any way—giving you intellectual permission not to believe, even if you so choose. It's only <u>your</u> "every other possible second of forever" you risk. Not me. I do not choose to face that inevitability in spiritual emptiness.

I believe.

I see no reason why you shouldn't too. I am merely stating the obvious; the truth that God chooses to feed into my brain at this late hour. Am I getting it wrong? Who knows? I sure don't. But God does.

Now you may doubt His existence agnostic, but we both know you have this kind of funny feeling way deep down inside that just maybe—you could be wrong! And what might the consequences be then? You set the odds on what you think the chances are that He is there in a place of inaccessible light that no one can prove exists. What do you think they are? A trillion-trillion-to-one? A thousand-to-one? A hundred-to-one? Ten-to-one? Fifty-fifty? What does it matter? If there is even the slightest tiny minute chance that all those billions who have proclaimed His existence and believed are right—don't you owe it to your immortal soul to at least consider it? If after all is said and done and He is He, are you prepared to sacrifice your soul? This might be a good time to mention that every day some 140,000 people die, and eventually you will too.

Can I positively guarantee you that there is a God and that you will ultimately meet him in the afterlife? Absolutely! Certainly! I'll do that. If I'm wrong, when you get the proof, feel free to sue me. Just in case you haven't yet made up your mind, to help you determine how you want to feel about God, I offer a few things to consider.

There either is or is not a god and if there is, you will ultimately find out whether you believe in Him or not.

If everything we see and do is all merely some evolutionary accident and there is no God, and you believe in Him in vain, you won't be disappointed because you'll never really know that He doesn't exist, so it won't matter anyway.

If there is a God, and you believe in Him, and that pleases Him enough to grant you the ever-lasting promise, everything is going to work out amazingly well for you.

It is therefore without question, far wiser and better—to believe in a God who may exist—than not to believe in a God who may not exist. Just think about the consequences.

It is obvious to me that it is far more comforting to go through life believing that when our bodies fail, as they all eventually do, our spiritual souls make their journey to that peaceful place where forever becomes reality.

After considering the above, it is evident that a person who chooses to believe in God is making the wisest choice, no matter what.

In case I never get the opportunity again, I do wish you well in your afterlife. I'd like to meet you there. I also wish you well in this one, because—God forbid—it may be the only one you ever get to experience. Let's both pray it's not. Better yet, let's truly believe it's not!

A couple of final thoughts and I am out of here. If God didn't create this dream we call life utilizing all the various miracles of evolution and His ultimate powers, then how did we get here? The inevitableness of time alone is more than adequate proof for me. We didn't just happen. Something had to start it all. What was here before there were stars and universes? They didn't just materialize out of nothing. What existed before, when there was only nothingness? I think it had to have been God. But mostly I believe in God, because every kind, loving, decent, gentle, caring human, including you and me, will ultimately pass. The thought that death is forever—the ultimate absolute end—is simply unbearable! God just makes sense. He wasn't merely borne into existence out of our need for Him. He was here before anything ever existed. He is then without a doubt—that which always was and always is and always forever will be. So—thank God for God!

Whether you are a pious and faithful believer without any uncertainties or insecurity; or harbor atheistic skepticism and ambiguity, you needn't worry for there will come a time when all doubts and beliefs will be validated—because we all meet our maker in the end. I just pray He likes me, and hope that there are some nice bike trails to ride in Heaven.

And oh yes... one last request—please remember me in your prayers.

FOR THE THRILL OF IT

Let me set this straight right upfront. I am no amusement park junkie. Somewhere along the line, it became obvious to me that they were building roller coasters and other thrill rides that exceeded my ability to enjoy the excitement offered. Sure, go ahead and think of me as chicken excrement if it makes you feel better. But I know and accept my limitations.

I discovered them one day at Magic Mountain. I was there with my eldest daughter and her temporary boyfriend. It was a sweltering hot summer day and we had just purchased the most delicious double-scooped waffle ice cream cones. Mine was Pina'colada flavored. I was attacking it with great aplomb and naturally distracted. My festive tongue was so involved with preventing a single drip loss that I paid little heed to the line we were standing in. I was in ice cream heaven and just slurping the last of it down and munching on the cone as we arrived at the entrance to some ride. In high sugar overload, I followed my lead dogs like sheep. We stepped into what appeared to be an open-fronted elevator. I started to suspect something was up when the bar closed in over us and they strapped us in. But it was too late. It shot upward at mach-something and left us staring out into space through the open door, which from the looks of things wasn't going to close. I looked at my daughter who was grinning wickedly and started to say, "they're not going to...aaaieeeaaahhh!

They did. We dropped in freefall from what seemed to me to be about a mile high, instantly surpassing the maximum velocity of falling objects and reaching the bottom in approximately one millisecond at which time our elevator immediately snapped into a horizontal position, leaving us laying on our backs and staring up at the open sky through which we'd just fell. As the elevator stopped I distinctly felt and heard all of the vertebrae in my back pop like rapid machine gunfire. It was tantamount to getting an instant ten-hour chiropractic full-spine adjustment. As I lay there gasping for air, while I hadn't had time for fear to set in, I did know that if I ever walked again, I'd never go on another amusement park ride. Somehow, I managed to keep my ice cream down.

Suffice it to say that after that little free-fall experience, I was determined to use temperance and countenance in all future amusement park participation. However, time heals all wounds, and we henceforward quite a few years, to a day whereupon I chance to notice that Disney Land was offering senior citizens a swell deal on a Season Pass to the park. Aha! I have always been nothing if not a kid at heart and naturally, being recently escaped from the rat race, with plenty of free time, I had to have it. After a short convincing plea negotiation with the Better Half—a.k.a. Peetie, I ordered us a pair. All the Disney Land we could stand for a year, without the hassle and expense of buying tickets.

We soon discovered that we both regressed to child-like behavior the minute we entered the Magic Kingdom. We had found our calling and became regulars. If laughter is good medicine and merriment is nourishment for the soul, we became healthy and were a couple of happy souls that year. We rode every ride, visited every attraction, and enjoyed every entertainment venue much more than thoroughly. It's a thing everyone ought to do at least once in their life if they have the opportunity.

We did it all. Every ride they had and most of them many times. But one ride only once and one ride never. I'll explain those later. Before that year was out we got to know many of the employees and I'm afraid that many of them knew us. Our adventures were numerous, and I could regale you with countless tales, but for brevity, I shall only point out a few of our more exciting (meaning embarrassing) moments.

On our first turn on the Big Thunder Mountain ride. Peetie started screaming the instant the mine car train took off on its lurching twisting heart-pounding journey. She hadn't expected it and gripped my right arm so hard that I believe I still retain some imprint of her fingers. Although we rode it several more times, it never again caught Peetie by surprise.

We marveled at such wonders as talented Michael Jackson's pre-molester days Captain EO and those harmless and amusing thug Pirates of the Caribbean. We took the Jungle Cruise often (Peetie screaming every time the hippo surfaced), and sailed to Treasure Island regularly. As a retired submariner, I had to take a regular cruise on the Submarine ride. Peetie, who has never driven due to bad eyesight became quite a speed demon on the Autotopia freeway.

Then there was the Rocket Jets ride. It consisted of small rockets that were suspended at the end of spokes radiating outward from a central column. The rider occupants sat in a small area in each rocket, one behind the other on a cushioned seat low on the floor of an open two-person cockpit, while sticking their legs forward into and under the body of the rocket for the duration of the ride.

We were standing in this long line and chatting amiably with the two gothic-looking dudes behind us. As we drew close to the loading platform, and not being small of stature, we naturally became concerned and wondered if the two of us would fit into that small cockpit area of the rocket, or if we should each take a rocket of our own. It looked like a tight fit for any well-proportioned adult, of which we were two.

Peetie, bless her kind heart, always willing to take advice from a stranger, no matter how dumb-looking, inquired of the two dudes as to whether or not they thought we would both be able to squeeze into the cockpit area of the rocket.

They quickly scanned us with their beady star-wars eyes and assured us that they had ridden the ride many times before and that we could easily ride it together. About that time we arrived at the loading area and in Peetie's direction, I squeezed in first, my long legs barely fitting under the nose of the rocket. Peetie attempted to climb in behind me, but wouldn't you know she didn't quite fit. But by then, she had somehow managed to get both feet wedged deep down inside the rocket and had started her sitting motion. Gravity had taken over and she was planted firmly behind me in a semi-standing half-way-sitting position. The next problem was, she began laughing. That ride had been designed with younger, slimmer, and more athletically capable riders in mind.

I feel I must digress momentarily here to explain that when Peetie laughs, she laughs. She truly gives it her all. She gets weak in the knees and loses all strength. I guess it's a woman thing.

So there we were. Jammed tight. I'm stuck and can't move, with both feet wedged forward into the rocket. Peetie is cackling away above and behind me, but incapable of moving. There are anxious want-to-be riders behind us, and they are beginning to get nervous. The poor kids assisting people on the rocket ride don't know what to do. They only knew that they must stop the ride until we were dislodged.

Suddenly there were all these hands trying to lift Peetie up and out. Another thing about Peetie is that when strange hands touch her she also laughs. I think it's a rampant giggle gene in her DNA someplace. So there we sat. The ride was stopped. The long line behind us wasn't moving. About a dozen people were trying to extract us, while those two weird dude advisors behind us were staring off into space.

Meanwhile, Peetie is giggling hysterically and offering up infectious one-liners like a hysterical standup comedian, "Maybe you should get a crane," "Does anybody have any oil?" and "Gee this is a fun ride" all of which was making the people trying to help us out laugh along with her. I was more or less helpless, only my legs were starting to cramp.

It took a while, but with Peetie still laughing all the way, they in some manner wrenched us out of there. I looked around for our two weird dudes' advisors, having it in mind to un-thank them, but they were long gone-having wisely decided to teleport out of the vicinity. Once out we thanked everyone profusely for their help and slinked away into the crowd, never to attempt it again. That is the one ride we never rode.

We usually visited the park about two days a week. We'd find a nice bench to sit on somewhere in the shade (usually in front of a store on Main Street) and just watch the people go by with frantic looks on their faces. They were all paying zillions of dollars for their day's visit to the park with their pack—and they "come hell or high water" were going to get it all in. Ha! We knew it was impossible. I have a theory that if one were to sit in one place at Disney Land long enough, they would eventually see everyone else in the world pass by. I felt a sort of smug superiority knowing that "They" would all be going home in the next day or two, while we had all the time in the world to sit back and observe them.

We methodically worked our way through the park. We sampled every ride and attraction to our heart's content. There were certain rides that we couldn't get enough of. For instance, I could ride the "Small World" ride every day a dozen times and still not get bored. It seemed to be built just for me. I became a Small World junkie, memorizing many of the lyrics so I could sing along loudly with the adorable little characters one meets on the ride, and accordingly to Peetie, often to the dismay of others trying to hear the music. It's playing through my mind right now.

Another infectious tune that will live in my soul forever is the music from the Main Street Electrical Parade. We never missed an opportunity to see those wonderful pixies and assorted Disney characters cavorting in strobe lights and fiber optics with all those amazing high-tech lighting effects. We regressed to the age of a young child each time we saw it. I occasionally still see it in my dreams.

I don't think we ever visited the park without first taking the Disney Land Railroad on a trip around the park. It seemed to set the mood. We also rode the Skyway to Fantasyland and Tomorrow Land. It was a huge thrill to go through the Matterhorn. I got a lot of personal enjoyment on the People Mover. I liked to wave at people below and loudly shout out some phony name as we passed over a crowd as if I knew someone. It usually got Peetie's goat, especially when they would invariably wave back. Peetie would sheesh me as if she was humiliated and embarrassed, but I knew she thought it was funny.

Another favorite of mine was the Haunted Castle. I loved the ghosts, especially the character that would get in the cart between Peetie and me smiling fiendishly as we zipped through the darkened interior. One of Peetie's favorite rides didn't move at all. It was the "Enchanted Tiki Room" with all those animated birds singing in unison. Every time we'd come out she would be singing: "Let's all sing as the birdies sing. Tweet tweet, tweet, tweet!" Peetie has a kind of bird thing.

We both just loved the stunning views in "America The Beautiful" which were shown in circle vision. It seldom ever had a long line and there were also games to play and things to do in the staging area while waiting on the ride to begin. I never failed to somehow talk Peetie into going on the Mark Twain Riverboat with me, even if it wasn't all that exhilarating. It also took plenty of charm and persuasion to cajole her into a visit to my favorite concession, which was the Carnation Ice Cream store. We generally stayed until after the nightly fireworks show and ended up straggling out with the last diehard park visitors.

That year the park introduced the Indian Jones Ride with much fanfare. Peetie and I didn't join the millions standing in line. We bided our time well, and on an off day (there is no such a thing in the world of Disney), we made our move. We only had to stand in line for about ten hours it seemed. One of the best things about Peetie is... that she doesn't remember a dang thing. She had completely forgotten the Indian Jones movies we'd seen and had no idea what to expect, only that it was a new and exciting ride.

There was a modicum of complaining on her part since her legs went numb after the first five hours of standing in line. But then we begin to see the light at the end of the tunnel, which proved to be a fairly accurate description of the ride. I saw a hint of displeasure on Peetie's face when they more or less herded us into that mock safari wagon. When it made its first jolting lurch and she was violently thrown against the hard side of the box, I had a hunch that it wasn't going to become her favorite ride.

The farther into the ride we got, the more that cart jerked and tossed us around. It was not a senior citizen ride. I strongly suggested to the attendant as we exited that they ought to have a four-foot "height line" at the entrance of the ride like they do on the little kid rides and if someone is taller than four feet, they shouldn't be allowed on that ride. Peetie proclaimed afterward that it had been the worst two minutes of her life, and she had the next day she had black and blue bruise marks to prove it. We never ventured anywhere near that ride again, and it is the only ride at Disneyland we only rode once. I can only hope that some Imaginationeer at Disney Land eventually realized what a tortuous ride they had created and modified the jerks with some sort of governors on those vehicles.

But the absolute most entertaining ride we ever had, and the one we still talk about and laugh about the most, was the first time we rode the Dumbo Ride. You remember Dumbo the elephant with those big ears who could fly. Yep, that's the one. It was a little kid's ride, that just went round and round in a circle. We took it simply because there was no line, which was too good a deal to pass up. We happened to be walking by, saw that we could get right on, and jumped into the first flying elephant that came along.

The ride started and wouldn't you know it—our elephant didn't fly. The rest of the elephants were filled with kids whose elephants were lifting them into the air and down again, but ours just floated along barely above the ground. It was not being fun. Peetie naturally assumed that our weight had somehow broken it, or was causing it to malfunction and asked something to the effect of "how come we got the only retarded elephant?"

I launched into a diatribe about how we really ought to go on a diet and how embarrassing it was not to be able to lift off the ground when all the little kids were flying. About then, Peetie got the schoolgirl giggles and began laughing hysterically at the situation. I laid it on thick as I could. We both began laughing as we sailed along just barely above the ground during the entire ride. On-lookers must have thought we were stoned or at least well-looped. Even the attendant couldn't contain himself because he was laughing and gesturing and pointing and shouting something at us every time we went around. Unfortunately, we couldn't hear him because both Peetie and I were laughing so hard we were emitting joyous pheromones.

I thought that ride would never end. While the little kids were going up and down, we went around and around and around and around, always barely above the ground. We had the lowest-flying elephant in the universe. The little kids all started to point and laugh at us, and people walking by stopped and laughed at us, and it became an unofficial laugh-off. People were having so much fun at our behest; I figured they would have to give us a prize or something.

Finally, the ride ended. The attendant rushed over to make sure we wouldn't do anything foolish, and as he helped us out of the ride, he politely pointed out the little lever that I hadn't previously noticed which makes the elephants fly up and down. I wanted to ride it again, but unfortunately, Peetie was still laughing so much that I figured discretion was the better part of valor and we slinked off to find a bench to sit on.

Thanks, Dumbo. You made our season pass.

COCKTAIL PARTY QUESTIONS

Want to make life interesting? Love to start emotional bonfires? Then here you are debate fans; a drunk baker's dozen of surefire controversial zinger subjects guaranteed to evoke argumentative responses. If you like magniloquent probing, lubricious witty repartee, callow teasing, and instigation, you might preface whichever subject(s) you opt for by saying: "Would somebody, anyone, please, pretty please, please with sugar on it—answer the following question(s).

Exactly what is the "National Debt?" Exactly who owes who all those trillions of dollars, and if it **US** (the taxpayers) owing ourselves, why don't we just mark the note paid and get on with business? And what the heck is the debt ceiling all about? Isn't it the Feds (banks) creating money out of thin air, and then loaning it to the **U.S.** (the taxpayers) assigning us the responsibility to us to repay it?

And in the same vein, who authorizes the printing of all that U.S. Money, and why don't they just print up enough to bail out the National Debt? Is that what monetizing means? Isn't that already what they are doing? It all defies logic.

Who is watching the people who spend all that money that the people who spend money order the printers to print up? I suspect it's nobody. Also, I was just wondering how someone gets the job of burning all that old U.S. Money and who watches them do it and are there any openings?

If I go down to the Post Office and send a letter off to a distant third cousin in Timbuktu, or some equally God-forsaken place, I am charged a certain fee for postage. The U.S. Postal Service then sends the letter to some town in Timbuktu, where a poor guy on a camel has to deliver the letter over the burning sands for three days to get it to the destination I chose. My question is, who pays the guy on the camel, and how? If he sends me a reply and pays 40 Druzmas for Timbuktu postage, and I am one of the lucky ones and the U.S. Postal Service manages to deliver his letter to me, how does the U.S. Postal Service manage to pay full retirement, with benefits, to the letter carrier that brought it to me? Ha! I bet ya' never thought of that.

Who in the H-E double L is running the ACLU and what on earth are they trying to accomplish? Have they no collective conscience, ethics, or personal integrity at all? Why don't they occasionally represent someone who deserves some legal help in obtaining or protecting their rights? How do they find the scumbags and scalawags they lavish all that money and effort protecting? And lastly, who gives them all that money, and why doesn't anybody publish their names and addresses so somebody can kill them?

What do those tattooed white dudes in prison think they are accomplishing by referring to themselves as the Aryan or Arian Brotherhood? Hasn't anyone ever bothered to inform them that "Aryan" refers to a member of an early people in the area of what is now Iran? Do those guys want to become Muslims? Or are they simply that dim-witted?

Who is the victim? (a) The father of the drug smuggler who did nothing to stop his son from a life of crime (b) The parole board who let him out of prison early? (c) The drug dealer who sold the drugs to the guy who got killed jaywalking (d) Those people who smuggled them into the country? (e) The drunk driver (f) The jay-walking drug addict he kills? (g) The bartender who sold the drunk driver the alcohol that got him drunk (h) The company that manufactured the alcohol (i) The government policymakers who allowed such a company to exist in their country or (j) The people who elected them?

Exactly what is this "dry heat" stuff that people love to mention when the weather gets too hot? Some say it is not bad because it's a "dry heat" and others claim that it's awful because it is a dry heat. I'm never sure which one is good. What do you prefer—wet heat or dry heat? Why?

By now, who among us believes that we will somehow manage to overcome thousands of years of Islamic tribal wars and hatred with an offer of democracy, and an opportunity to become a part of the global community? Please raise your hands.

If anybody thinks mankind will ever find true peace on earth, please at least explain why on earth the supposedly civilized Catholics and Protestants can't find some way to peacefully coexist in Northern Ireland.

How come the birth rates of the more affluent industrialized nations where the citizens can afford to have children are declining, while the birth rates in the poorer poverty-stricken third world countries are continuing to crank out babies as fast as they can beyond any reason?

Since less than half the voting-age Americans cast ballots in the last few presidential elections, what would have to occur in this democracy before the apathetic fifty percent of seemingly non-caring, non-voters would find area reason to educate themselves politically by reading newspapers or periodicals and find the strength to get off their lazy butts on election day and go down and cast an intelligent well-thought-out vote for the individuals they want to run the government? 9/11 didn't do it? What will it take?

Why don't we expel all those lazy "it's the only life I've known" preferring individuals who are currently camping out in the overcrowded prisons at tremendous cost to us taxpayers? How come they get early retirement and a free ride? Why don't we force them to get a job and pay for their keep—in addition to paying a big fine? Is it because that might deter them from committing further crimes? How come our collectivistic modern-day society isn't smart enough to use our penal system to only confine those who commit violent crimes and deserve to be there?

How many of the Forbes 400 Richest Americans, who are all Billionaires, do you think tithe ten percent or more of their earnings to their church? What percentage of their annual earnings do you suppose they give to charity on average? How many of them practice tax avoidance schemes or cheat on their taxes?

And lastly, your freebie, and possibly the most controversial of all—what is the best ice cream flavor, and who makes it?

COMPATIBILITY TEST

Feeling lonely lately? Been looking but not finding it? Are your cell phone minutes going mostly unused? Are your Saturday nights spent at home over-eating pizza and rocky road and watching the tube? Do you just need a gosh-darn hug? Those are clues, my friend. If they apply to you, then by golly, we can help, by extending the following free compatibility test to all lonely hearts. Just answer the following fifty questions to determine your perfect match and what sort of creature you ought to be snuggling up to.

Note: This test will be treated with paramount confidentiality. No one but you, and our impulsive blabber-mouthed evaluation panel will ever see your answers. You will be graded on honesty. So don't cheat!

Which would you choose—a non-running fast motorcycle or a semi-operational beat-up minivan? Pick one.

Would you prefer a free tattoo or a complementary body piercing?

Have you ever been to a hangin' and if so, did you become aroused?

Do you drink regularly or just at night?

Have you ever et' frog legs? Raw?

What is the largest farm animal you ever dated? Please explain.

Is your neck size larger than your waist? Really?

Do your ears flap in a breeze and/or do you snort while laughing?

Can you whistle excruciatingly loud by putting two fingers in your mouth?

Have you ever accidentally robbed a convenience store?

Would you rather shoot holes in highway signs or blast cans off a fence?

Do you have more than two cousins named Bubba?

Can you make a loud popping sound by smacking your lips?

Do you enjoy pitching horseshoes more than cowpie-throwing contests?

Do the stars amaze you, and if so which ones?

Has there ever been any temporary insanity in your pants?

What are the most hard-boiled eggs you ever ate in one session? What was the next day like?

Is there gunfire on most of your birthday celebrations?

Can you spit farther than 14 feet? How much farther?

Have you ever plowed more than 50 acres in one day? Tractors or mules?

How many times have you woken up in a hog trough? Does that also describe the ugliest pig that you ever slept with?

Is there any truth to the rumors about you on the Internet? Which ones?

Do you believe that Superman is allergic to Kryptonite, or is that just something they made up to make him look bad?

How loud can you pass gas?

Have you ever laid a penny on a railroad track, and after a train run over it, drilled a hole in it once it was flattened, and worn it on a chain that turned your neck green?

Do you have buckteeth? Do you like them on others?

What are the most warrants you have ever had out for you at any one time?

What is the largest amount of bail anyone ever posted on your behalf?

Have you ever felt "the" urge?

Do you miss John Wayne?

Would you believe a lie if someone gave you money to believe it?

Have you ever had a Mohawk haircut?

What is the highest grade you achieved? Have you ever tried Pike's Peak? What were you driving?

Do you frequently become aroused during slasher movies?

Do you own any actual serial-killer trophies?

How many belt buckles do you own? Describe your favorite.

Do you know who Fatty Arbuckle was? No kidding?

Would you kiss a frog to get high? French?

Can you yodel romantically?

Have you ever chawed tobacco? Brand?

Would you prefer to drink a single pitcher of pond scum or five 8-ounce glasses of pond scum? Why?

Can you dance better when you get drunk?

How far is it from where you live?

How many times have you been camping in one week?

What's the least you would take for your car? (If you do not have a car you may skip this question and go directly to question number 26.)

What kind of body odor do you prefer?

What're the most you ever made in one poker hand? Were you bluffing?

Do you always read whatever writing you happen to come across on public bathroom walls? What's the best thing you ever read or written on one?

Have you ever voted? For whom?

What's your favorite kind of egg?

That's it. It was easy eh? But do not be misled. It's amazing what these simple little questions will reveal about your hidden personality and getting laid potential. To obtain your free UADESJD evaluation and dating profile report; once you have thought out your answers to the foregoing questions, simply write them down, or write them down simply, in crayon please, on whatever sort of paper you have handy. Then kindly send them to our Unofficially Appointed Dating Expert Senior Judge and Designate Mr. Donald Trump, Trump Tower Building, NYC, NY (Never mind the zip code as the P.O. knows how to find him).

P.S.: It may take a little while for Mr. Trump to get around to evaluating it since he has other interests. So please be patient—and in the meantime keep on hunting for that special someone. You probably deserve them. We thank you for your participation. Good luck.

TEN MOST AMAZING MEMORIES

There are countless beautiful things in this world and I feel blessed to have experienced my share of them. There are doubtless hundreds of memories I could write about—like the fields of spring bluebonnets that blossom by the immeasurable acre in Central Texas, standing on the west rim of the grand canyon at dawn, seeing the real Havana before Castro cast it into stagnation, trade winds rustling palm trees growing out of black volcanic rock overlooking a secluded pristine Hawaiian lagoon, the Key West sunset ritual, riding snowmobiles in the surroundings of Yellowstone Park in December, a humid summer evening in the Garden District of New Orleans the way it was before, Christmas Eve ice skating in Central Park, an early autumn houseboat cruise on Lake Powell, boating a Roosterfish off Cabo San Lucas, riding a tramway through the Costa Rican rain forest, a reflective rainy summer night in downtown Seattle, a motorbike tour of Bermuda, the subway in Tokyo, becoming a Shellback, etc. You get the idea.

Most people see some amazing things in their lifetime—things that they may tell others about when the moment is right. Not many of us ever get around to putting it down on paper though, which is what I hope to undertake here. I promise to spare you and not make it merely a travelogue, so I'll keep it to the United States. I also won't include any military experiences, family events, religious epiphanies, creative or financial successes, and gambling turns. Those are each a story unto themselves. I simply want to share a few of those unanticipated moments where time and fate conspired in some unexpected way to blow me away. One almost literally did.

Number 1 – An Encounter

One beautiful summer day I was sea-trialing an incomparable Sea Ray yacht for a family in the process of purchasing it. We were a few miles off the Southern California coast and everything was going superbly. The prospective captain was at the helm and I sat beside him, coaching him on how to properly operate the craft as we skimmed over the shimmering sea-green water. His wife and two children were seated on the aft deck, enjoying the ride. We had just fallen off the plane and were coasting to a stop, where I intended to demonstrate the proper use of the boat's electronics. I had gotten my customer to shift both engines to neutral, so the props weren't turning.

At that very moment, without warning, a Blue Whale gracefully breached just off the starboard side of our yacht spouting a twenty-five to thirty-foot high plume from its blowhole. The sound of its exhaling was piercing, and the prevailing breeze carried the misty spray of whale spit directly over us like falling rain, causing a great deal of excitement on board. I was utterly astonished by the sudden appearance of that immense creature that I estimate was 90 to 100 feet long. Due to its unbelievable size and smooth dark blue skin, I knew immediately what species it was, and to my way of thinking, that giant knew we were there before it came up. It had spotted and/or heard us and intentionally surfaced way-to-close-for-comfort to get a better look. My mind immediately raced as I considered the options.

I had learned to properly identify whales while in the Navy and had experienced close encounters with them before while on recreational boats. They had mostly been with the much smaller Gray Whales and an occasional Finback—in late winter and spring months during their annual migrations. I'd even spotted some Orcas (Killer whales), and a few Humpbacks and Minke in Southern California waters. But none of them had been anywhere near as imposing or ominous as that 100-ton creature, suddenly making our luxurious yacht seem very small. That cantankerous leviathan was quite obviously checking us out. It seemed curious and remained there with its blue and gray mottled head poking out above the water, carefully scrutinizing us with saucer-sized eyes over its huge protruding snout. I was praying the Goliath had no evil intentions and was merely giving us the once-over.

The man and his wife were stunned, while their kids seemed to be just highly stoked. I knew the Blue could swamp us in an instant if it wanted to, or even by accident if it were not careful. I did my best to appear calm and managed a weak smile in my best effort to not create panic mode. I said the first wisecrack thing that came to mind, which was: "I sure wish we'd brought some fishing gear". The man smiled half-heartedly, but his wide-eyed wife wasn't impressed in the least by my dark humor.

Then like a diving submarine, with a little flick of its huge tail fin, the whale quite intentionally but non-violently, splashed our boat as it slowly submerged. Was it a threat or just the whale's idea of a joke? I had no idea. But its disappearance had startled me almost as much as its arrival because the wash it created caused the boat to heel a bit. I immediately sprang into Moby Dick-mode thinking we might capsize and that the monster could return and devour us human beings one and all. My heart was beating so loudly that I thought surely everyone on board could hear it.

Fortunately, the kids began to chatter excitedly, verifying with each other what they had just experienced. If you'll forgive a banal pun, they were having a *whale* of a time, and eager for it to return. I was strongly inclined to engage the engines and get the heck out of there. But, not wanting to potentially jeopardize my pending sale, I remembered the first rule of boat salesman-ship, which was to be cool—so I didn't do anything. I just froze and we sat there bobbing around. I endeavored to look calm while we waited for the whale to return and do with us what it willed.

Sure as heck, the beast was in no hurry to leave, for after we sat a few minutes listening to waves gently slapping against the hull, it surfaced nearby again and swam within about fifty feet of us, eyeballing us for the second time. My brain was beginning to try to rationalize that the beast harbored no ill intentions. Carrying on with the mission at hand while silently gulping air, I, being the consummate salesman—confidently assured my now enchanted customers that we were quite safe. The truth was—I was still concerned as heck about the safety of my customers and the *very expensive* boat and me, in that order. After satisfying itself with a much too-close-for-comfort encounter the whale became bored, for it simply lowered its head beneath the water and raising its colossal tail, with a thunderous slap of its enormous fluke, quickly disappeared from whence it came, back into the depths of the Pacific.

I heaved a silent sigh of relief and immediately launched into an extemporaneous whale familiarization speech, trying to sound like an expert. I explained how spotting a huge Blue was quite unusual; because the majority of whales "us" recreational boaters encountered off Southern California were the much smaller Gray Whales. I elucidated how whales such as the Blues, Wrights, and Humpbacks were baleen types that dined exclusively on a small shrimp-like crustacean called krill, and how a feeding Blue could eat about 4 tons a day. I told them how whales are the only mammals other than manatees that live their entire life in the sea, and how they use their blowhole to breathe.

I explained that Blue whales were the largest living creature on Earth and how the larger females could be as much as 100 feet long and weigh up to 200 tons. I conveyed how they were found in oceans all over the world and lived as long as humans, confessing that mankind was the only enemy they had ever known and how we had almost hunted them into extinction. I told them how scientists estimated that there were over two hundred thousand of them before the 1800s' when whalers began hunting them, but that their number was thought to be only around ten thousand, with a couple of thousand of them found off the California coast. I explained how the blue whale's hearts are the size of a Volkswagen beetle, that their voices could travel thousands of miles, and that they can recognize each other's voices.

Both grinning kids and their parents listened intently as I made clicking noises to demonstrate how the smaller-toothed sperm whales used echolocation to locate their prey much like dolphins, and illustrated with my hands how they often battled giant squids under hundreds of fathoms of water far out at sea, swallowing them whole once the battle was won. I made high-pitched squeals and tried to appear nostalgic and make it as interesting as I could while describing how we nuclear submariners had often listened to Humpbacks singing their eerily complicated thirty-minute-long low-frequency love songs deep in the sea.

Being much more familiar with Grays, I enlightened them as to how they make the longest migration of any mammal, traveling from 40 to 80 miles every day during their annual 10,000-mile two-to-three month pilgrimage from their cold-water feeding grounds in the Bering Sea each year to mate and calve in the shallow warm water lagoons of The Gulf of California. I proudly stated that each year from December through March, about 25,000 whales were swimming past us just offshore, which, of course, meant that "we" Southern California boaters spotted them quite regularly. I gave them my best *this kind of great stuff happens all the time when one owns a Sea Ray* look. I guess they bought that because they bought the boat. I made the sale and found myself a whale of a memory to last.

Number 2 – Starry Skies

In these days of rapidly increasing light pollution, when two-thirds of the people in America can't even see the Milky Way from their back yards, I'd like to tell you about some unspoiled star gazing in a time and place when I first became aware of the cosmos. In my teens, every summer my brothers and I, along with a feckless few neighborhood rapscallions, enjoyed sleeping in the back of dad's old pickup truck, parked in the yard behind our house. Mom graciously lent us one of her prized well-stuffed feather beds, which fit the truck bed perfectly and allowed a boy to sink into a great softness such as few people have ever known. For added gratification, the sweet fragrances emitted from nearby growing honeysuckle and night-blooming jasmine wafted through the warm night air.

You can't begin to imagine the majesty and brilliance of the Milky Way Galaxy unless you have observed it as we did then—seemingly only a few feet above us—while we lay there enfolded in the great darkness of those warm Texas nights. The stars looked to be so close it felt like we could almost reach up and pluck one out of the sky. Being star-minded those many decades before Star Trek, each night, we'd verify the time of the year, as if to make sure the planet wasn't shifting its orbit, by noting the position of the Big Dipper (also known as the Big Bear or the Constellation of Ursa Major) as it poured into the Little Dipper (also known as Lesser Bear or Ursa Minor), whose outermost star was Polaris or the North Star.

At the time, I felt like it was quite a scientific achievement being able to quickly find Polaris in the sky by locating the Big Dipper and following the bottom star, (Merak) to the star at the tip of the cup (Dubhe), which points directly to Polaris, the last star in the handle of the Little Dipper. Many think the North Star is the brightest in the sky, but it's not very bright at all. It does, however, remain in a fixed position in the sky throughout the year, while all the other stars and constellations appeared to revolve around it. Opposite Polaris and the dippers are a sort of squashy "W" which is the constellation Cassiopeia. I knew this was all very useful information if a guy would ever get lost in the woods or at sea. At least he'd die knowing which way North was, which also means he'd know which way West, South, and East were. It always made me want to get lost. Unfortunately, I was never able to.

I was awestruck by the uncountable stars in the universe, and even then knew I was only able to see a small fraction of them without a telescope. I often wondered if there were more stars out there than all the grains of sand on all the beaches of the world. That great sparkling expanse of the heavens was unbelievably spectacular for kids whose heads were still full of growing up. The shooting stars were beyond wonderful and more than amazing. Magnificent meteorites would create lightning streaks in the darkness as they blazed across the firmament. During the annual Perseid Meteor Showers, they would sometimes shoot across the sky by the dozens at a time. The amorous fireflies tried to compete with them in the darkness but stood little chance.

We often saw heat lightning ripping through the night so far away that we wouldn't ever hear the thunder. We'd lie there for hours talking about little or nothing at all to entertain ourselves. The younger boys tended to crash early and as soon as they started sawing wood, we nearly grown-up guys found time to discuss the things older boys find important to talk about. I'd lie there listening to my friends talking over the nightly serenade of a billion crickets and creek frogs competing against the distant calls of nighthawks, owls, doves, and coyotes as my mind got lost in the winking infinity above.

I'd stare up at the stars in the Milky Way and the amazing constellations, making promises to myself of things I intended to do as an adult, some of which I kept. Being of stalwart willpower, I'd normally manage to hang on till the others fell asleep, and subtly the breezes that caressed the night would wash over me and bear me to sleep as the imaginative dreams of a child began. Those were truly wonderful times to store in the memory bank.

Number 3 – The Seafood Buffet

I am exceedingly fortunate to reside on a southwesterly facing beach where every day is overwhelming and each sunset paints its work of art upon the sky. Late one typically pleasant fall afternoon I happened to discern an extremely large number of seabirds congregating along the shoreline. It was a soft day with a placid offshore breeze and cumulus clouds to the west indicating that the sunset was going to be breathtaking.

During that time of year, many flocks gather on the sand for their daily sunset worshipping ritual of birds socializing and feather care. But this was different. There were too many birds and far too much commotion. I grabbed my digital camera and headed down to the water to see what all the turmoil was about. What I stumbled on was beyond belief.

As I trudged across the sand the western sky held a passionately warm orange glow and the cool sea twinkled with reflections shimmering on distant jade. Catalina Island appeared as a huge dark cloud-ship floating on a white mist, and there was an electric feeling in the air arousing my skin and making the hairs on my neck and arms tingle. The closer I got to the water, the more I realized just how many birds there were—innumerable birds of every type: gulls, pelicans and sandpipers, cormorants, terns, and every other species of seabird known to Southern California. Their excited cries competed with the roar of the rolling waves.

As I crested the small dune created by the tidal surge I immediately saw the source of the great chaos. Deposited on the wet sand by the waves were countless thousands, or perhaps millions, of dead or dying baitfish. They were scattered everywhere, as far down the beach as I could see. The birds were in the throes of the most incredible feeding frenzy I have ever seen—enjoying the rare smorgasbord provided by nature. They were, to put it mildly, in the process of literally gorging themselves. It was a panorama of total pandemonium. I began snapping photographs and in my mind, each scene was a potential National Geographic Cover.

The beach was bathed in an eerie and magnificent twilight glow such as I have never before or since witnessed. The sinking sun was just starting to change its rays from orange to red and the wet sand was the color of purple mud. All along the shore the silver scales of the baitfish, most six to eight inches in size with some up to twelve and sixteen inches, twinkled in the sunset glow. I was in photographic awe. The reality of the situation was unimaginable. Some of the birds were already overstuffed to the extent that they could hardly fly anymore. They stood around on the wet sand with a dazed look and the majority had a fish in their beaks that they couldn't swallow.

The vibe in the air was beyond description. Dusk had become magic-time and through the viewfinder of my digital camera, I could see that each picture I snapped was going to be fantastic. All along the beach, the seabirds chattered and gulped fish down as fast as they could. The air was filled with raucous satiated birds and others stalked around on the sand like the crazed but overstuffed gluttonous creatures they were.

Birds that would normally be skittish completely ignored me, and I was able to walk right up without spooking them. The pelicans and gulls cavorted around comically in the foam as each wave delivered more of the fry. If two birds averred a particular delicacy, there would be an instant of territorial challenge, and the smaller bird would immediately surrender and grab the next available trophy. There was simply too much food to be fought over.

As the sun grappled the horizon, the frenzy began to wane. There was a kind of metaphysical feel to it all—an almost spiritual aura that compelled me to keep shooting. A short distance away the Newport Pier was silhouetted against the most startlingly intense sunset I have ever seen. As an eminently qualified sunset observer, I am happy to say there have been many. I even included those viewed in Hawaii in the years I lived there.

I raced about, taking pictures of birds in the air and walking around on the sand with fish in their beaks—waiting until their gullets could handle the load. I took pictures of the piles of stranded baitfish lining the shore, and photos of birds from every possible angle, stalking the shoreline like a madman with a camera. Astonishingly, only a few other beach strollers had stumbled onto the enchanted situation and were aware of what was going on.

As the lights in the oceanfront homes began to flicker on one by one, I was sad to realize that the darkness would soon claim the day. Still, with twilight shadows deepening to rosy purple, each wave shimmered ashore with more baitfish. It was becoming obvious to both the birds and me, that they would not be able to devour them all.

Some of the bloated birds began to take off for night roosts, and others simply sat on the wet sand staring incredulously at the inedible sea of dead baitfish. It was later surmised that the die-off was the consequence of the baitfish following their food supply into the underwater canyon just off the Newport Pier. It was believed they had unexpectedly swum into shallower water where they encountered a sudden temperature change, which depleted their oxygen supply. The seabirds didn't care.

Number 4 - A Homage

This amazing thing is a retrospective and perhaps wouldn't have made my list were it not for the horrible events of 9/11. In the late 70s, I was in New York City on business and on a whim decided to visit the recently completed World Trade Centers. I will admit that I have never been much of an admirer of tall buildings, but at that time the recently completed towers were undeniably the ultimate icons of the Big Apple and I just had to visit them.

I had been to the top of the Empire State Building before and found it to be a memorable but not particularly enjoyable experience, which was not too surprising for a structure that was opened in 1931. To me, everything seemed to be far too rustic for a modern skyscraper, and as the elevator bounced around on the way up. I imagined it to be precariously suspended by a rusty old untrustworthy cable being cranked by a big strong guy down in the basement somewhere. At least it felt like it, as we ricocheted all over the place while being wrenched upward.

Allow me to digress and explain. The truth is—in any high building or man-made structure, I usually feel a touch queasy the nearer to the edge I am. I don't appear to be bothered by natural wonders like cliffs or mountains, probably because I have more confidence in nature than in man. Nor do airplanes particularly vex me. I suppose that's because if one is the least bit pragmatic they realize airplanes are a necessary and statistically safe mode of transportation. By that same token, I confess that I have never had any ambition to go up in a stunt plane.

I was once cajoled into spending an anxious couple of hours sitting in an outside seat in the revolving restaurant at the Crowne Plaza in San Antonio and somehow managed to get through the evening and keep my meal down. I've been to the Top of the Mark in San Francisco, the Space Needle in Seattle, and The Sears Tower in Chicago. The altitudes were great, but my attitude generally wasn't.

Naturally, I was a bit surprised at myself when for some reason completely unbeknownst to me; I suddenly developed an impulse to go to the top of the World Trade Centers. But I went while I could and I'm so glad I did. They were fantastic. From a distance, the towers seemed monolithically cold and sterile, but the closer I got, the more imposing they became.

Upon arrival, it became clear that there was a heck of a lot more than two slim skyscrapers. The sheer immensity astounded me. The tower lobbies by comparison made the lobby of the Empire State Building seem like a hot dog stand. The site itself took up 16 acres of lower Manhattan, and the towers had around 10,000,000 square feet of rentable space, occupied by about 50,000 people, not counting tourists, with restaurants that could feed 20,000 at a time. The Centers were getting about 80,000 visitors a day

Standing before the tallest buildings in the world and peering up over 1,300 feet to the top felt something akin to standing before God.

They were massive. Not just in height, but in sheer size. That slimness I had expected was gone, replaced by the most amazing and colossal steel and aluminum structures anyone had ever seen. Yet, it was all somehow impressively functional, reminding me in many ways of the nuclear submarines I was stationed on, due to the magnitude of shiny metal and innovative engineering.

An information booth attendant informed me that because the World Trade Centers were constructed over landfill, the foundations went down more than seventy feet to bedrock. To withstand strong winds, they were built to sway about three feet from the center during storms. There were 21,800 windows in each tower and every floor offered about an acre of rentable space.

In addition to several other buildings around the site, I was surprised to learn there were also seven underground levels connecting the WTC to the NYC subway system. One World Trade Center had the ultra-elegant

"Windows of the World" restaurant and Two World Trade Centers had observation decks. Everything was organized and ultra-modern. There were stores and shops of every kind. It appeared to me as if a person could have lived there, obtaining everything they wanted or needed, without ever leaving the site. The towers were a small city unto themselves.

My mind was boggled while standing in the Plaza level of Two World Trade Center and staring at some of the 104 avant-garde elevators zipping people to the various 110 stories. I hesitantly stepped inside and instead of experiencing that carnival ride feeling I'd encountered at the Empire State Building, I felt as if I'd just gotten into the Teleporter on board the Starship Enterprise. I was ready to be beamed up.

I was in the express elevator of the sky lobby system and headed for the 107th floor at warp speed. It took less than a minute, which was much smoother and faster than I'd expected. I hardly had time for trepidation to kick in before we were there. Quick as that, I was on the promenade on the roof of the Observation Deck which was the highest observation platform in the world, from where I could see about 50 miles in any direction, except—as a local informed me, that distance was often limited to whatever visual penetration the smog/fog/haze level permitted.

On my visiting day, the air was reasonably clear with faint blue skies and distant clouds. It was a good day for viewing. I am happy to report that I suffered no vertigo up there. It was too darn high. I could see for almost forever but because of the height, everything below somehow seemed almost unreal. Amazingly, the normally gritty aura of the urban jungle below gave way to the height and metamorphosed into a soothing and cleanly washed city that appeared visually dazzling.

There was no wind in the face, because glass partitions protected the sightseers, possibly to prevent would-be suicides from taking the big leap. The observation deck was huge with throngs of visitors milling about. It looked to me like a football game could be played there. Peering almost straight down I gazed at the Financial District and Wall Street, where all that money was at play, and metaphorically imagined it to be reduced to the size of a monopoly game. To the east lay the East River, Brooklyn Bridge, TriBeCa, China Town, Little Italy, and Soho. It was like a game trying to

locate buildings and/or places I could identify. Further down I spotted the
Manhattan and Williamsburg Bridges. They looked like ant trails with tiny
vehicular-ants in continual motion. Broadway was reduced to a pulsing vein
that ran out to Battery Park.

For a long time, I stared over midtown Manhattan, checking out Central
Park, reduced to a small patch of green with light reflecting off the ponds.
Greenwich Village, Murray Hill, the Garment District, and the Upper East
and West Sides seemed like a distant world viewed through a window screen.
I could see Harlem, Morningside, and Washington Heights. The Bronx
across the water was merely a hazy matrix of box-like dwellings.

Near midtown, just past the theatre district, I spotted the Queensboro
Bridge and Roosevelt Island. I became engrossed in marveling at how
Manhattan had become some distant world, populated by tiny insect-sized
creatures that scurried about below. Out past Upper New York Bay, the
backdrop of Staten Island and the New Jersey Coastline stretched to infinity.
Past the Bronx, the Long Island Sound was silver reflections of the sky, and
Westchester was a distant mirage that blinked on and off. Beyond Brooklyn,
I could see plane traffic for JFK over Jamaica Bay. I felt sort of like an
astronaut.

After tiring my eyeballs, I went over to the other tower with an associate
for lunch. We enjoyed a terrific meal at the aptly named "Windows of the
World" where the view was every bit as spectacular as the food. We lingered
as long as we dared, and by the time we were ready to leave, I'd gazed down at
the ordinary world from space long enough to feel completely free of vertigo.

During lunch, we ironically discussed the possibility of a plane running
into one of the Towers by accident, as had happened to the Empire State
Building. We both felt confident that if that ever occurred to one of the
towers, it would do little damage except in the immediate area of the crash.

I never imagined that anyone would dare to endeavor to bring down
the great buildings, as was attempted when the bomb exploded in the
underground parking area of Tower One in 1993. I was angry and
emotionally devastated when that tragedy occurred. But the noble icons had
persevered, proving to be indestructible.

I would have never prophesied what was to come for those majestic
structures and how many lives would be lost on some terrible future day—or

what wrath their recollection would now conjure in the minds of all who remember them as I do. I wouldn't have believed how many lives were lost or changed forever on that horrible day. It touched so many people, even me. The parents of our next-door neighbors were on American Airlines Flight Number 11 which crashed into the World Trade Center. They were flying from Boston to Los Angeles to see their recently born first grandchild,

Nowadays, every film or photograph I see containing the Manhattan skyline is instantly dated in my nostalgic bank. Like you, my heart aches whenever I see an image of those majestic structures towering above our greatest city. I have no answers to the obvious question: how did those evil people who committed that atrocity ever think this country would react passively to such aggression? They had no comprehension of the American psyche.

Number 5 – La Jolla Kelp

Some of the nicest experiences I've had were underwater. No, I don't mean on a nuclear submarine, although there were plenty of those. I'm talking about the magnificent adventure of scuba diving. Until one has been exposed to the aquatic world and that marvelous ecosystem, they have truly never known the wonders of this planet. The experience of being weightless and encountering creatures that few people ever get to see in their natural element is beyond compare.

Thanks to my Uncle Sam, I have been able to dive in the waters of Florida, the Caribbean, Hawaii, and even under the arctic ice. But the most amazing probe I ever made into the undersea universe was in an amazing forest.

I was stationed in San Diego and on a nice summer day, I went with several shipmates to scuba dive in the world-famous kelp beds just off La Jolla. It turned out to be a remarkable adventure. The water was clear and typically cold when we fell backward off our dive boat's swim platform into the Southern California Pacific, and into that silent turquoise world where the sound of our regulators became our link to survival.

My diving partner and I swam around a bit allowing our wet suits to work their magic in the chilly water, checking our equipment, and gathering our thoughts. Once ready, we submerged, to a comfortable transiting depth of about twenty feet and started swimming toward the kelp as we slowly descended. My temp gauge said the water was 64 degrees until we hit the thermo-cline where it dropped about ten degrees. The closer we got, the more immense the forest appeared to be.

I had never seen anything like the huge jungle of giant kelp, the largest of all marine plants, known to grow up to two feet a day. The normally cold upwelling California coastal waters continually bring in the nutrients that allow such kelp beds to thrive. I had heard that the thick forest harbored many different varieties of sea life and marine species by providing food, habitation, and protection, and I was excited to see it. But I had no idea.

As we approached the dense green kelp, undulating in the currents, my heartbeat was fast as my diving buddy and I peered into the seemingly impenetrable rainforest-like jungle. It looked foreboding and mysterious. The dancing stalks or stripes were so close together that many of the ribbon-like branches wound around one another. The massive trunks or *holdfasts* were rooted firmly in the bottom and the kelp grew 60 to 80 feet clear to the surface, where some of the leaf blades floated on top of the water. For buoyancy, the blades contain gas-filled sacs called pneumatocysts. The kelp requires sunlight penetration since it exists by photosynthesis and it can grow in water as much as 200 feet deep.

I had thoughts of becoming entangled in the constantly swaying vines, but my partner had no such reservations and motioned for me to follow as he swam directly in. I apprehensively followed into another world. It was breathtaking undersea flora—nothing less than spectacular, with giant kelp towering above and sunlight streaming through the fronds creating an eerie, almost spiritual glow all around us. The kelp added an entirely new dimension to diving, making us want to explore the entire column of water, rather than merely gliding around near the bottom.

The fronds caressed me as I swam, pushing it away and brushing against it with my flippers. Moving about was no problem, except that it was astonishing because the bright sun above refracted down in countless light strobes and wavering shadows. It was much like the experience of walking through the California Redwoods for the first time—only the redwoods don't undulate and sway as kelp does. Diving conditions were excellent with good visibility in the 20 to 25-foot range. I could see all kinds of fish congregating in and around the kelp, many of them staring at us.

The beds housed a plethora of sea life within its sheltering garden. I immediately spotted a small school of Perch camouflaged in the dappled sunlight. Shortly thereafter we encountered a huge school of fast-moving silvery iridescent Sardines darting about as one body. We'd only been in the kelp a few minutes when this massive Sheepshead swam right up and peered into my faceplate like a curious puppy. As I was to find out time and again that day, because the area is a protected ecological preserve, the local denizens were not leery of our presence as one might expect. Instead, they seemed to know no harm would come to them. Most of the fish seemed downright   inquisitive   about   the   strange   rubber-clad,   one-eyed, bubble-making creatures from the world above who had entered their domain.

We began seeing numerous flamboyantly brilliant orange Garibaldis, the California state fish, which are highly territorial Damselfish, on the protected list as an endangered species. Knowing we presented them with no danger, they would nosily swim right up and some let me pet them. I had never encountered such tame fish before. There were myriads of Senoritas and Kelp Bass swimming around among the swirling masses, and we once encountered a school of Yellowtails hunting the kelp.

Up above, near the surface, I noticed a large shadowy apparition slowly nosing its way through the kelp. It was a Leopard Shark and probably looking for dinner. I nudged my buddy and saw his eyes widen as I pointed the shark out to him. We were glad to see it move off, probably to select from the massive schools of juvenile fish that continually darted around in the forest.

Near the bottom, we rousted several bull Calicos from their camouflaged lair. We also saw some rather large Stingrays, a couple of Angel Sharks, a few barn door Halibut, and some bright blue Rockfish. There were red and blue colored Lobsters, Moray Eels, Squid, Octopus, vividly decorated Nudibranchs, Tube Anemones, Kelp Crabs, flashy orange Sea Snails, and Abalone. We even stumbled upon a beautiful coral formation adorned with colorful Starfish and Sea Urchins.

The downtime passed too quickly, as there had been so much to see. As we began ascending and depressurizing on our way to the surface, a mischievous Harbor Seal started making friendly passes near us like it wanted to fool around. As amazing as that was when we surfaced a small pod of genial Dolphins that was cruising by began leaping and playing all around us. It was like Neptune didn't want us to leave. I felt like I had visited a scuba diving paradise. I hated to quit, but unfortunately, our waning air supply dictated that it was time to get back to reality. It had been the most enjoyable underwater experience of my life. Sometimes if I get a little tense I close my eyes and envision the beauty and wonder of that most amazing day.

Number 6. – An Unbelievable Wedding

All names in this piece have been changed to protect the guilty. It's the 1980s and a couple of my very casual friends were getting married. Sure, I'll go to the wedding I promised, not reasoning through what that might entail. The pair was unusual, to say the least. They had left yuppy-ville far behind and been traveling a road many people wouldn't set foot on. That's not to say they were loose, or even drifty. They were just phenomenal, in that they had been there and done that, whatever it was. When they informed me that the affair would be nude to casual, I didn't flinch. I was hip and curious. It was the eighties. What the hey?

The wife and I received directions over the phone and on the big day dressed about as casually as we knew how. Our spirits were high as we proceeded from our home a long way into the secluded, rustic outlands of the Antelope Valley. We arrived fashionably late and there were several cars parked alongside the gravel road leading to the isolated ranch. I guessed the temperature to be about 98.8, which may be fine for bodies, but not so cool for the weather. I was glad I'd taken the invitation literally and down-dressed with casual shorts and a tee shirt. The wife hadn't been so uncouth and would be paying a sweaty price for her quasi-wedding attire.

As we left the car and ambled toward the ancient-looking rock house, located near a babbling creek that ran down from nearby mountains out in the middle of nowhere, the unexpected roar of a lion raised our eyebrows. We were courageously not deterred, even at the sudden sight of the flock of scantily and no-clad characters skulking around in front of the place. We didn't know a soul but could see at first glance what they were made of—so to speak.

We strolled through the throng feeling way over attired but determined to see it through. My friend the groom and his bride-to-be, who had already been sampling various stupor-inducing substances greeted us on the porch. They were a sight for sore eyes. He was wearing—I kid you not—a perfect olive green Robin Hood outfit. His appearance took me back to Earl Flynn's days as he stood there proudly in a tunic with metal studs and a waist-tied, light green lace-up gauze shirt with matching twill pants, and a faux suede peasant hat with a feather. His betrothed was adorned in full-length see-through white gauze-thick brocade Maid Marian dress with line-drop sleeves over a widespread see-through petticoat. Her hair was woven into a crowned braid and her face was draped by a fine sheer veil.

By their side stood our host, a way past nobly endowed and ruggedly handsome well-tanned old dude, I must say. He looked like a weary soul who had been reincarnated too many times. He wore solely, an Indian-type braided belt, with several of what he proclaimed were eagle feathers, dangling from it with two more at the end of his long braided ponytail hair hanging from the back of his mostly bald cranium. The ponytail's host-mate was a nubile little natural blonde fox some thirty-odd years his junior. She too was, as wifey-poo liked to say, depicting nude-front, except for an Indian-type braided band of beads around her head, but with only a single eagle feather dangling. She was gorgeous with a capital G, but I kept my eyes gentlemanly averted, especially when my wife wasn't.

I won't go into the assortment of characters and their various non-disguises. But they came in all forms of weirdness and were mostly from another time and place zone. I seriously doubt if such an eclectic group had ever been assembled en' masse on this planet, or any other for that matter. Most were sans clothing. A few were concealing but most were revealing. It was a voyeur smorgasbord. I began to feel weird being clothed but knew that I would have felt much weirder without my protective garments, skimpy as they might have been. Needless to say, to keep the mood flambeau, there was plenty of smoking and snorting being partaken of.

Before commencing the pre-marital celebration, we managed to get a tour of the place. Yes, the old ruggedly handsome had a pet male lion, which he'd raised from a cub. He told me it was as tame as a dog, but even so, to keep it, he'd been forced to move from his old home near civilization to the isolated ranch, because of his neighbors complaining about the lion's roaring at night.

The beast was housed in a rickety old barn with a small padlock on the door and fragile-looking bars on the windows. I peered through the window into his huge lion eyes only a few inches away, thinking he could come right through those aged boards and skimpy bars if he took a mood. I knew right away who was the lead dog. He looked docile enough, but being an astute lion evaluator, I immediately surmised that feeding him and taking him out for a daily romp must have been pretty interesting.

I was surprised to hear that the house had no electricity, but there was a generator powering a bubbling hot tub located on a deck in the back of the house. However, there were so many naked people squeezed in, there couldn't have been very much water. Our host proudly informed us that the delicately soft water for it, as well as all the household water, was mountain rainwater and snowmelt pumped from the down-flowing creek, which ran year-round. The ranch house proper was filled with unnatural wonders like stuffed wild animals standing around looking unnatural and other mounted animal heads staring glassy-eyed out from the walls. There were scented candles lit to compete with the strong incense aromas wafting around the confines. Most of the furniture looked bizarre like it had been handcrafted by drunken leprechauns.

The host and his mate slept on an old crudely fabricated massive wooden bed, using actual animal skins for sheets and blankets. There was an old, large, well-worn enough to be a Goodwill store antique ranch-hand dining table, a wood-burning cookstove, and other relics. I spotted one large bowl chock full of de-snaked rattler rattles, and another filled with arrowheads. There were also bowls of assorted ranch-style hors d'oeuvres, casually placed around for the guests. There were lots of other interesting things about the place, but the most noticeable was the isolation. There were no neighbors to be eaten.

After our tour and many quickly forgotten introductions, the wife gave me her secret nod and we promptly found an adult beverage to consume and a place to park out of the spotlight where we could sit back and take in the strange. The group was virtually fascinating due to the sundry-stew factor alone. The party conversations raged and rambled about things I'd never even thought about before, much less discussed in public. The only prerequisite for jumping into the conversation seemed to me to be having the ability to effectively postulate some unreasonable position. They spoke in vividly enthusiastic terms about oxymoronic topics like enforced pacifism, peaceful war, and whether the Earth was heating up or cooling down.

One smiley-faced chap wearing only an exceedingly huge handlebar mustache spoke at length on the benefits of homegrown herbs as he passed out samples of his productive gardening efforts, no doubt to expand his clientele. The guests seemed to be on the cutting edge of reality as they debated such esoteric matters as paranormal intelligence to spirit medicine. The atmosphere reeked of strange vapors and melancholy vibes. The smoke rose and the revelry continued as the sun lazed across the desert sky. The abundant snacks slowly disappeared, as many attendees developed serious munchies. At the first significant lull, a couple of previously incognito folk-musicians broke out their string instruments and started up a spaced-out hoedown on the front porch. By then, nobody appeared straight enough to dance, but there was some sociable *sing-a-longing.*

Then about an hour before sundown, it was time. Our host summoned the suitably well-mellowed-out attendees to come together in front, for the unification ceremony to commence. I couldn't help but notice that he was leading his pet around on a leash. Following the host's directions, everyone gathered in a big circle under the shade of a colossal ancient oak tree a slight distance from the rustic old ranch house. The lullaby of gurgling water sounds from the ever-babbling nearby creek helped establish the mood.

We were directed by the host to hold hands for the ceremony. I figured that the reason for that was so we could hold each other upright, as some in the group would have had difficulty standing on their own. We stood there semi-circling the host as he settled himself on a small pitcher-like mound in the center, his four-legged master-at-arms on his left and his adorable little pixie-mate toeing the dirt just off the mound to his right. The effect couldn't have been more overwhelming than the prominent demonstration of authority affected by the sight of that leashed king of the beasts tamed down to housedog status while his master's gallantly displayed manliness swayed in the breeze. It was a humbling moment indeed. The bride and groom stood respectfully before him, holding hands and occasionally giggling. I couldn't help but notice that Robin was carrying a proper bow with a quiver full of arrows slung over his shoulder. He was really into the thing.

I stood there with my wife on one side and this bizarre-looking wild-eyed woman on the other. She was tall, bulimically lean, and buck-naked except for her cowboy hat. The poor girl sported a recently acquired sunburn to her breastorial region. She also had the sweatiest hand I've ever held. It felt like it had been dipped in glue. Now and then she gave me a little squeeze. I couldn't decide if it was drugs, a grimace of pain, or merely to show she cared.

I have to admit, it was a beautiful setting with that ancient oak providing welcoming shade on that still very warm afternoon. That huge tree even held a small flock of chirping birds that provided background music. Rays of sunlight filtered down through the canopy and dappled us with a sort of spiritual discothèque lighting effect. For some inexplicable reason the words to that old Porter Wagoner song, which goes: "They'll all come to see me... in the shade of that old oak tree... when they lay me 'neath... the green... green grass of home..." kept running through my mind.

The host performed the rites in his best deep voice, his incredible pet standing motionless alongside him, restrained only with that dog leash being loosely held in his left hand. On his right he held a staff, much like the one Charlton Heston, a.k.a. "Moses", used in the Ten Commandments movie. At the time I thought it might have even been the same one. At least the imposingness of our host was equal to that of Moses. During the ensuing ceremony, I kept glancing nervously at the lion and he appeared to me to be casually licking his lips while he panned the group as if picking out dinner. Those great hungry-looking eyes seemed to pause whenever they fell directly on me and it concerned me deeply that he seemed to be taking more than a casual interest in my body fat content. The idea of becoming prey held no appeal.

Our host used no script while improvising his impressively solemn and truly original one-of-a-kind ceremony. He thanked the Supreme Being for the generosity bestowed, for the privilege of living his current life, and for the stars and the galaxies, the wind, the cosmic consciousness, the universal energy vibrations, metaphysical meditation, and other things I knew practically nothing about. He spoke of the collective heartbeat and rhythms of life. Then he launched into the touchy-feely aspects of committing as soul mates and about how the plighting of troths was a sacred right granted to the children of the universe by the benevolent creator.

It seemed long. Our Moses rambled all over the map, talking about the bride and groom, and the Indians who used to camp on that very same land, and how they did things, and from time to time drifting off into tangential tales of life as he knew it. He quickly seized the opportunity to comment on a small butterfly that circled Maid Marian's head during the ceremony, declaring that it was a spiritual emissary. When a wandering distant cumulus momentarily passed between our group and the setting sun, he proclaimed that as a sign of cosmic acknowledgment.

The sun was fading fast and so was our circle. Eyes started to roll and legs begin to wobble. When our host sensed rebellion, he reluctantly secured the couple's pledges of undying love and promise to remain bound forever. He finished up by giving them some worldly advice to remain true to one another and respect the sacred vows they were taking. He finally tapped them both gently on their noggins with his staff and proclaimed them married, timing it all to end just as the sun slipped below the tree line. Robin slipped an arrow into his bow and fired it off into the dusk somewhere. It was all very touching. It was almost magic. I was particularly glad the lion never ate me.

Number 7 - The Demon

I was a newsboy in Waco, Texas that spring day in May of 1953. Right after school I proceeded to the Tribune-Herald building on Franklin Street and picked up my newspapers. It was a little before four in the afternoon. It was lightly sprinkling and the thick aroma of ozone floated on the humid air, which smelled kind of nice. My only worry was preventing the rain from getting my papers wet, which were tucked into the front and back pockets of my over-the-shoulders bags. The temperature was stifling and as far as I was concerned we needed a good soaking, to cool us down and help us get over the ongoing drought.

To the south, I noticed very dark green burgeoning clouds with what looked like too-full cow's udders sagging beneath them. They were towering cumulonimbus mushrooms, oozing about like moving mountains, sliding and stirring akin to a sleeping giant rising from his slumber. But, being young and naive, I thought little of it as I started making my rounds.

From the gathering clouds, I kind of suspected that some serious rain was coming and I was obsessed with getting my papers delivered before it started. I paid little attention neither to how the green sky was turning ominously darker—nor to the suddenly gusting wind that tugged at my newspaper bags, practically lifting them off my shoulders as I entered the Bird Kultgen Ford Dealership at 10th and Franklin where I had several customers.

I had no idea that at that exact moment, there was a newborn monster closing in, already whirling and thrashing, uprooting trees and tearing up farmhouses in Lorena and Hewitt to the South of Waco. The menacing storm was gathering pebbles and rocks and other ammunition, gaining strength for its onslaught on our unsuspecting town. It was rushing toward us at about 30 miles an hour and would soon arrive at the traffic circle at 18th Street in South Waco. It was two blocks wide as it began assailing its way toward the center of downtown Waco, spitting out huge hailstones, ripping up telephone poles, exploding power line transformers, and making cars fly.

I'd finished my rounds in the dealership and was about to leave the building when I heard what sounded like up-close shotgun blasts coming from the ceiling. I looked up to see large white balls smashing through the skylights and showering everything inside the building with splinters of falling glass as they exploded into parked cars, concrete and whatever was in their way, causing everyone to run for cover. I'd seen hail before, but only the size of pebbles. Nothing like the frozen baseball-sized bombs raining down from the sky. They scared the heck out of me and all I could think of was to get out of there as fast as I could. I foolishly dashed out the side door to escape from the onslaught and started running across 10th Street. The day had turned dark as night and I was nearly struck by a speeding automobile that was trying to outrun the demon.

Luckily, I managed to dodge the car and had almost made it across the street when I felt something smack the newspaper bag hanging over my back like I'd been hit with a baseball bat. I stumbled and fell face forward onto the pavement. All around me, I heard the sound of the hailstones smashing into parked cars, rooftops, and the pavement. I felt something lift me and realized a big man in a business suit had run out from under the eves of a doorway and snatched me up by the newspaper bag. There was a frantic look on his face as he quickly yanked me across the sidewalk and pulled me up the two steps and under the shelter of that doorway, as the giant hailstones smashed down into the pavement before us exploding like white cannonballs.

Suddenly the hail stopped and there was only silence. The man still held me close. I looked up into his eyes and saw terror. I struggled to push myself away from him. He shook his head from side to side strongly indicating "no" and pulled me even tighter as he peered in fright into the darkness surrounding us. I'd thought it was over but I couldn't have been more mistaken, because all at once the great blackness enveloped us as a roaring began and it almost seemed like the whole earth began to spin out of control. The overpowering noise sounded like a runaway freight train coming right at us. The world seemed to be coming apart. Within a few seconds, that roaring grew in intensity and became as loud as I imagined a jet engine would be if you stood right next to it. My head throbbed and my ears began to pop. I pressed my hands to my ears to block out the noise, but it became inexorable.

The furious raging wind began to pull at me! I clung desperately to the man as it tried to suck us both out of the entranceway. He had to let go of me with his right arm to use it to cling to a handrail. I felt my feet being taken out from under me and my legs started to fly away, but somehow that man held me tightly clenched with his left arm wrapped around my chest, which was made even more difficult by the bags of newspapers slung over my chest and back. I could feel it trying to rip us both loose and out of that doorway, I knew it would have if the man had let go of that metal rail that assisted people up the steps into the building. The walls around us seemed to move in and out.

I looked northward and saw the car that had almost hit me lift and sail towards Austin Street—its rear wheels several feet above the road. Flashes of lightning began exploding all around us. My ears kept popping and it was hard to breathe. The suction pulled the very air from my lungs. Huge hailstones smashed into the pavement and ricocheted off like rifle bullets. It sounded like a million demons beating down as the man pulled me as tightly to his chest as he held on to that rail for dear life.

I was frozen in shock, as hailstones, tree limbs, bricks, sheets of metal, bits of glass, roofing material and splinters of wood hurtled through the air past us. I clung to the stranger desperately as the barrage of objects flew past our little niche. I choked and coughed as the howling grew ever louder and I felt myself being lifted into the air and settled down several times.

Every newspaper I carried was sucked out of my bags and went shooting off into the maelstrom. The empty bags instantly filled with air like a parachute as the wind tried to claim me. Fortunately, the bags ripped open at the seams and flapped in the air like a captive wild bird whose legs were being held. When the bags ripped apart it allowed the stranger to pull me closer to his chest. I buried my face in his coat and put both arms around him, hugging him with all my strength. I could feel both of our hearts pounding. Only the strength of his right arm kept us anchored.

It sounded like screaming demons and I recall a fleeting thought that it might be Judgment Day and that we were already in hell—or the place bad people go when they die. There were cracking sounds of timbers breaking, and the falling crashing noises of buildings imploding and falling. There were brilliant lightning-like flashes and explosions as electrical transformers blew up, and above it all the ever-constant howling wind.

Then, as quickly as it had arrived, the screaming began to dissipate, leaving behind only the noise of the pounding rain, which was coming down in buckets. Over the rain, I could hear the roar moving away from us. Through his wet clothes, I could still feel the rapid heartbeat of the man clinging to me. His face was whiter than I imagined any ghost could ever be. Abruptly, he came out of his trance and patted me on the back, and released me. Neither of us had said a word. I had no idea who he was and I started to thank him. But, before I could, he sprang down onto the sidewalk and began running.

I yelled loudly out to him "Thanks, mister!" and he stopped promptly, turned, and gave me a quick smile and a little wave. Then he ran as fast as he could, south toward Franklin, away from the black whirling monster, which was now heading down Austin Street into the main downtown area. I never knew his name.

That F-5 tornado practically destroyed downtown Waco. It was the most destructive and deadly to ever strike the center of a large city during business hours, and nothing like it has happened since. I pray to God it never does. The things that happened to the people of Waco during and after that vicious tornado were simply mind-boggling. If you want to read more about it, and how the people of Waco dealt with that immense tragedy, I've covered it in detail in my book "**F-5 – Assault on Waco** - *When the Legend Died.*"

Number 8 - A Horror Show

Picture this. Because the vast majority of my adventures have been vicarious, I felt as if I should include at least one movie event. There have been so many it was not easy to narrow it down to one. My favorite film would probably have to be "Gone with the Wind." It came out the year I was born and nothing much better has been made since. I conclude that Stanley Kubrick's "2001" based on a short story called "The Sentinel" by Arthur C. Clark who is one of my favorite writers, would be my second choice. I saw it in the cinema dome on Sunset Boulevard when it debuted and it was a mind-expanding and awesome experience. When Strauss's "Alsa Sprach Zarathustra" began and those primitive apes went ape—I was there! When that fantastic space shuttle begins to rotate and slowly close on the space station in perfect synchronization to the other Strauss's "Blue Danube" soul-stirring waltz—I was there!

I suppose my third, fourth, and fifth choices could be a toss-up between three fantastic, but different westerns. They are "The Wild Bunch." It was without question director Sam Peckinpah's and actor William Holden's best film. Frederick Loewe's and Alan Jay Lerner's "Paint Your Wagons." Who would have ever thought Lee Marvin and Clint Eastwood could both sing? And of course, Mel Brooks "Blazing Saddles" was the best dang funniest cow-punching picture ever. Mongo bad.

Six through twelve would be the original version of "The Out of Towners" with the hilarious Jack Lemon and Sandy Dennis, "The Exorcist," which made the hairs stand up on my neck, "The Sound of Music," with perfect casting and amaranthine music, the first Christopher Reeves "Superman," "Out of Africa" an inspirational and unforgettable film, and the great director Sir David Lean's "Dr. Zhivago," which has that classic soundtrack and a love story for all time, and "Jurassic Park," where dinosaurs became real. Let's make thirteen "E.T.," fourteen "Close Encounters of the Third Kind" and fifteen "Star Wars" just to come to some sort of reasonable end. You could probably mix those all up in any order and I'd still be happy. Just don't feed me that old line about "Citizen Cane" being the best movie ever made.

Oh, wait! I forgot one. I must mention it. It would fit in near the top someplace, but in the interest of getting on with it, let's just say it's a holiday add-on. I'm talking about one of the funniest and most heartwarming films ever made: The Christmas Story. I've seen it at least once every holiday season since it first came out and it has never lost a bit of its entertainment value.

Anyway, the fore-mentioned movies were all groundbreaking, ahead of the curve, and terrifically entertaining films. I'll watch reruns anytime anyplace. I could give you another fifty to go with them, but I've got to get on to my choice as the "**most amazing theatrical experience**" I've ever had, which is different from being one of my favorite films.

It was a cheaply made R-rated film, distributed by 20th Century Fox in 1975, although it was initially released in the UK in 1973. Jim Sharman directed it. Say what? Yes indeed. It's a sort of horror, sci-fi, comedy, and musical fantasy motion picture experience. It starred such well-known actors as Meat Loaf, Susan Sarandon, and Barry Bostwick. Lots of singing and dancing. Got it yet? Okay, last hint. It also starred a relatively unknown actor Tim Curry who played a doctor. Of course, that's it—a gay transvestite Doctor named Frank N. Furter.

I had missed the movie when it first came out and was invited to see it many years later in Hollywood by some close friends who didn't tell me what to expect, except to bring my sense of humor. I naively dismissed the phalanxes of plastic raincoats as some bizarre clothing fad, for which I had missed the boat. The line itself was a convivial adventure. Intoxicating odors were being emitted by the semi-crazed-looking pot-smoking weird-assemblage of attendees who were attired in all sorts of bizarre costumes. They were looking La La Land fabulous and way beyond 'Holly-weird' freaky if you know what I mean. There were girl-boys in masculine drag and boy-girls in heavy makeup and assorted other virile weirdos of ambiguous sexuality. Many were something of a crossbreed between various Star Trek and Bella Lugosi characters. They all were carrying bags of some type and partying Hollywierd heavy. By the time we got into the theatre even those who weren't indulging had a contact high. Nobody was feeling any pain.

The fun began with the credits and didn't stop until they swept us out long after the movie was over. At first, dumb old me was trying to understand the plot like I always did in a movie and wasn't prepared for the audience participation. People were jumping up and down annoying me. Then they started going onto the stage and mimicking the film script. I began to get the idea.

When Brad appeared everyone yelled "A-hole!" only in the two-letter-longer version and when his new bride Janet appeared everyone yelled "slut!" When they came out of the church as newlyweds everyone dug into their bags and began throwing rice up into the air. When Janet threw her bouquet I caught one. When it began raining out came the water pistols. When a toast was proposed there was bread sailing all over the theatre. When the troubled Brad and Janet saw a light in the darkness, everyone lit a match or flicked on a lighter. It went on like that with a continual mimicking and exchanged dialog between the screen actors and the audience, along with interaction using items such as confetti, rubber gloves, ringing bells, newspapers, toilet paper, and various other things. It was FAN-tastic!

I had no bag of props, but got into the spirit anyway and began booing villains and standing up to sway when the audience did. By the time the Transylvania Time Warp began, I was up with my friends dancing in the aisle. At last, I understood and set my inhibitions free becoming one with the Rocky Horror gang. It had taken a total reprogramming of everything I'd thought I knew about what made a motion picture great. But, I'd discovered that it's not the film itself at all, but rather what the audience allows the film to do to their minds. The experience had been psyche-expanding and utterly gratifying. By the time it was over I was emotionally drained and wholly converted. I almost couldn't wait to see it again.

After we partied our way out of the theater, I stood there with those who had shared that night's experience. We were all fully stoked and still riding our Rocky Horror Picture Show high. So right there on busy Hollywood Boulevard, with a steady stream of strollers and cars rolling past, we began to extemporaneously perform—loudly singing and synchronously dancing the Time Warp: "Jump to the left... a step to the right... with your hands on your hip... bring your knees in tight..."

Number 9 – Where Indians Trod

Since my paternal grandmother was a Native American, I am obliged to include something here to recognize that part of my being. Therefore I shall describe that spot where I have felt the most spiritual closeness to the Indian culture.

It's a place of extreme temperatures where secluded canyons hide from the day—one of the most miraculous places to be found in North America. It's a world of huge granite monoliths, towering sandstone spires, and natural wonders ringed by majestic mountains—a region of intensely blue skies where sunshine heats the desert air and rain dances seldom work. After all, it's only a hop, a skip, a jump, and a short car ride from there to Death Valley.

The temperature is hot with a capital "H" as in Hell and the humidity is mostly none. It's the kind of blast-furnace slap-you-in-the-face heat that softens sunglasses and melts the fillings in teeth. The wind comes at you like a hairdryer blowing extra hot, singing your nostrils, and making it hurt to breathe. It's a terrain where coyotes prowl the dark of night and Big Horn Sheep watch from the high country of the surrounding mountains; where scorpions and rattlesnakes warm their blood in the early morning sun. It's a locale where little has changed for eons. It's where I took a journey back to the time when my ancestors hunted plentiful game and lived in contentment in their American oasis.

The Palm Springs Indian Canyons, settled centuries ago by the Cahuilla Indians are now under the control and protection of the Agua Caliente Band of Cahuilla Indians. It's open for visitors during the fall and winter and is near Palm Springs, California. It is reached by driving through city streets and forests of Joshua Trees. At first glance it doesn't seem like much—you cross a couple of dry washes, and proceed up a secluded canyon toward a bunch of trees. Then you arrive at a parking area where you park your car and as soon as you open the door, you receive a furnace blast in the face. You stand there gasping for breath and hoping your car tires don't melt.

The first time I went, the temperature was hovering a tad over the century mark. As soon as I got out of the air-conditioned car, and stood in the fried sunlight for a few seconds, my clothes got sticky and my mouth began to pucker up as an old prune left too long in the sun. I felt like an overheated Gila Monster. My tongue was quickly petrifying and badly in need of something wet. I would have paid big money for a snow cone. Every breath was like being stuck in an out-of-control sauna. Then panic set in when I realized I had to make an exerting stroll up and over a small hill. I dug deep for courage and trudged up the dusty path in the stifling heat wondering why I was doing it. When I got to the top of the hill and saw the welcoming oasis, I was amazed.

The temperature seemed to drop twenty degrees the instant I stepped into the shade of the countless palm trees. I recall vividly how the air suddenly became cool and sweet to breathe, mingled with hints of sage and palm. That's because, as one proceeds along the moderately graded trail a short distance, they are completely sheltered by innumerable tall palms, which stand in breathtaking contrast to the surrounding rocky gorges and barren desert lands. It is a 15-mile-long tranquil canyon of indigenous flora and fauna. Hidden in the middle of all that dryness and panorama of red-textured rocks and green cacti is a small slice of paradise.

One can't help but feel overwhelmed by the metaphysical energy like Indian ghosts are watching from the shadows as they walk the same path where so many moccasins have trod. Hundreds of plants and animals are found within the area. The Indians and Spanish Explorers called the area "*La Palma de la Mano de Dios*," which means "The Hollow of God's Hand."

The reason for the name was simply because of the springs, which flowed there. The main requirement for survival in the desert was water, which attracted game, and permitted the growing of crops. Consequently, the early Indians lived a fairly contented and easy life there, and as you traverse the oasis, you will discover evidence of their precedent habitation.

They were intelligent and gentle people with a love of family and nature. The white man's smallpox and measles nearly wiped them out, and it was mostly their isolation in the secluded canyons that allowed the Agua Cahuilla to survive. I think they are now getting even with gambling casinos and through the richness of their landholdings. Speaking of which, there are many Indian artifacts, jewelry, and other tribal relics to be seen or purchased afterward in the trading post.

Along the trail up the canyon, there are picnic tables and the perennial Andreas Creek, a babbling brook that produces the lush oasis. The hike is well worth the effort. There is wildlife there, although it may be hard to spot at first. You will see various insects, butterflies, lizards, and lots of birds, and perhaps even catch a glimpse of a rabbit or squirrel as you stroll along beside the creek in the shade. I don't know about drinking the clear and cold water from the creek so if you should happen to go—take plenty of your own.

If you persevere and negotiate the scenic foot trail all the way, you will be rewarded with a beautiful sixty-foot waterfall and a pond that your feet will beg to soak in. About then you will begin to notice the intensity of the colors, or the way the sunlight dances with the tree shadows. You might spot some quail playing in the nearby brush, catch a glimpse of a Big Horn Sheep, a wild pony, an American Gold Eagle, or a Red-Tailed Hawk soaring above. You may even experience spiritual enlightenment, feeling the psychic energy of your ancestors, and want to do a little Indian dance there in the secluded oasis—the way I did.

Number 10 – Alaskan Wonder

And lastly, I recall one day of a very special voyage to Alaska. Cold right? Lots of snow and freezing wind in your face? Wrong! It was the Fourth of July and an El Nino year. The temperature was in the nineties and it was hotter than blazes. We cruised up the Inland Passage and did all the usual Alaska tourist stuff.

On the way, we'd ported at Victoria on the southern end of Vancouver Island and enjoyed high tea at the world-famous Empress Hotel. At Juneau, we'd taken a seaplane flight and viewed the fantastic vistas from on high. The day after, our ship had already carefully maneuvered around the huge icebergs and made its way into the icy waters of Glacier Bay where we saw an amazing variety of wildlife, including such creatures as orcas (killer whales), minke and humpback whales, bears, seals, and countless birds such as bald eagles, cormorants, and gulls.

We had also witnessed the spectacular 200-foot high ice cliffs of tidewater glaciers cracking and crashing, or "calving" into the bay.

On the 4th our ship was in Skagway, a picturesque little town with a bare foothold on the edge of the immense Alaskan wilderness. A fireworks display was scheduled for midnight; that hour was chosen because the sun was going to bed late that time of the year. The biggest local attraction was our cruise ship and the passengers wandering around in the streets of the quaint little town. It was really weird, seeing all those women strolling around in shorts and halter-tops in Alaska because of the unusual weather.

That morning I'd ridden the White Pass Railway train up to the top and take a mind-bending mountain bike ride back down in the company of a number of my fellow passengers. It was fantastic. At first, my brain had been trapped between *terrorized* and *thrilled* as the momentum carried me faster and faster. Although I'd been riding bikes since I was fresh out of diapers, I was pretty much a virgin at flying down mountains. It didn't take me long to realize that without continual gentle braking, I would probably become airborne. I imagined the sensation must be akin to skydiving with the brakes serving as the parachute.

If you've never ridden a well-maintained mountain bike down an actual mountain, through a virtual paradise, it would be almost impossible to describe how stupefying it was. We zipped along applying the hand brakes as necessary, restrained only by our tour leaders who kept us from attaining warp speed. Time began to blur as we descended, and I started cataloging the fleeting visions in a fraction of a second.

The hot weather was working overtime on the accumulated snow-pack and creating an unusually heavy thaw. The abundance of runoff was producing miraculous waterfalls that cascaded off cliffs and hills and took the path of least resistance as it raced downward through the mountain passes. What with all that water and sunshine, the copious forests of evergreen trees on either side of us, made a happy chorus singing to the tune of mountain breezes.

It was an incredible feeling with the wind rippling our light jackets and brushing us with the myriad scents of mountain wonder. The high meadows and valleys were teeming with beautiful wildflowers sparkling in the alpine sun. Squirrels and birds played in the trees and scores of bees and butterflies darted from flower to flower, collecting precious nectar.

Now and then someone would spot an animal, pointing and crying out its location. We'd usually fly past before anyone else would confirm it, but they were there. I saw some of them myself. We'd zip silently around a curve and be unexpectedly splashed by the icy spray of a newly formed waterfall, cascading down from a sheer granite cliff, often creating a rainbow through which we'd race. Despite the heat, the refreshing high coolness pressed against us. Amazingly, our rapidly descending ride required little effort other than braking. My kind of sport.

We got back to the ship just in time for lunch, which if you've cruised much, you know is always way more than merely extraordinary. My average weight gain is about a pound per day on cruises. It's a sacrifice I am willing to make. After a leisurely lunch, with a double dessert on account of the holiday, I stuffed myself into my fast-shrinking bathing suit and hobbled up to the on-deck spa to soak away the strains of my arduous mountain bike ride. Like huh? Well... just go with me here.

The water was steaming and luxurious as I slipped into my neck, carefully positioning myself so one of the jets was directed onto my upper back. It was Heavenly. I sighed contentedly and gazed up into a sky as clear blue as any God ever created. The only other occupant of the spa was a retired pharmacist whose sparkling eyes, toothy smile, and thin mustache kind of reminded me of David Niven. He had partaken of more than adequate libations and smiled at our blatant self-indulgence making a comment about it being a hard life but how somebody had to do it. I readily agreed with him.

A moment later, a nattily attired white-coated bar boy came along and the pharmacist ordered a refill—insisting on treating me as well. I graciously accepted. A little while later as the two of us lazed in the spa partaking of our cool refreshments, something caught my eye in the sky above. Then I spotted another and another. There were three, then I spotted a fourth and realized that there were about a half dozen American Bald Eagles up there, slowly circling our ship.

They were riding the wind currents, gliding effortlessly in circles over the harbor, searching for fish prey in the water below. We lazed there in the spa, enjoying our drinks and being entertained by those majestic symbols of our country. Now and then one of them would dive down into the water and scoop up a fish. Could anything top that? Just wait.

During dinner, we enjoyed the mood music of a perfect stringed quartet. We started with caviar and champagne, followed by an excellent cut of prime rib with all the appropriate accessories, including an Alaska-sized Baked Potato with everything possible on it. It was far too many calories for mere mortals. Somehow, I made room for Baked Alaska. After the wine and cheese and stuffed like a desperate man on death row trying to forestall his execution through endless eating, I managed to stagger to the health spa for a relaxing massage and sauna before joining the little woman (don't tell her I called her that) in the lounge, where I saw the absolute funniest thing I've ever seen on a cruise ship.

It was an Elvis impersonation contest made up of un-volunteering passengers, drafted by spouses and/or the hilariously funny cruise director who was the MC for the event. It was won by a slightly past middle-aged, height and weight-challenged, practically baldheaded, large-nosed, black-framed glasses-wearing, rather grim-looking fellow. He beat out several other far-more-handsome contenders, including one that remarkably actually resembled The King. The little Elvis impersonator was a riot. He somehow managed to simultaneously duplicate the exact Elvis lip quiver, eye twitch, and thigh shake, as he brilliantly lip-synced the King. Then with perfect timing, he popped several buttons off his shirt with an impulsive passionate chest expansion as he slid in one stunning movement across the stage on his knees while crescendoing Jailhouse Rock, thus protruding his bare and extremely robust non-Elvis-looking belly (even in his most fat period) into the roaring audience's faces, immediately bringing us all to our feet in a spontaneous standing ovation. He won hands down.

Then it was time to grab a drink to go and head up to the aft deck and secure a comfortable lounge chair to observe the fireworks display. When nature wants to amaze it has amazing ways. The sun was setting and the northern sky clung softly to a fading pink glow. The horizon slowly metamorphosed to cobalt as Mother Nature—as if in the encore—begin another aerial display by sending ions streaming toward the Earth. The particles were being caught by our magnetic field and pulled toward the North Pole. The northern hemisphere was glowing with ribbons, bars, and waves of spectacular illumination. Emanated in the dark sky were splashes of green, white, red, and purple, flashes and strobes, continually stretching and receding in a hypnotic kaleidoscopic of the wonderful Northern Lights or aurora borealis. We forgot all about the pending fireworks as we gazed in childlike awe at the unexpected phantasmagoria.

Slightly before midnight, the starry sky was lit up with an ostentatious display of man-made fireworks. We sat there yawning and watching like sleepy-eyed children seeing such a phenomenon for the first time. It too was an incredibly eye-dazzling demonstration, and yet somehow almost anti-climatic. But, it served to cap off the most amazing Fourth of July I've ever experienced. All I could say at the end of the day was God Bless America.

THE LAST OF THE MACKSIMS

A borrower who can and will make the payments on time does not need a co-signer.

If you aren't happy with what you've got, chances are you won't be happy with what you want either.

If you are wondering whom that person staring back at you in the mirror is, you probably need to cut back on something.

Colleges only give you schooling. Your real education is acquired on the street.

Uncontrolled enthusiasm is as useless as a ship without a rudder.

The very worst place to get seriously ill is in the hospital.

The soul dances when the spirit is free.

The best help you can give a charity is to eliminate the need for it in the first place.

A novel is like a mistress—only more demanding and time-consuming.

Committees mainly postpone.

You never hear anybody complain about the way the ball bounces if they catch it.

Nothing is faster than passing time.

A wounded conscience is often fatal.

Start earlier and go slower and you'll be more likely to get there.

If you can't dance be a musician.

The fun of teasing fades, but its victim's memory won't.

The faster you run, the more they are going to chase you.

Be careful with abysses.

You can't force trust.

A wise man never argues with a fool because people watching won't know which one the fool is.

The best possible way to get rich is to make a whole lot of money doing something you enjoy.

Halfway depends on who is doing the measuring.

You can't learn what you think you already know.

If you marry someone you meet in a bar don't be surprised if they turn out to be a drunk.

A painting is the permanent capture of someone's dream.

The amount of life insurance you carry is directly proportional to the odds of being murdered by your heirs.

The best way to resolve a disagreement is to figure out what's right instead of who is right.

As a general rule, never have any operation you don't need to prolong your life.

Never allow anyone to mess with your soul.

Men of few words usually don't have to eat so many.

If you want to live a few years more than you ordinarily would, at least twice a day take a few minutes off and do some deep breathing.

Folks who look down on others usually live on a bluff.

Whenever you go to the bathroom, always take some kind of reading material.

You have already won the one-in-a-hundred-million lottery by being the fastest sperm—don't expect to win another one for cash.

The real season isn't over until the last paycheck is cashed.

Anyone who can be bought is cheap—no matter what the price.

Better to be hurt by too much anxiety than ruined by too much confidence.

Profit is what's leftover from the waste.

Every omelet requires a chicken's help.

Middle-aged bachelors are either too fast to get caught or too slow to be worth catching.

A book is only part of a wasted tree unless someone reads it.

One great poker hand is better than a hundred fairly good ones.

There is no right way to do something wrong.

Leaving lots of money to charity in one's will proves you would have taken it with you if you could have.

Charm is the art of getting someone's mouth to say yes when their brain is thinking no.

Success is concealing your defects while discovering and capitalizing on other people's weaknesses.

A cynic overflows with emptiness.

If you can't take advice, you ought not to ask for it.

Making it too soft for your children is the surest way of making it hard for them as adults.

A philosopher may think something is true but a scientist must know it is true.

The economy rides a horse named capitalism, on a racetrack identified as credit-ridden by a jockey called character.

Much is feared when much can be lost.

When a war ends in a tie, both sides win.

No matter how difficult the climb to the top—the bottom is only one careless slip away.

The ones with the right to boast usually don't.

Heroes are generally no different than ordinary men, except for that few minutes of foolhardiness.

We all sweat the small stuff.

The one who has the least to lose often wins the argument.

Certainty is an illusion that gropes for trouble.

Living in a lie is like dancing in fire.

Character is lost when honor is compromised.

It would be smarter for society to build far more schools and far fewer prisons.

Be proud of what you are, not what you hope to be.

To deny God is to deny yourself.

Character is what others think of us.

If it has always been done that way—it was probably being done wrong.

The real heroes are the ones who face everyday life without complaining.

In the end, the only thing that matters is what we accomplished.

Pimples and adolescence will both vanish if you outwait them.

Experimental planes ought to be flown only by well-paid test pilots.

Arguing with a fool is like shining a flashlight on the path of a blind man.

The harshest critics seldom do anything themselves

An open mind is a well full of things that can't be explained—only accepted.

Sometimes it's better to have a big problem than a small one. A big problem will force you to take action, while you are maybe able to endlessly endure the little one.

It's smarter to tell them what they want to hear, and not what you want to say.

Anything good is enjoyed more by occasional abstinence.

Treating an animal like a human is as unkind as treating a human like an animal.

Dependability is the best ability.

The outfit makes the man and the man makes the outfit.

A man must learn to do what he can do, and forget about the rest.

You can't conquer your fears until you learn to rule them.

Don't break things that can't be fixed.

Rotten apples fall hard from the family tree.

Make time to savor time and time will savor you.

A person who can get angry over anything can also get angry over nothing at all.

Rage blunts the brain and sharpens the tongue.

A person can be accurately measured by the size of the thing that gets them angry.

Atheism is more misunderstanding than denial.

The best way to appear well-dressed is to wear a neat smile on your face.

It is a fool that not only expects the worst but also goes out in search of it.

Anxiety is the end of success and the beginning of doubt.

It is far better to look foolish than to be foolish.

When you are talking bows, remember the director who got you there.

The best way to win an argument is to take the other person's side.

Every book is a gift to its writer's soul—an attempt to buy immortality.

Starting is easy. Maintaining is hard.

Souls have no color but lots of spirits.

Speeches given in anger will be remembered in regret.

The weaker their position—the more they are interested in negotiation.

If you have a clear conscience perhaps it's because you've never used it.

It's axiomatic that politicians will spend all the money they can raise.

The colder the shoulder, the less bold the beholder.

A slip in crime—begets time.

The worst thing that could happen is more horrible than you can even imagine.

Fools with power are weapons of mass destruction.

Almost every great thing started as a dream or an accident.

Money compensates.

We are all responsible for our happiness, sadness, and weight.

Little decisions lead to big consequences.

A book is never truly finished. People just get tired of editing it.

The difference between a novel and a movie is lots and lots and lots of words.

Abusers are users and typically losers.

Don't air your dirty laundry in front of someone who knows where all the bodies are buried.

The mean justifies the end.

The best part of sleeping is the dream.

Merely "having" potential is inconsequential.

Innovation follows determination.

The wind will prevail for the sailor who best sets their sail.

Very few people are exactly what they appear to be.

Apathy is an...er...uh...oh... who cares!

Sometimes you just can't.

THE BEST FREE THING IN LIFE

Suppose I offered you a free education with unlimited knowledge and no limitations. It could be on any subject you wish to study, allowing you to progress as far as you want. Would that interest you? I am going to make that offer. The only caveat is that you must be willing and able to read. Ah—there's the rub. You've got to read.

I was bitten by the reading bug at the tender age of nine. My favorite hangout was the newsstand next to the Waco Theater, where they had an extensive selection of comic books. Even though there were "NO READING ALLOWED" signs conspicuously posted, due to my naturally curly red hair, abundant freckles, charming personality, ardent persistence, and obvious joy in reading, the kind lady who owned the stand took a liking to me. She would allow me to take a seat in the rear, out of sight from her customers, and read to my heart's content.

I started off giggling at simple comics for fun, like Donald Duck, Casper the Friendly Ghost, and Mighty Mouse. But soon that wasn't enough. I began spending more hours there taking part in the amazing adventures of Batman and Robin, Superman, Green Lantern, Hawkman, Flash, Plastic Man, and the Captains: Atom, America, and Comet. I read Archie, Wonder Woman, and Sheena progressed to Space Adventures, Weird Science, Strange Tales, and Classic Illustrated with stories like The Invisible Man, King Solomon's Mines, and Rocket to the Moon.

I developed a ravenous reading appetite and began to read the newspapers I was selling every day. I also undertook what I considered to be more serious reading such as Look, Life, The Saturday Evening Post, Field and Stream, and other magazines. I was so captivated that when I wasn't wandering around selling papers, I could generally be found there. I invested inestimable time for several years, contentedly sitting in my private chair devouring the printed words, being extremely careful to keep the comic books and magazines looking new and unread so they could still be sold.

I figured it was my calling and destiny to read them all and for a while, I think I pretty much did. Without a doubt, the time that I spent at that newsstand was one of my life's most transforming experiences. Now, I'd like to offer you the opportunity to make that same transition. You see, it took me a good while after discovering that fantastic newsstand to make a bigger and better discovery about free reading materials. It was and is the ***best source of all free knowledge***. I shall now pass this amazing secret on to you. And yes, it can change your life greatly, or at least as much as you want it to.

My secret place to acquire all the knowledge you could ever want, is none other than—(Are you ready for it to be revealed?)—***The Public Library***. Yes! That's it. Don't be disappointed. Libraries are without a doubt just about the best free thing you can avail yourself of in life. There is practically no limitation on what you can learn there. There are books on every subject known to man, and the amazing thing is: THEY ARE FREE!! THEY ARE FREE! All you need is a library card, which takes merely a few minutes to fill out and you are then officially qualified to check out free books and lots of other things from the library. In most libraries, you can get up to fifteen books and keep them for two to three weeks. If you need to keep one longer, unless someone else is waiting for that particular item, they will usually allow you to extend the loan period.

The most amazing thing about a library is that they contain most of the knowledge collected by all mankind, assembled over the ages, and made available for you to consume at no charge. At the library there are books on all matters, from biology to bananas, gardening to painting, fishing to quilt making, cooking to history, travel to English, math to astronomy, professional to an amateur in practically everything, funny to horror, fiction, non-fiction and anything you can imagine. It's all there for you and up to you how much you want to learn. You can get an education, or merely read for pleasure. It's your choice. And I can't say it often enough–IT'S ALL FREE!

You can research anything you want, and if reading is not your thing, do you know you can check out books on tape at the library? All you have to do is listen. You can also get CDs at the library. That's right—with a wide variety of great music on them. You can also get VCR tapes and DVD movies at libraries too. Most libraries offer a large assortment of current and topical magazines and newspapers to read in the quiet surrounding, while ensconced in the comfortable chairs provided for guests.

There are law books, reference books, and books on just about every possible hobby or occupation. There are books on travel, exploration, and the history of every country, person, or thing. If you are having personal problems or just want to improve your life, there are thousands of self-help books written by the world's foremost authors on just about any subject. There is practically nothing one can't learn at the library.

It's very important that one's education ought not end when one finishes formal schooling. If you are not a library person, I urge you to reward your mind by immersing it in that vast sea of literary knowledge. Your life will be remarkably enriched and you will not feel the guilt of allowing that marvelous brain you've been loaned to atrophy.

Beyond the thousands of free non-fiction books, there are countless thousands of fiction books and novels available for reading enjoyment. There are books for every educational reading level from pre-school to post-graduate. In most libraries, there are even computers that allow you free Internet access to browse online, send e-mails or help you look up things.

Libraries have a warm and friendly atmosphere and are peaceful places of tranquility. If you are not a book person or library literate, you need not be afraid or hesitant. Every library is staffed with helpful and friendly people who will gladly give you an introductory tour and help you find anything you desire. They are some of the nicest folks you will ever meet. I guarantee you that a few visits will make you feel comfortable and at home. There is as much education and/or entertainment available there as you could want. And the most amazing thing of all — (one last time) —IT IS ALL FREE! How can you beat a deal like that?

IF ELECTED I WILL SWERVE

Dear Friends:

Please permit me to capriciously prostrate myself in front of you in sardonic insipidness. I have been doing some serious soul-searching lately on matters of grave consequence. I have recently established a one-person (me) exploratory committee to explore whether I am as wonderful as I think I am. I am thrilled to report that I am even more exceptional than I thought, is not only talented and gifted but also charming and extremely charismatic. I am proud to state that I have been a human being for a good many years now, and I am committed to enhancing this world we live in, and making it a better place to work, play, eat, sleep, watch TV, and exist. To achieve the foregoing, I have chauvinistically investigated many of the troubling issues and uprooting problems of our planet. Therefore, I have decided it is of utmost importance.

To that end, after much apathetic effort on your behalf, with great guile and jingoistic calculation, I have come to the concise conclusion that I must brazenly beseech you to bestow a Herculean honor upon me. You see folks, there is only one face equipped to cope with the issues we now face, and I am not ashamed to admit that mug belongs to me. I deduced this through exhausting hours of superfluous contemplation, frowzy pretension, and heartfelt meretriciousness. I shall therefore strive to enhance myself at all times bearing in mind that you, my constituents could not possibly have the intuitiveness to grasp the intricacies of a man of my good standing and aberrant stature.

Therefore, to ensure the continued progress of mankind and the protection of our species, I humbly ask for your support. This is a matter of great magnitude with consequences inconceivable to you simple working persons, so I don't expect you to comprehend the complexities and ramifications of giving me your trust. All I ask is that you believe me when I boastfully proclaim that this is the only way I can establish a balanced fiscal policy and maintain continued economic prosperity on my behalf.

Truly educated individuals and good-looking people will readily understand and appreciate my experience and recognize the need for my kind of desperate leadership. Getting this world straightened out will require persistence and someone willing to make hard choices. This is a big planet we live on and it will take a big man to run it. I go around 190, and maybe after a really good buffet.

I am a proven magniloquent winner. I have been a newsboy, professional dishwasher, sailor, boat salesman, business manager, member of various advisory committees, and President of my third-grade Home Room Class. Qualifications such as mine are not found under every rock.

I will represent my fellow men with discursive pedantry and persiflage, endeavoring to govern in amity with liberty and free cheesecake—yes cheesecake for all. There will be no merely plain cheese given out under my administration. I will work with all local, state, and federal officials as well as kings and potentates of other nations attending as many official steak dinners as necessary. I will lead the effort to clean up whenever and wherever I can, setting high standards for all from trash collectors to condominium conversion committees, accepting nothing less than the maximum kickback in all eventualities. You say you want specifics. All righty then!

I will ban crowd surfing at Tony Bennett concerts and all Barbara Streisand Farewell Tour events as well as all other draconian music events. I will propose legislation to mandate a maximum of four servings at Chinese buffets, or maybe six. I will ride herd on and control all television hucksters, demanding fair and reasonable shipping and handling charges, including all home shopping networks. I will restrict park dueling until at least 10 AM so that more people might observe without being forced to get up before dawn. I will establish an Official Lobbying Fund Acceptance Office (OFLAO) and serve as the chairman. I will restrict all excessive salaries for overpaid professional athletes and lower the admission fees for all sporting events. The same goes for actors and actresses and theater ticket prices. I will find all rap singers $25.62 for every profanity uttered on their CDs and each subsequent airplay. I will define clear-cut definitions between poetry and prose. I will mandate that all overnight RV campers in Wal-Mart parking lots be provided with a coupon good for every member of their party for morning bathroom privileges and a free breakfast at the Wal-Mart fast food court.

I will closely oversee the tourist industry by personally traveling to all luxurious destinations and sampling their cuisine and any adult beverages they serve. I will help protect the future of the farm and food industries as I enjoy eating well and most animals, finding them to be delicious. I will make sure that all-natural landmarks are scrubbed and polished regularly by convicted child molesters and that all tourist visas are paid promptly including all defalcation charges due. I am also concerned about the environment and will check to make sure it is okay by frequently going outside. I have lots of other clandestine plans, which I cannot reveal at this time, as you people are not on a need-to-know status.

My policies will be great! You will be able to place your entire future in my capable hands and sleep soundly at night because when I am elected, I intend to make sure everyone gets a legal prescription for the sleep aid of their choice.

I am sure that it will be a rewarding, Lucullan, and insightful experience... and much, much more. I could go so far as to say that it may even be life-changing, allowing me to interface with many business leaders, dignitaries, and other rich persons.

I could go on, but you can see that I am a man of great vision and unprincipled turpitude so you may rest assured and be comfortable by giving me your vote of confidence. I am a man you can look up to especially if you are six feet under. I am just like one of you ordinary people except that I am a leader who knows how to stand on the tissues, and properly use them as well.

One of the few difficulties I have found with my amazing abilities is that my greatness cannot be under-exaggerated. You might therefore assume that I will require a fancy title or job description. I'm pretty humble but... well... okay—but only to help you out. I won't demand much of a salary. Anything in the mid to high seven-figure bracket will suffice. However, I will need plenty of perquisites, as the job could be somewhat demanding.

I will be pleased to improve the quality of my life and enjoy spending the funds you entrust me with. In noble admiration, I, proudly proclaim that enthusiastic unprofessionalism has never stifled my complete incompetence. I thrive on discursiveness and inanity. I will be everything I think I am and more than you could dare to dream. I will share my passion with all those of the proper persuasion whom I come in contact with. In fact, as a token of my great appreciation, once empowered I shall forthwith appoint everyone who voted for me as my official myrmidons.

Therefore, it gives me profound pleasure to announce that I am willing to accept the position of Supreme Universal Commander & Head Of Planet Earth or (SUC & HOPE), along with all possible perks and benefits. My friends, if you harbor any doubt at all about bestowing me this awesome power, simply ask yourself just one question: "Could I possibly be worse than your presently elected officials?"

I would like to thank you in advance for your support and understanding. I shall now bid you farewell—trusting you will all do the right thing when you go to the poles—either of them.

What Now?

ABOUT THE AUTHOR

Vernon 'Mack' Mahoney Jr. was born and raised in Waco, Texas and currently lives in Newport Beach, California.

Mack is a retired U.S. Navy Chief who served on nuclear submarines. After the military, Mack became a salesman, manager, and owner of marine retail dealerships in Southern California. He has also been the Vice President of Marketing for several new product development companies.

He was a columnist for various newspapers and magazines and for several years wrote and published boating books for marine dealers throughout the United States. He has written three fictional novels, a screenplay, and three non-fiction books.

During the last nineteen years, he has created over 8,000 original greeting cards containing his artwork, photographs, and poems. It is the largest such collection in the world.